HANDSHAKE:
CODE OF THE WEST

An Autobiography
by
Clayton Jennings

Copyright © 1993 by
CLAYTON JENNINGS
& CAROL JENNINGS
Box 436
Highmore, SD 57345
605-852-2001

Library of Congress
Catalog Card No. 93-94149

ISBN 0-9638624-0-5 (Hardcover)
ISBN 0-9638624-1-3 (Paperback)

Printed in United States of America

PINE HILL PRESS, INC.
Freeman, S. Dak. 57029

Table of Contents

	Dedication to Ted	v
	Dedication to Carol	vii
	Love and Appreciation	ix
	Preface	xi
	Foreword	xiii
Chapter 1	Beginnings	1
Chapter 2	My First Job	4
Chapter 3	Pirates	5
Chapter 4	Sex – A New First	8
Chapter 5	Cattle Train to Chicago	9
Chapter 6	Trapping and Bootlegging	10
Chapter 7	Man's Work	12
Chapter 8	The Silver Dollar	15
Chapter 9	Basketball	16
Chapter 10	The Pig Story	22
Chapter 11	Boots Gregg	27
Chapter 12	Feeder Cattle Excursion	32
Chapter 13	Branching Into Feeder Cattle in South Dakota	35
Chapter 14	Brown Hotel	42
Chapter 15	My Sheep Story	45
Chapter 16	Another Sheep Story	53
Chapter 17	Restocking the Drought Areas	57
Chapter 18	Miller Livestock Auction Company	61
Chapter 19	Frazier Vs. Jennings	66
Chapter 20	Diamond A Cattle Company	69
Chapter 21	Against the Wall	73
Chapter 22	Navy Days	75
Chapter 23	Letter to Mother	90
Chapter 24	Buying and Developing the Hyland Angus Ranch	98
Chapter 25	Hyland Angus Ranch Crew	109

Chapter 26	Dorothy – My First Wife	116
Chapter 27	Artesian Well	118
Chapter 28	Cattle Business in Old Mexico	121
Chapter 29	Winter of 1951/52	126
Chapter 30	Champions	134
Chapter 31	Denver Bars And Girls	152
Chapter 32	Judging Major Shows	157
Chapter 33	Purebred Herds	161
Chapter 34	Bulls – Montana Bound	164
Chapter 35	First Sale at the Hyland Angus Ranch	167
Chapter 36	Copenhagen	173
Chapter 37	Discipline	175
Chapter 38	Eloise – My Second Wife	180
Chapter 39	Rocks Galore	182
Chapter 40	Sugar Loaf Scot 913	185
Chapter 41	The Big Move	188
Chapter 42	Black Angus Heifers by the Trainloads	195
Chapter 43	J & J Ranch	203
Chapter 44	Beef Friesian Cattle From Ireland	212
Chapter 45	The Cow Palace	221
Chapter 46	Cast a Little Bread	227
Chapter 47	Claymore Field Day	231
Chapter 48	Carol	233
Chapter 49	1979 Halloween Storm	236
Chapter 50	Our Little Country Ranch	238
Chapter 51	Fancy Bull Sale at Brown Palace	243
Chapter 52	Hall of Fame and Other Honors	246
Chapter 53	Bankruptcy	250
Chapter 54	Alberta Clipper	251
Chapter 55	Manic Depression	253
Chapter 56	Religion	254
Chapter 57	South Dakota Has Been Good to Me	255
Chapter 58	Glimpses	259
Chapter 59	Reminiscences From Old Friends	288

JENNINGS BROS. Owners   HIGHMORE, SOUTH DAKOTA

Dedication

Dedicated to my brother Ted who has given so much to so many people and to this country. He has given to me and many of you his heart and soul.

Western Headquarters For Quality Angus Cattle — Registered & Commercial

P.O. Box 436
Highmore, South Dakota 57345

CLAYTON JENNINGS
HIGHMORE, S.D. 57345
RES. 605-852-2001

Dedication

Dedicated to my wife, Carol, for the very being of *HANDSHAKE, Code of the West*. Without her I would not have written this book. The massive research required from coast to coast and to have facts, figures and humanity accurate and in perspective was a challenge she thrived on. Please believe me when I say there would not have been a book without her encouragement and relentless dedication.

Love and Appreciation

I have "known" Clayton Jennings for many years, and never in my wildest dreams did I ever expect to meet him and getting to know him was beyond any and all comprehension. But I did meet him in 1978 and getting to know him as I have, has been a learning experience ever since. Clayton lived two-thirds of his life B. C. – Before Carol! I have written this with love and appreciation to my wonderful husband, Clayton, for living such an illustrious life and giving me an opportunity to relive the personal events with him through his stories, while helping him with this book. Ours is a wonderful sharing, caring relationship that would be difficult for anyone to equal!

Now I have a story to tell!

When I met Clayton, Maud was the family dog. She was a large St. Bernard with lots of age and was good for nothing but to love. She always met you with a gleam in her eye and her tail wagging. Maud had trouble moving about in her later years and one day we feel that she laid in front of a visitor's car. When they started the car to leave, she could not move fast enough and was run over and her back was broken. We hoped her back wasn't hurt that much, so we let her lay around a couple of days. Each day we hoped she would get up and walk around, but it didn't happen. Clayton called the local vet and he came right out. He examined her and told us she had a broken back and the humane thing to do would be to put her to sleep, which he did.

After the vet left, Clayton worked all afternoon burying Maud. He dug a grave for her in the grove of trees just north of his home (where he lives now). It was all he could do to get her body moved to the grave, as she must have weighed 150 to 200 pounds. He covered her with dirt, then he hauled rocks from the pasture in the trunk of his car to cover the grave. When he finished with the rocks he came to the house and said to me, "Come with me. I want to show you where I buried Maud." He took me to the grove of trees and showed me the grave. It was a masterpiece! He said, "I buried her under these trees so the sun will shine on her first thing each morning and she will be in the shade during the heat of the day!"

What a beautiful thing for this famous, powerful, flambouyant man to do! I knew right then that there was much more to this complex man than first meets the eye!

I love you, Clayton!
Carol

Preface

Why *HANDSHAKE, Code of the West?*

In 1932 when I came to the Pierre, South Dakota area and west as far as you wanted to go, I found the code of the west. Ever since the pioneers settled in that vast country, an agreement of any kind was finalized with a firm handshake. It was the tradition of the land. These people didn't feel it was necessary to draw up a contract. I had negotiated the terms of my first cattle deal with a west river rancher until we both agreed on everything. This rancher then reached out his big hand, grabbed mine, shook it firmly and said, "That's a deal, boy!" It was a great inspiration to me so I have followed this tradition to this day and will continue always.

I am writing this book because of the many livestock people who have kept asking me why I didn't write a book. These are people I have dealt with over the years, some are third generation. This had been constant for the past four years and I always laughed it off as I had no thoughts of writing a book. How could I write a book? I wouldn't know where to start and besides who would want to read it? The classic response I got was, "If you write a book and tell all the truth about your life, it couldn't help but be a best seller!"

The pressure had been hot and heavy, so I reluctantly agreed to take a whirl at it. I feared it would be drudgery. Never did I realize what a challenge and inspiration writing this book would be.

This autobiography "Handshake" covers eighty years and I'm giving you all the red meat of my life. I am more interested and am trying harder with this endeavor to make it a worthwhile project hoping that it will leave a lasting impression on all of you.

All of my life I have been a dreamer. My dream now is that all of you who read my book will find some quotes or stories that will make you smile or laugh or shed a tear or two and maybe some of this book can be applied to your life. I have taken a whole lot out of life and if I can give some little thing of consequence back to others I will be fulfilled.

This is my book and I am writing it. I am exercising my right and privilege to show and tell you about me! I have written it entirely from my memory and with my own words. If you think I have written in a braggadocio manner, please forgive me and read on. I know of no other way I could have given you the facts, figures and events of my life. This book is me!!!

Foreword
Clayton Jennings a Cattleman for All Seasons

We can hear and see it now even as we reflect back in memory for more than three decades. The year was 1961. The place was Chicago and the scene was the International Livestock Exposition. The occasion was the International Angus Bull Sale. The memory of that happening is vivid indeed! Dave Canning was sale manager for the event and the noted Colonel Roy Johnston cried the sale. In the corner of the ring stood an especially distinguished looking gentleman. He wore an expensive Western hat and a sheepskin lined coat. He was approaching middle age at that time and he did cut quite a figure. Yes, that was the Clayton Jennings of an earlier era. He was at the very zenith of his power in those days. The sale was being conducted under the so-called Berth system where the consignors had the right to reject the final bid if they felt it was inadequate. Clayton Jennings did place the opening bid on nearly every bull that entered the ring that day. If memory serves correctly, he did purchase a fair number of bulls on that occasion.

That was a typical role for Clayton. He was the consummate cattleman in those days and rarely was his judgment questioned. He was of great assistance to Dave Canning in those days, always present at the Great Atlantic Bull Sale and other like events. It was Clayton who started the bidding and put a "floor price" upon cattle of some value. In the process, many well-bred and excellent Angus bulls were shipped to the Hyland Angus Ranch. Of course, Clayton handled a lot of cattle in those days. A few of the elite bulls from these groups were used in the purebred herds at Hyland Angus Ranch and a larger group was utilized in the vast commercial herds.

Some bulls were resold to other ranches and a number of these bulls did find their way into purebred herds in South Dakota.

It is well to remember that Clayton Jennings enjoyed the respect and confidence of many of his fellow breeders. No one was more highly regarded in the Angus world in those days than Clayton. He did fulfill many important roles within the Angus industry. It is a well-known fact that during the so-called "middle period" of Angus history many of the good Angus herds were to be found in the East. At the same time, the greatest opportunities for expansion existed in the vast cattle country of the American West. Clayton Jennings often bridged the gap between these two worlds. He gathered together groups of good Angus bulls in the East and took them to the West where they were really needed. It is impossible to emphasize too strongly the role of Clayton Jennings in the expansion of the Angus breed in the western country.

Clayton Jennings and his good friend Ralph May believed that "a herd bull is where you find him." Clayton found herd bulls in all sorts of places. He believed strongly in the Raona Bardolier cattle and many of them came West from the Raona herd in Michigan. Interestingly, this blood figures strongly in the background of the "Sky High" bull and also in the background of the cattle at Gartner-Denowh Angus Ranch. Also, if you trace back the pedigree of the immortal "Cracker Jack" you will find Raona's Bardolier 2nd. Clayton also believed strongly in O Bardoliermere 53rd, the so-called "Rump Bull." Many of the "53rd" sons found their way to the West under the influence of Clayton Jennings.

Clayton was a close friend of the late Jim McGregor. Many will recall that Jim McGregor was the final proprietor of the famous Glencarnock Stock Farm at Ada, Minnesota. Clayton did work closely with Jim. (In fact, his son Jim Jennings was named for Jim McGregor.) It was largely through the influence of Clayton Jennings that the latter day Glencarnock cattle did experience such broad distribution.

Earlier in this narrative, we alluded to the fact that a number of these good bulls did find their way into purebred herds. A number of breeders over the years have confided in this writer that they could always count on Clayton Jennings when they were in a "tight spot" for a herd bull. If your old bull had been injured or if you were a bit pressed for money to acquire a new herd bull, Clayton was the person you contacted. Almost always he could come up with a well-bred bull at a price the breeder could afford. It is a matter of record that many of these bulls did contribute to breed progress.

Yes, Clayton Jennings has, for several decades, been the "cattleman's cattleman." For decades he was one of the eminent and dominant figures within the Angus breed. The fame of Hyland Angus Ranch spread throughout the continent and for a variety of reasons. Many top feeder cattle were produced there and feeder calves from Hyland Angus Ranch did win many prestigious feeder cattle shows. The Hyland prefix was also noted in breeding cattle circles. Many great breeding bulls, such as Hyland Marshall 7, were produced in the purebred herd at Hyland Angus Ranch. For a number of years Hyland Angus Ranch sent out a formidable show herd that competed successfully at the broad range of shows. The imprint of the Hyland Angus bloodlines upon the breed was considerable in the '50's and '60's and on into the '70's.

It is during this era that Clayton Jennings did achieve considerable distinction as a judge. He served in that capacity at a variety of shows. It was a matter of no small import to win under the skillful eye of Clayton Jennings. Many of us recall watching him sort over 300 head at the 1962 Iowa Futurity.

Over the years, it has come to be generally known that Clayton would often come through when things were a bit on the tough side. One such occasion comes immediately to mind. A production sale was being held for Albert Beck near Artas, South Dakota. The cattle were certainly good enough. (Many important cattle were produced in the Beck herd including the maternal grandmother of the many times champion High Voltage.) However, conditions were rather dry and cattle prices were somewhat depressed. The crowd which gathered was extremely small and people didn't seem to be in a buying mood. A phone call was placed to Clayton Jennings with the assurance that the cattle were good and needed buying. The net result was that Clayton ended up buying most of the offering which included bulls and females of varying ages. Many other such instances could be cited. Clayton often saved the day!

It is well to remember that Clayton has remained loyal to the Angus breed through many periods in its development. His faith in the breed has never wavered and his confidence in the Angus has remained consistent. As we enjoy the present pre-eminent position of the Angus breed within the beef cattle industry, it is appropriate to recall those who worked on behalf of the breed when Angus were less popular—and promoted the Angus breed when it was not in the majority. These were the men who built the Angus breed.

Yes, it is well to occasionally call the roll of those breeders, for we are much indebted to them. High on any such list must appear the name of Clayton Jennings!

Al Conover, owner
Conover Auction Service
and
"Mac" McKeag, staff writer
Conover Auction Service
Baxter, Iowa

Chapter 1

Beginnings

I was born December 13, 1913, in the same bedroom of the same farm home where my two sisters and brother were born north of Boone, Iowa. I was named Charles Clayton Jennings. My father was Charles McClellan Jennings, born December 18, 1884, in Boone County, Iowa. Dad was a successful livestock dealer. I admired my dad. He was highly respected and everyone liked him. He loved to laugh. He farmed extensively and fed fat cattle, which he shipped to Chicago. He also raised fat hogs which he shipped to Wilson Packing Company, Cedar Rapids, Iowa. Dad knew how to make money, but he didn't know how to preserve it!

Dad married Mary L. Vogler on May 2, 1906. She was born December 28, 1883, in Boone County, Iowa. Mother was an absolutely beautiful woman and had a striking personality. She was a very neat, swift and accomplished homemaker. Everything she did was for home and family. She felt her work here on Earth was done when her children were raised and on their own and her husband had passed on. "There is no need to live any longer," she said to me quite often. Mother suffered a heart attack before Christmas and died gracefully in the Miller, South Dakota hospital in mid-afternoon on January 8, 1954. All four of her children were with her. I adored my mother.

I have very few recollections of my young years on the farm near Boone. I do remember attending first grade in a country school in 1919. I had a pony that I rode the two

Charles M. Jennings and Mary L. Vogler wedding, May 2, 1906.

Charles and Mary Jennings with children Ted, Margaret, Clayton and Nadine. About 1914.

miles to school every day. I'm told, my teacher had her mind on getting married and not on teaching. Consequently I had to take the first grade over. We moved into Boone in 1920, so I attended the first four grades there. Dad had quit farming and was dealing exclusively in cattle and hogs.

Chapter 2

My First Job

My first job was highly rewarding. I was about ten-years-old and we were living near the outskirts of Boone, Iowa. I had a great desire to earn some money. The owner of a commercial strawberry patch about two miles down the road was hiring pickers for the season. I walked to the patch and talked with the owner. He had 20 or 30 older or mature people picking on the ten-acre patch. He offered me a chance to pick the strawberries at three cents a quart, working from daylight till noon. At noon, all the picked berries were delivered to Boone and sold to the grocery stores. He said I could start anytime. I started right then!

As I recall, I worked at a pretty good pace, picking and filling quart containers and placing them in the walkway of the patch. When I had the quarts all full, I carried them to

Ted and Clayton Jennings. Clayton is on the pony. About 1923.

the center of the patch, where they were counted and I got more empty containers. Then I went back again to the patch and filled more containers. I worked about 3 hours the first day, checked in and found that I had picked 16 quarts and made 48 cents. We were paid in cash each day. What a great feeling it was to reach into my pocket and jingle the money all the way home!

Each day I learned a few things. I found I could pick with both hands. I put my basketball pads on my knees. It was a lot easier and I could pick more. Each day I increased the amount I picked by five to ten quarts. The final day, I turned in 103 quarts, which was my record. I thought I was a millionaire jingling the $3.09 in my pocket as I walked all the way home!

Chapter 3

Pirates

While living in Boone, I bummed around with two boys about my age. We were between eight and ten-years-old and we had all read books about pirates. We decided we wanted to be pirates. We must have a cave to keep our wares and precious possessions in.

We built this cave eight feet square and eight feet deep. It must be covered the same as the surrounding terrain, so no one could detect it. There should be only one entrance, not a walk-in, but we would burrow a hole approximately 18 inches in diameter and about four feet long from the ditch to the cave. We could crawl in, then camouflage the entrance with some old canvas, so no one would be able to see it.

We decided to build this cave on the edge of a field by a gravel road, about one fourth mile from my home. We found the tools to do the cave work — spades, shovels and picks. We found it took a lot of work to dig a cave of this dimension. The deeper we dug the harder the ground became, but we did it, and thought it was a masterpiece.

We mortised in a foot of dirt on the top so we could set some old barn doors a foot below the ground for the roof, and then put dirt on top to the level of the ground so no one would suspect a cave. When we finished the digging, we scattered all the excess dirt thinly over the field. Our entryway worked very well — crawl in on your belly and out the same way. We were really proud of our endeavor and felt we were geniuses.

Now we had to acquire some booty. All three of us went to Woolworth's in Boone. We separated in the store and put anything in our pockets — like gum (Yucatan, BlackJack and Juicy Fruit), candy bars of all kinds, peanuts and lots of marbles, all sizes and colors. When our pockets were full, we filed past the counter to pay for one or two items we had in our hands. We did this several different days. We would put the loot on a shelf in the cave. Why we never did get caught, I don't know. All of us must have had a lot of natural ability for thievery.

We put all we had lifted in the cave. We lined it up, so it was a beautiful sight to behold. We didn't tell anyone about us being pirates. Fall and winter came and the weather kept us from frequenting the cave, except on occasional days. Then came spring and a catastrophe!

The man who owned the field where we had dug our cave was discing for spring grain crops with a heavy disc and four sorrel Belgian horses weighing nearly a ton each. When they came over the top of the cave the four horses crushed the top and fell into the cave. This was the worst sight of entanglement of horses and harnesses that I had ever seen. The horses were kicking and squealing and the harnesses were snapping and breaking all over. It could have been worse. If we three kids had been in the cave — that would have totally ended our lives! But for the grace of God, we were walking on the road to the cave and were within throwing distance of the catastrophe.

The farmer looked over the indescribable mess and jogged across the field to his farm for help (lots of it). He came back with two men, more horses, a fresno (a horse-drawn dirt excavator), chains and shovels. One of the men used the team of horses and fresno to remove dirt on one side of the cave to create a good slope, so the horses could be dragged out with chains and ropes on their legs. The other two men had knives and worked furiously cutting all the straps and tugs that were not already broken.

The horses were upside down, on their bellies or on their heads or rear ends. They continued to flounder around and squeal with pain and fright. Yes, it was frightening to watch, but we did.

In about an hour the man backed up the team as close to the slope as possible. The other two men put a slip knot on the hind leg of one horse and handed the rope to the man on top so he could tie it to the single tree. This was done swiftly. It took several attempts and all the power of the team to pull the horse out to safety. They used this same procedure on the next horse. The last two they haltered, and they climbed and struggled up the slope to get out. They led the horses home. Two were really lame and all were skinned up on all parts. They had big welts from the kicking and floundering.

We headed home and we knew the worst was yet to come. We all had been so proud of the cave and the pirate-like thievery. Now, we knew the episode was all over, except the correction. Why, oh why, did we do any of the things that created this catastrophe?

When I got home, I had a lot of stress and fright, so to relieve my soul I told my folks everything from the beginning. They believed me, but wanted me to show them the place. I felt that they were shocked. They saw the loot on the shelf and scattered in the rubble on the floor of the cave. They sent me back to the house for a bushel basket, and upon my return I had to pick up all the loot. They didn't scold me any on the way home, but I could feel they had plans for me.

My dad and I went over and settled the damages with the neighbor. We then went to Woolworth's. I told them what we three boys had done, and made settlement there, also. But the worst was yet to come. On my plate, at every meal, was a stick of Yucatan gum. Before I could have one bite of food, Dad made me chew the stick of gum, which I did without question, during which time I suffered much humiliation and embarrassment. It seemed like a lifetime!

How many days would it take to chew a bushel of gum — one stick at a time?

The humiliation and embarrassment may have saved me from getting into worse trouble, as my two buddies, whose parents did not discipline them, ended up in reform school a few years later!

Chapter 4

Sex—A New First

We moved to Livermore, Iowa, in 1924, when my uncle W. O. Jennings, who held the hog buying contract with Wilson Packing Company of Cedar Rapids, Iowa, was moving to Chicago. He had purchased a livestock commission firm in the Chicago stockyards. This gave Dad the opportunity to take over the contract with Wilson Packing Company.

I liked Livermore. I had made some friends, and we played basketball together or went to the pool hall, but my parents were quite strict, and I had an evening curfew that I knew I'd better not miss.

As I recall, I was about eleven years old, and one moonlit night, as I was hurrying home from the pool hall, I met Geneva, the sixteen-year-old neighbor girl who was on her way downtown. We met near the M. & St. L. Railroad right-of-way. We stopped to talk. We walked hand-in-hand, then arm-in-arm. All of a sudden she stopped and kissed me like I had never been kissed before. She gracefully pulled me down on the grass.

I knew I was over-matched. The sensation ripped through me like a tornado. I didn't know what was happening to me, but I knew it was fantastic!

Hurrying home, I had mixed feelings about what had happened. I wasn't proud of this incident, but I wasn't ashamed either. This was my first time, and it was an indescribable experience!

Chapter 5

Cattle Train to Chicago

During the years between 1924 and 1930, we shipped numerous carloads of cattle to the Chicago stockyards. We averaged eight to ten carloads a month. Sometimes Ted or I accompanied the cattle, as Dad's health kept him from making the trip. We would leave Livermore on Saturday evening and arrive and unload in Chicago on Sunday evening.

The caboose ride was a horrible shake, rattle and roll experience! It was a "hell bent for election" situation! When the freight train started to move, it was a jerky affair, shaking us all over the hardwood benches. Those of us who rode the train, named the caboose "the torture chamber."

In the winter the coal furnace had to be kept fired up — it was either too hot or too cold. In summer it was terribly hot.

If we wanted to sleep Saturday night we had to lie on the hardwood benches. The train blew its whistle, loud and clear, at every crossing from Livermore to Chicago (about 500 miles), making it impossible to sleep. We were subjected to the train's starting and stopping at all stations along the way, all night long. It was continual up and down and all around, jerking, clanging and squealing all the way. If you could still smile when you arrived in Chicago—you were tough!

Our cattle were always consigned to my uncle, W. O. Jennings & Company. I'd meet him in his alley with our cattle and have them ready for sale on Monday morning.

While in Chicago I attended whatever professional sports that were available. In summer it was either the Chicago White Sox or the Chicago Cubs baseball games. In the fall it was Chicago Bears football. We scheduled the trips to coincide with the games, sometimes we would see two or three games in a row. My uncle always had tickets for every game. I truly enjoyed these games, which made the hardship of the trip more bearable.

The railroad issued passes for us to go with the cattle on the freight train to Chicago. We also received a return pass on a passenger train, which was very pleasant.

Chapter 6

Trapping and Bootlegging

When I was about 12-years-old, another kid and I decided to trap some small fur-bearing animals. We lived within two miles of the Des Moines River, where there were considerable mink, skunk, muskrat, and weasels.

We borrowed a bunch of traps from a friendly old trapper. The old trapper told us how to set traps and where to set them, which helped a lot. He also said he would sell the pelts for us, as he was very experienced. We walked to and from our trap sets every day. Our catch was sporadic—some days we had good luck, some days not so good. The first week we caught a few and the old trapper did sell them for us. We were very pleased with the money we got.

One day we decided to branch off on an old side road where there was almost no travel. There were two culverts and it looked like there had been animals coming and going. As we got ready to set the traps, we saw a new paste board box pushed back into the culvert. We pulled it out. We opened it and found 48 half pint bottles of 190 proof alcohol. We looked in the other end of the culvert and found another 48 bottles. What a discovery!! We knew that some bootlegger had planted it there, until dance night in Livermore. These bootleggers would sell it on Saturday night. Why couldn't we peddle it? Those were prohibition days and 190 proof alcohol was more in demand than any other liquor. And besides that, everyone knew that Livermore was a favorite spot for bootleggers. In fact, it even had the nickname of "Liquormore."

We took the boxes home to our barn for safekeeping until dance night. These were big dances. We took a box uptown and hid it in an alley. We put two bottles in our pockets and mingled with the "big boys." We had decided to sell these half pint bottles for 50 cents each. We didn't have any trouble getting rid of every bottle, as we were undercutting the bootleggers. We sold the two boxes for $48.00, which we divided, each of us getting $24.00. We swelled up like toads. We thought we were big operators!

While I was out in the alley bootlegging, my sister Margaret, was in the dancehall. Big bands played every week. A dance contest was held at most dances to pick the best dancer. Margaret was a special dancer and she won many first prizes in these dance contests. She knew them all—foxtrot, Charleston, waltz, two-step and big apple. We never found any more alcohol stashed away. The bootleggers must have wised up. So we went back to trapping.

We set traps on each end of the culverts on the same old side road. We felt really good about these traps and wanted to get back early the next morning to check them. As we neared the first culvert we could see that we had something in the trap or that it had been tripped. The trap was pulled inside the culvert. I got on my hands and knees and took hold of the outward end of the chain and pulled, so we could see what we had. There was considerable resistance, so I knew we had something, and in a second or two, I saw a bushy black and white tail and a spray hit me squarely between my eyes and on my head. The spray immediately totally blinded me. I turned the chain loose, I knew it was a skunk because there is no other animal in the world that smells like that!

I was totally blinded and smelled worse than anything I can describe. The pain in my eyes was unbearable—never had I felt such pain. My friend led me by the hand and took me home to my mother. She scrubbed my face and hair for several hours. Finally I was able to get my eyes open and I could see only blurry objects. My mother and sisters washed and brushed with all kinds of soaps and deodorants. They continued this ritual for several days. In about a month my eyes were all right and the odor had disappeared. It seemed like it took forever to get the odor out and away from me.

To this day I can see that tail flash up and can feel the sting of the spray in my eyes—probably the most horrible situation I have ever been in.

Folks, you have not totally lived, unless you've been pissed on by a skunk!!

Chapter 7

Man's Work

When I was about fourteen-years-old, I thought I was big enough to handle a man's job.

John Wonderly of Livermore had a small construction company. He hired about six men. Wonderly's company was known as the best to construct big, tall cement block silos and to shingle the highest of barns.

Clayton (15) and Ted (17) Jennings.

I went to visit John and told him I was looking for a job. He asked me how old I was, and I told him that I was nearly fifteen. John said, "Well, boy, I can use one more man, if you can handle a man's job. The work is heavy and it is steady and I would want you every working day." He said I could try it a few days and if I could stand the work, he'd pay me a man's wage of $1.50 a day.

The crew had already been on a job building a big tall cement block silo and wood shingling an enormous hip-roof barn. I was to start on Monday morning.

We all reported to work and rode in the back of an old pickup about eight miles to the work site. We carried our lunch with us. One of the men showed me the various jobs I would have to do. First, he showed me a big water tank filled with bundles of wood shingles that had been soaking all night. When I wasn't working on the silo, I was to carry a bundle of wet shingles on my shoulder to the barn, up a ladder to the eave, then on up the roof to where the shingles were being placed. These bundles were very heavy, but I thought I could do it.

The silo was being made of cement blocks and "mud." We had a tripod with a pulley and heavy rope, which we hand-over-hand pulled five gallon buckets of mud or a number of cement blocks to the high point of the silo. As we laid the rows of cement blocks, the tripod was raised higher and higher, we continued to hand-over-hand the cement blocks and mud.

This was the heaviest work, of any kind, I had ever tried. I started getting tired a little before noon, but after we stopped for the lunch hour and rested, I felt refreshed. My strength and energy held up pretty fair until the middle of the afternoon. Then it was the longest three hours until quitting time that I can remember. I was so tired and the ache in my muscles was so severe I could hardly breathe. In fact, on the way home in the back of the pickup, I promised myself that I would never go back to that place to work.

When I got home, I just wanted to go to bed and never get up. But the next morning my sister Margaret called me at 5 a.m. I told her I couldn't get up, I was too tired and too sore. Margaret encouraged me. She got me breakfast and persuaded me to try it another day—maybe it wouldn't be so tough!

I remember my sister faithfully getting me up in time to do my chores at home, which was to milk two cows twice a day, and then off to work. With her encouragement, I kept on the job and I made it through the summer.

John paid us every week and as he promised, he paid me a man's wage of $1.50 per day. I'll never forget how gratifying it was to be able to work with men. He was a great man in our community and I'll always remember the courtesies and kindness that he showed me.

But all the time we were doing this heavy manual labor in the Iowa heat (up to 115 degrees) I thought, "There must be a better way to make a living!"

Chapter 8

The Silver Dollar

I had heard a lot of talk about the big west of which Denver was the central point for livestock. I thought I would go there to experience the far west for myself. This was the first time I had ever stayed at the Cosmopolitan Hotel in Denver and to me, a kid of 17, it was fantastic.

I decided to walk around all of the big buildings in downtown Denver and observe all the humanity that came and went. As I walked down a street I noticed a brightly lit sign ahead of me about a city block. It was high on a two-story building and it read "Silver Dollar." I kept looking at the sign and wondered what it might be. I walked on to the next corner. I looked back and saw the sign. It made me curious so I walked back until I got to a wide flight of stairs that went up directly under the sign. I hesitated but I decided to go up and satisfy my curiosity. There was a large room with plush furnishings at the top of the flight of wide stairs. A matronly lady wearing a beautiful long gown came into the room. She asked, "Would you like a beer?" I couldn't say anything, but I nodded my head yes. She said, "Have a seat and I'll be right back." Soon she returned with a bottle of beer and said "That will be one dollar." That was high for those days.

As I took a couple sips of the beer, two beautifully dressed girls came into the room. They sat down and smiled at me like they had always known me. Then it dawned on me where I was. To say the least, I was shocked and embarrassed! I set my beer down and excused myself saying, "I'll be back later!"

Realizing that this was a "House of Ill-Fame" not a "Hall of Fame," I ran down the stairs taking two steps at a time, hoping all the time that no one had seen me!

Chapter 9

Basketball

When we moved to Livermore, I was in the fifth grade. Several boys in my grade wanted to play basketball. One of the fathers, Jack Sykes, was the janitor at the school and gymnasium. If nothing else was going on, he was glad to let us practice basketball. He would even give his son the key on Sundays and holidays. We lived in the gym and played by the hour. We became more advanced in basketball handling and shooting than any other kids in the surrounding towns.

By the time we reached high school we had togetherness in team play that not many could match. Our senior year (1931/32) was the climax for all of us. We had played and nearly lived together for almost eight years.

We studied the play and tricks of the top players of the top teams before us. We were all team-wise confident and feared nothing of any other team. We went through the season beating everyone. We worked our way through four tournaments to earn a berth in the state tournament. There was a total of 1093 schools to begin with. At that time, all teams regardless of their class played in the one state tournament, which consisted of sixteen teams.

My father was an invalid and walked with two canes. He was welcomed to the state tournament games with a special chair placed at the center edge of the playing floor.

We won our first two games and the majority of the sports writers and the other teams rated our team "unbelievable and fantastic" to have beaten Diagonal and Mason City. I feel confident that we could have won the entire tournament, had we not run out of gas in the third game because of no substitutions.

Our coach, O. J. Cayou, did not use substitutions, except in emergencies. Consequently, our starting five played every second of every minute of every game. Coach Cayou felt that

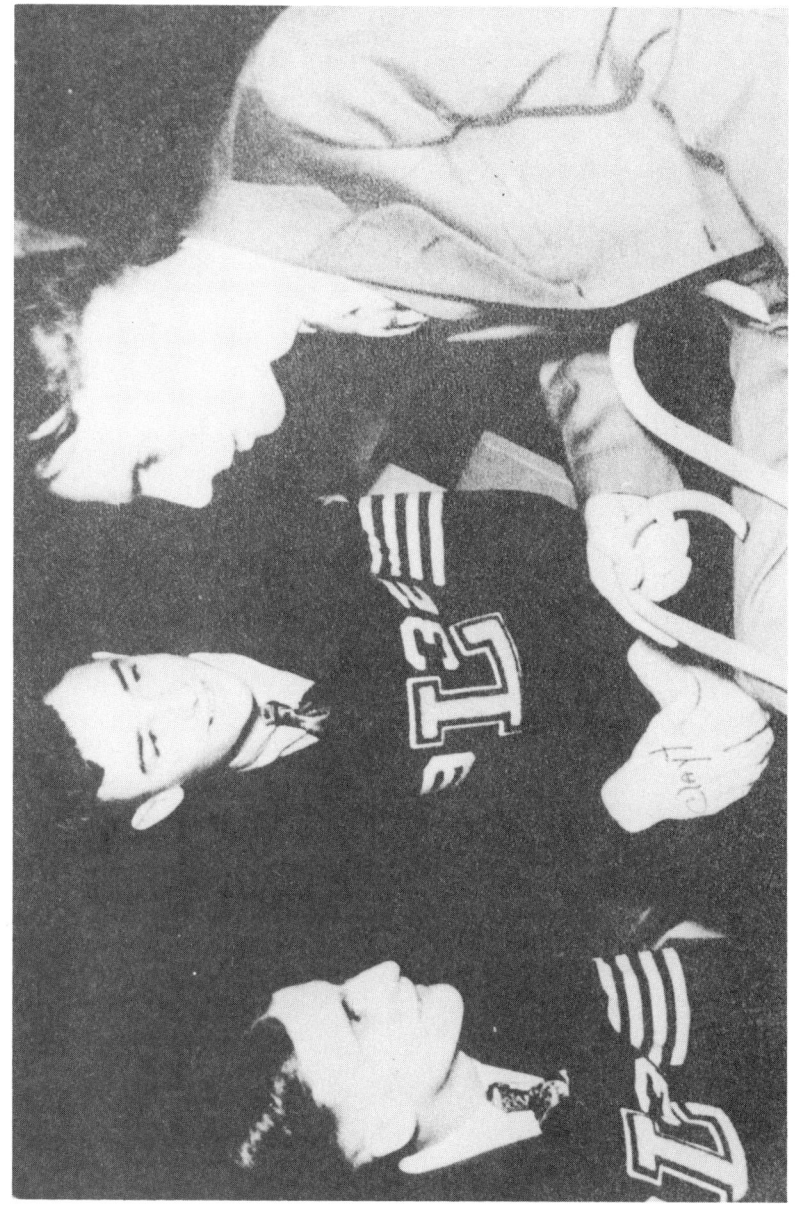

Ted and Clayton with their dad, Charles Jennings.

1932 Livermore, Iowa team. Front row l to r: Clayton Jennings, Gene McPherson, Herbert Raney, Merlin Baker, Buster Sykes, Coach O. J. Cayou. Back row l to r: Shultz, Baker, French, Sweeney and Hood. We are ready for the state high school basketball tournament in Des Moines, Iowa.

our second string boys were too young and too immature to play in a game of this calibre.

When we went to the state tournament, all five of us boys were in superb condition. I weighed in at this tournament at 132 pounds. Four days later, after the games, I weighed 116 pounds. It took several months for me to get over the tired feeling.

The game with Central High of Sioux City, Iowa, a class A school, was our final. As customary, when we went to tip-off and started the ballgame, we always shook hands with the opposing player on the other team. I came up to shake hands with Chuck Bernard. He shook my hand pretty heavy and said, "Hotshot, you've been making a lot of points up to now but I'm not going to let you have any points today. In fact, I'm not even going to let you shoot."

I was at a loss for words, but I did say, "You are going to be damn busy!!" He weighed 225 pounds and I weighed 116. He had been all-state in basketball and football the previous two years.

After the tournament I was named to the All-State basketball team and 20 years later I was still named on the All-Time All-Iowa team.

Following the tournament I received lots of fan mail. Some was from girls who wanted to get acquainted with me. I didn't want to disregard them, but there were too many to acknowledge separately, so I made carbon copies and sent each girl a letter, not realizing how improper this was. I heard from several of them, but I was unable to follow up as I went to South Dakota on livestock business as soon as I graduated.

Herbert Raney and Clayton Jennings. A combination hard to beat!!!

LIVERMORE WINS CLASS B TOURNEY

Livermore 23 — Mason City 20

With Clayton Jennings scoring 13 points in a miraculous exhibition of shooting, Livermore's quintet of basketball players gave the crowd what it [...] Friday afternoon [...] startling upset [...] class A five, 2[...]

Jennings was nearly the whole show for Livermore. His shots were uncanny, every one of them being from far out on the court and the first, which opened the scoring, being of the one-handed variety.

Jennings alone made 11 field goals and one free throw for a total of 23 points. This was the individual high score of the tournament, including both class[es].

The little hotshot of the fighting Livermore outfit, Clayton Jennings, has totalled 18 points in two games. Jennings, of course, was the big hero. Thus it was that [Livermore] grabbed the lead on Jennings' shot.

Livermore ousted the powerful Mason City quintet from the running with a sparkling 23 to 20 victory featured by the spectacular shooting of Clayton Jennings, a slender little forward.

DES MOINES, March 19.—With Clayton Jennings scoring 13 points in a miraculous exhibition of shooting, Livermore's quintet of basketball players gave the crowd what it had been aching for Friday afternoon by turning in a startling upset of Mason City's class A five, 23 to 20.

The folks up in Livermore should arrange a reception for little Clayton Jennings. This youngster has won two games for his team here this week. Against Diagonal Thursday he shot the winning basket with less than 30 seconds remaining and against Mason City he drove home six field goals and a free throw to account for 13 of the 23 points credited to his team.

Jennings Scoring Ace

Livermore 24 — Diagonal 23

A little forward named Jennings, who shoots baskets for the Livermore team, won an important state championship tilt from Diagonal at the Drake fieldhouse Thursday afternoon by looping a long one in from the side in the last 15 seconds of play.

Jennings' shot gave his mates a 24 to 23 victory and snapped Diagonal's string of 35 consecutive victories, claimed to be a state record.

The winning goal was made after Beal of Diagonal had almost made a hero out of himself by putting the losers on the long end of a 23 to 22 count with but 20 seconds to go. It was a sensational one-handed effort. On the next tipoff play the ball was tossed to Jennings who sank the deciding bucket.

LIVERMORE WINS FINAL GAME AT MASON CITY

The shining stars of the day's hostilities were Jennings, the little Livermore forward, and Marcellus McMichael, Roughrider center, who counted 15 of his team's points and scored the winning basket [...] the overtime with [...]

PRAISE FOR LIVERMORE

"Jennings, midget Livermore forward, had a perfect evening at scoring and won high honors with a total of 12 points. Three field goals and six free throws out of six tries was his record"

Livermore—24	fg.	ft.	pf.
Jennings, f.	3	6	0
Baker, f.	2	1	4
Raney, c.	1	0	3
McPherson, g.	0	1	0
Sykes, g.	2	0	3
	8	8	14

Tourney Sidelights

Livermore 57, Humboldt 19.
Livermore 33, Renwick 11.
Livermore 18, Coldfield 21.
Livermore 16, Mallard 25.
Livermore 33, Havelock 11.
Livermore 34, Titonka 14.
Livermore 18, Ware 12.
Livermore 51.
Total points—Livermore 760; opponents 338.

Chapter 10

The Pig Story

Dad had a contract with Wilson Packing Company of Cedar Rapids, Iowa, to buy fat hogs in volume on a commission basis at the rate of 10 cents per hundred weight, regardless of weight or kind.

Livermore was a big hog producing area and most of the farmers depended on their hogs to pay the mortgage. They had quality hogs and in volume numbers. Saturday was always the big day as people brought the hogs into Bode, Livermore or Hardy in wagons, sleds or bobtailed trucks. Some even drove large bunches of hogs to the stockyards at the three locations. Ted received the hogs at Livermore, Phil Wilson at Hardy and I was at Bode. We loaded all the hogs from the three locations on the Rock Island Railroad on Saturday evening and shipped them to Wilson Packing Company, which was about 200 miles southeast of Livermore, with no less than a trainload each week. The average trainload from the three towns would be from 30 to 80 cars, depending on the season. The hogs arrived at Wilson Packing Company on Sunday evening and were slaughtered on Monday. We had a beautiful working relationship with Wilson Packing Company. Never once did we have a disagreement of any consequence.

Ted and I followed Dad step by step in the sorting, weighing and paying for the hogs. Dad was afflicted with arthritis in the early 1920's, when Ted and me were 13 and 11-years-old. He got to the point where he could not do much because of the pain. He was bedridden for a year and a half or more. It was necessary for Ted and I to take over the business with Dad's council.

In 1932, the banks all over the territory were having a lot of trouble, and many were closing their doors. Some of the farmers had checks that couldn't be cashed because of the bank failures. All of the farmers were skeptical and had a right to be. They had to be careful about taking checks. Some of them would not accept checks from anyone, even if they called and the check was good. Many times by the time they got to the bank, it was closed.

Ted and I decided to run a cash exchange, so we leased the Farmers Savings Bank building at Livermore. We made a deal with Wilson Packing Company to forward us cash for the proximity of each Saturday's shipment of hogs. We would give them a call on Friday morning, telling them how much we needed. They would send the cash with one armed guard on the Saturday morning passenger train coming from Cedar Rapids. We met the train at the station in Livermore and escorted the armed guard to our cash bank. The guard would catch the evening train back to Cedar Rapids.

We were probably the first and largest cash payer for hogs in that part of the country and it made our business flourish. Everybody from every direction wanted to sell all of their hogs for cash. Our business became highly lucrative.

We hired our sister Margaret to handle the cash. She worked out of the vault of the old bank building. We gave each farmer an invoice for his hogs with weight, price and total. He took the invoice to the bank and Margaret paid him the cash. Every

Kenneth and Margaret Howard. My sister and her husband. Taken in 1935.

seller was happy. It was a mostly German community and they liked their beer, which they made themselves. It was easy to believe they brought some to town, as they knew their neighbors were selling hogs also. They enjoyed getting together, having a beer and a laugh or two. They told everyone how great it was that they got cash for their hogs. It, no doubt, raised our prestige throughout Iowa, because we were able to pay cash for these hogs.

During the summer of 1932, Ted and I heard about the same situation in South Dakota from the continuous radio reports over WHO Radio. South Dakota was having a severe drought and bank failures. We talked it over and agreed that I would go to South Dakota and look over the situation. I took $2500.00 in cash with me, just in case I could buy some pigs.

I drove to the Sioux Falls, South Dakota public stockyards, where I thought I could get information on the bank and drought situation. The stockyards were full of cattle and quite a few butcher hogs. There I met Hans Hansen. We walked around and talked about the severity of the drought further into South Dakota and the banking conditions.

Hans Hansen was a farmer from Salem, South Dakota. He was highly interesting and congenial. He told me about his area. He knew all the farmers in his county and adjoining counties. He told me that every farmer in that area had pigs weighing from 100 to 150 pounds and had no feed for them and no way of getting money to buy feed. All of them wanted to sell. He said everyone was scared of the banks, and if I had the cash I could buy every pig in the territory. He would personally go with me to each farm.

I arranged to meet him at a cafe in Salem early the next morning. He was waiting for me when I pulled in. We stopped at the first farm on the road and asked the farmer if he wanted to sell his pigs. His answer was, "Hell yes, if I can get the cash for them." I told him "no problem" as I had the cash with me. I would pay the farmer when the pigs were delivered to the railroad stockyards. We went on down the road and it was the identical situation – almost the same words spoken. We did this most of the day. We kept track of the numbers as we went along. We were about out of money. I told Hans we'd better quit. We ordered stock cars on the next freight train going east and south to Livermore. We paid all the farmers and I had a little over $150.00 left. I told Hans to line up more pigs and I would be back with another sack of money.

When I traveled around the country with Hans, we were in the worst drought in South Dakota history. Dust was blowing in the air from the hot winds that prevailed. It was thick and blowing in all directions. The dust would get into the radiator of the car and the engine would heat, causing the radiator to boil dry. We'd have to stop and walk a mile or two to get water to fill the radiator again. We quickly learned to carry several cans of water in the trunk. It was inevitable that our car would heat several times a day. The dust blew so hard that we could seldom see the sun. It was so dense that you would have the same feeling if you were in a heavy fog or blizzard. These were dirt blizzards! In reality, these dust storms were more nauseating, with the dust in your nose and lungs, as compared to a snow blizzard, which is refreshing.

Typical dirt and dust of the "Dirty Thirties."

I went back to Livermore, unloaded the pigs, and they truly pleased Ted and me. When I showed him what they cost he said, "Get your ass back up there, and buy all the pigs you can find." So that I did, and Hans was waiting for me. We probably bought more pigs out of that area, in a shorter time, than had ever been bought before. We went through the same procedure of getting the pigs on the way to Livermore.

I was getting low on cash money, but I had enough to pay Hans a decent commission for his time and sincere efforts. When I counted out the money to him, he smiled and shook my hand and said "I just wish you were my son."

I guess this was when I started liking South Dakota, because these were real men, yet so polite and decent in dealing with me, a kid of 18!

Ted and I planned to fatten these pigs. We contacted the creamery in Algona, Iowa, and made a deal with them to take all of their buttermilk every day. We had a 500 gallon water tank on the back of a bobtailed truck and could haul 2 or 3 loads a day. We had the pigs on self-feeders of shelled corn and the buttermilk. We had a woven wire fenced creek with flowing water and lots of timber. This was an ideal spot for any kind of pigs.

Livermore to Have Cash Stock Exchange

1932

Jennings Brothers, stock shippers at Livermore, have leased the Rossing building in that town, and will open a cash stock exchange office there. The building was formerly occupied by the Farmers' Savings bank. The establishing of this office will enable the farmer to get cash for his stock on the day of the sale.

Margaret Jennings, who is at present employed at Orleans, plans to return to Livermore to take charge of the office work. Jennings Brother plan to open for business on Tuesday of this week.

—Jennings brothers shipped thirty-two carloads of stock out of Bode and Livermore during the past week, and during the past month have shipped a total of one hundred and three car to marketing centers. As energetic a stock buying firm as that is a great benefit to the town in which it operates.

SHIP 57 CARLOADS OF CATTLE, HOGS, DURING PAST WEEK

(Republican-Independent News Service)

LIVERMORE— Jennings brothers, stock shippers for Livermore, Bode, and Hardy, shipped 57 carloads of cattle and hogs during the past week.

In the long period of time that Jennings brothers have shipped from this vicinity, this is the largest number of cars they have ever sent forward over a one week period.

There were fifty-four cars of hogs, and three cars of cattle.

CLAYTON JENNINGS, youngest member of the firm of Jennings Brothers stock buyers of Livermore, returned last week from two weeks spent in South Dakota where he purchased livestock. He bought four carloads of pigs and shipped them to Livermore. They have been sent to a farm south of Livermore. Young Jennings is not yet 19 years old.

NOTICE — For Sale

1000 vaccinated thrifty spring pigs. These are good boned pigs and of good quality. We will sell these pigs in any number to fill your order.

JENNINGS BROS.

Phone No. 69   Livermore, Iowa

We had planned to fatten these pigs to top weight, but we had an opportunity to sell them now!! We had only owned them two or three weeks. The price of fat hogs had slumped to a new low and the government came out with a program to help save the hog industry. The government decided to buy the pigs delivered to a major packing house where they would electrocute them to take them off the market. They were paying 13 cents per pound. Our packing plant was Wilson Packing Company at Cedar Rapids. We had given a cent to a cent and half per pound for these pigs, and sold them for 13 cents per pound. The pigs averaged about 110 pounds, and the net profit on them was a little over $10.00 per head. We delivered 2,650 pigs. That made our net profit $26,500.00, which was an unheard of profit in those days.

The government got the word out about this program and the farmers found that they could sell at any major packing house, thus bringing an end to the farmers' need for me or my cash!!

Chapter 11

Boots Gregg

The year was 1935. I was working the area around Pierre, South Dakota, buying calves, when I heard of a rancher 23 miles south of Harrold, who had some calves he wanted to sell. I drove to the ranch near the Missouri River, and there I met "Boots" Gregg. I discovered at this first meeting that he was a veteran cattleman and that he had a great personality. A red scarf was always around his neck.

He saddled a horse for me and we rode though his cattle, going almost to the Missouri River, seeing almost 75% of his calves, which was enough for me, as I was very impressed with his herd of cattle. We talked about price as we rode through the cattle. He said he always liked to sell by the head, instead of weighing them. That way he didn't have to worry about shrink if he had to drive them very far for delivery. He said he would deliver them to the Chicago and Northwestern Railroad stockyards at Harrold, South Dakota, for $27.00 a head. I told him I did like his calves very much, but that was more than I could pay, and he came back with, "Well, shoot me a deal!" Before we got back to the ranch he had sold me the calves at $25.00 a head for the steer calves and $22.00 a head for the heifer calves, and he would deliver them to the railroad stockyards at Harrold. The deal was for some over 500 head of Hereford steer and heifer calves which I would load on the railroad cars and ship to Livermore, Iowa, where my brother Ted would receive them and sell them to buyers around there.

This was one of the greatest, most eventful times of my life up to this date. Boots was a professional in all respects of the livestock business, and he has gone down in my book and many others, as a legend and one of the greatest ever in his line of business. I was feeling good that I could deal with a man of his calibre.

When Boots said he would drive the calves to the Chicago and Northwestern Railroad stockyards in Harrold, I couldn't quite understand how he could do this, but he said he would get them there, and we would count them after they were delivered to the stockyards. There was to be some over 500 calves. I couldn't believe those bawling, ranting calves that had just been taken off their mothers could be driven 23 miles to Harrold. So I asked Boots how he was going to drive that many bawling calves that far. And he said, "Well, boy, I've got the best of eight top men and horses lined up and we will bring them in one evening, and cut off the calves that are going to Harrold, and leave them penned next to where the mothers are penned. Then at daylight, we eight men will start out, open the gate for the calves to head north." He said, "Don't you worry. It will be tough, but nothing's easy when dealing with calves. We will get those calves delivered safe and sound to Harrold. They will be wild as hell the first few miles, but after that they will walk into the stockyards with their heads down. They will be as gentle as kittens. Any loss will be my loss. You just pay for what I get there in good sound condition."

I held doubts. I thought a lot about it, but the fact was it was his responsibility to deliver them to the stockyards and mine to pay for them after we counted them in the stockyards. So we set a date a few days ahead so he could gather every cow and every calf he had on the ranch. On that date, at plumb daylight in the morning, he would start out with the calves.

Well, we were there, ready and waiting for it to get daylight. He had all the calves sorted off that were to go on the shipment. The eight men on horseback fanned out to the west and the east and behind the calves, and the gate was opened when everyone agreed they were ready. It reminded me of a wild west rodeo, and in lots of respects it was better than any I have ever seen. When the gate was opened, the calves poured out of about a twenty foot gate, and kept pouring out and heading north. When they all got going, the dust was so intense in the air it was worse than any fog I had ever been in. I was truly shocked, but it seems like after they got out about so far, the dust thinned out and the calves

The start of the round-up of the Hereford cattle on the Gregg Ranch.

kept going. The cowboys intentionally spooked them so they would not stop and try to turn around. They all went on the run for some time. Then some slowed to a trot, and then to just a walk. After the first five miles they were broke to drive without any problem. They arrived late that evening at the stockyards. The calves were exactly what Boots had told me they would be, gentle as kittens. They didn't run. They didn't trot. They just walked squarely into the corral where we penned them. That is something that I had never seen before nor have I seen it since.

We proceeded to count the calves. There were some over 500 and that was the pay number. Boots' responsibility had been fulfilled. He had delivered these calves to the Chicago and Northwestern stockyards without a fatality. Yes, they were tired as hell. They walked slowly around the corral, and within thirty minutes nearly every calf was lying down. They were dogged and tired, but they were clean, except for some dust. They would be shipped by rail the next day to Livermore.

All rejoiced at having the calves penned. They were no problem now. They were gentle, with no injuries. We all took

Boots Gregg with his horse on his ranch.

out for town to eat. We ate heartily, laughed and joked and we all had a little bit of booze—Old Granddad it was.

Everything was fine as the calves had settled down for the night, but tragedy struck during the night. A through train blew its whistle and spooked the calves. They all started running and hit the east end of the corral. The corral was flattened, and the calves scattered every direction. I discovered the disaster early the next morning. Thank God! Boots and his cowboys had left their horses in the stockyards for the night. They saddled up and began searching for the calves. They were found in bunches of maybe 40 or 50 heading back to the ranch. The calves were bunched together and trailed back to the stockyards at Harrold where it was discovered that we were short eight head, which were never recovered.

The cattle cars had been parked on the sidetrack near the stockyards. We used a pinch bar (a manual source for moving freight cars) to pinch the cars down the track to the loading

1960 - Boots and Ann Gregg.

chute. We pinched a loaded car away, and then pinched another car into place at the chute. Boots helped load the calves on the cars and helped pinch each car into place. He was singing all the while and nipping on a jug of whiskey. I was very impressed by his singing. Each time Boots wanted me, he yelled, "Hey, boy." Later I heard that he had told his neighbors that he had sold his cattle to a "kid" and he wondered if the deal would be good! The deal was good—Boots was satisfied. We sold the calves for a reasonable profit, and all the buyers in Iowa were very pleased with the calves.

Chapter 12

Feeder Cattle Excursion

Because of the drought, money was tight for most people, prices were low and feed scarce. But there were plenty of opportunities if you happened to be in the right place at the right time.

In 1935 or 1936, Ted and I had heard over the radio that there would be extra large runs of cattle from the drought areas of Nebraska and South Dakota at the Sioux City, Iowa and Omaha, Nebraska, public stockyard markets on Monday morning.

Ted arranged for quite a bit of money in case we were able to buy some of these cattle. Since there was going to be so many cattle, maybe the price would be favorable for buyers.

Ted would drive to Omaha from Livermore, and I would drive to Sioux City from Miller, South Dakota. I was to call

Paul, Mary Margaret, Dean and Nadine Robinson. My sister and her family.

him at 12 noon at a telephone in one of the livestock commission firms, and we would discuss the prices and kinds of cattle at each location. I called him and found that he had already bought several hundred cattle at a price much below our expectations. I told him I had found a like situation and had already committed myself to buy about a like number at prices I thought were considerably under the money.

Ted had an automatic mind and within minutes he had figured the amount of money to pay off, and we found we had spent considerable more money than we had made arrangements for. We quickly agreed that we would head to Livermore and sell cattle to somebody to stay within our financial agreement. We paid for the cattle and left shipping instructions at both locations.

We both arrived at Livermore a little before dark looking for buyers. My sister and her husband, Paul and Nadine Robinson, had a nice farm at Bradgate, Iowa. They had good yards that were empty. We sold them three carloads of Hereford heifers, which got us off the hook. We sold them for our exact cost, which was $3.30 per hundred weight, and they weighed 480 pounds — good quality, but thin.

These heifers did exceptionally well during the six months they owned them. They weighed 1,020 pounds when sold, and brought $10.50 per hundred weight, finished cattle price. They doubled their weight and more than tripled the price per pound. This gave Paul and Nadine a real boost in their farming and hog operation.

Following the sale to Paul and Nadine, I headed back to South Dakota, the country I was learning to love...

Chapter 13

Branching into Feeder Cattle in South Dakota

With the profits we had made in the pig business the previous year or two, Ted and I felt we could expand into the feeder cattle business in South Dakota.

In September 1933, South Dakota was still in the midst of a severe drought. The farmers had little chance of a feed crop, and many of them would have to sell their cattle.

My good friend Frank Reding and I drove up to the cattle country around Aberdeen, Leola, Ipswich, Eureka and Long Lake, South Dakota. These communities were complete mixtures of many nationalities.

Frank was a little older than I, maybe 22. He suffered from asthma, so he volunteered to go with me just to get out of the intense heat of Iowa. He would drive part of the time but asked for no pay. He weighed about 230 pounds and looked the part of a bodyguard, which I needed. It took a lot more money to buy a carload of cattle than it did to buy a carload of pigs. We had to carry a lot more cash to pay off. We divided the cash into five or six packages and hid them under the carpeting of the trunk and under the car seats. We hoped we could possibly avoid a hold-up that might take all the money.

Within a day, the word was out that a kid was buying cattle and paying cash — in full. The farmers got the word and looked me up. We went with them to look at their cattle. It seems that we bought nearly all the cattle that we looked at, on a dollars per head basis, delivered to the railroad stockyards at their nearest town. The cattle were counted and paid for then.

The cattle we bought were sold before they were unloaded. Over the phone, I would describe to Ted the different bunches of cattle and the cost. Ted was an artist at selling cattle, sight unseen, to customers in Iowa.

I always tried to buy the cattle at a low-risk, reasonable figure. Ted would sell them at cost, plus a decent profit. Volume was the name of our game!

The next year we branched out into the big cattle country, west, north and south of Pierre and Fort Pierre, South Dakota. Practically all the cattle shipped out of this area was by the Chicago Northwestern Railroad. I had regular shipping dates, where I would have a bunch of stock cars ordered so we could get special service to the corn belt.

I was fortunate to find a spotter, Earl Sonnenschein, who knew every road or trail every direction, north, south and west. He also knew all the ranchers by their first names. Earl was a rancher on the mouth of the Cheyenne River, which was about 25 miles from the Mission Ridge country. I always bought his cattle and he was on the drive each year. We were the same age and we became the very best of friends and have remained so all our lives. He went with me wherever I went in that whole West River country.

One day, when Earl and I were in Fort Pierre, we ran into Tom Berry, former governor of South Dakota. Earl knew him well, so he made us acquainted. Besides having been governor, he also was a prominent rancher at Belvidere, South

Earl Sonnenschein

Dakota, and ran a couple thousand cattle. He invited Earl and me into a little saloon in downtown Fort Pierre where we spent the afternoon visiting and getting better acquainted. He invited me down to his ranch to look at some big steers he wanted to sell. He was one of the most interesting and witty men I have ever met. This has got to rate as one of the most fantastic afternoons of my life. It was nice to meet a man of his calibre and be able to call him friend!

I developed a very good business with a lot of these ranchers year after year. All of the ranchers had the same operation They didn't sell any steers until they were from two to four-years-old. They also marketed their dry cows along with the steers. There were no young cattle sold. The ranchers liked to sell their cattle for so many dollars per head, delivered to the Fort Pierre railroad stockyards, usually around September 1st.

The entire group of ranchers in a given area would go together and drive their cattle to the railroad stockyards at Fort Pierre, which was a distance of 30 to 50 miles. They would slowly graze them into town, taking four or five days for the trip, and when they got to Fort Pierre, they looked

Clayton Jennings at the Ft. Pierre Railroad Stockyards.

better than when they left their home grounds. These big steers drove and trailed easily, somewhat like horses, with a slow even gait. The ranchers would have one chuckwagon and cook to feed the crew. The cowboys ate well and had an enjoyable trip, getting better acquainted with their neighbors.

It was quite a spectacle to see the total herd of cattle, 1,000 to 1,500 big steers, trailing into the stockyards. Everyone joined in to sort the cattle for ownership and I paid them on this count. They helped load the cattle on the railroad cars. Then I normally took everyone to downtown Ft. Pierre for

Memorial to Casey Tibbs, Ft. Pierre, South Dakota.

Livermore Stock Dealers Map Buying Campaign

Special to the Republican—

LIVERMORE— Jennings Brothers have decided upon a stock buying expedition in western Texas and Clayton, youngest member of that firm, left Livermore Wednesday where he will spend some time in that locality.

If prevailing conditions are found favorable in Texas the buyer expects to purchase approximately 2,500 head of stock cattle during the months of April and May.

Most of this number will be shipped into the western part of South Dakota and North Dakota where ranchers and cattle concerns have been forced during past seasons to dispose of their herds because of the scarcity of feed.

Clayton visited with many dealers and traveled through those territories and booked many orders for May delivery.

Beginning with the year of 1934 Jennings Brothers started buying cattle through the drouth stricken areas of the Dakotas and thousands of head have been shipped into Livermore where they have been cared for during the pasture season. Clayton spent the better part of last summer in those states, while Ted, other member of the firm handles the local territory and weekly shipping of hogs and cattle which mounted to around 300 car loads out of Livermore during the past year, these shipments going to commission firms and packing plants. There is considerable demand for cattle here due to the increased government seedings. It is the plan of Jennings brothers to ship into this territory again this spring twelve hundred head to supply this demand.

The record that Jennings Brothers, both young men graduates of the Livermore high school, have been outstanding in their line of work, has caused state wide attention due to the fact of their keen buying and selling talent. It was several years before Ted had finished his high school work that he was carrying on with this line of work before and after school hours and Saturdays.

They are sons of Mr. and Mrs. Charles Jennings who are wintering in California.

Clayton will meet George Wermerson of Miller, South Dakota, who is connected with a cattle firm of that place, and they will travel through Texas together.

Youthful Iowa Livestock Buyers Do Big Business

Jennings Brothers Started Early in Life.

(The Register's Iowa News Service.)

LIVERMORE — Two of north Iowa's largest livestock dealers also are believed to be the youngest.

The boys, Theodore and Clayton Jennings, 22 to 18, respectively, annually handle thousands of dollars of livestock. In the past month they have shipped a total of 103 carloads of cattle and hogs from Livermore and Bode.

Theodore stepped into the business at the age of 13 when his father's health failed.

Accompanied Father.

Business competitors and farmers soon learned they were dealing with no novice in the business for the boy had accompanied his father on buying expeditions for several years prior to that time.

The youthful stock buyer once purchased a shipment of livestock worth $12,000 in Humboldt county, and offered the farmer a check for that amount.

Before an astounded banker in an adjoining town would accept the deal as bona fide, he telephoned Livermore to find that the transaction was absolutely final and that the check written "by the kid" was "good as gold."

Basketball Player.

Both continued the business throughout their high school careers, buying stock before and after school hours. They also found time to participate in athletics and Clayton was a member of the Livermore team at the state basketball championship tournament.

The boys believe they have inherited a part of their business acumen in livestock buying. Their father, Charles Jennings, prior to his illness, had been buying livestock in Livermore and vicinity for many years.

An uncle, W. O. Jennings, was founder of the W. O. Jennings Co., a livestock commission firm in Chicago.

Brings Back A Train Load Of Feeder Cattle

LIVERMORE, Aug. 5—Clayton Jennings of the Jennings brothers stock firm here returned to Livermore Wednesday with a trainload of cattle, coming from Pierre, S. D., where he has been stationed since April.

The train left Pierre Tuesday at 6:30 a. m. and arrived at Livermore at 3:30 p. m. Wednesday. It was not necessary to unload and feed during transit.

The cattle were all unloaded here and part of them are already sold, and Jennings brothers expect to finish out the feeding of perhaps half the shipment and resell.

The cattle are not the ordinary class of feeders that come in for a resale but are big fat cattle, with a possible two weeks' fattening necessary.

Clayton Jennings, youngest member of this firm, has made an enviable record for himself as buyer, in view of his age. He and Ted, the older member, were both buying strong while they were still high school students here, working diligently after school hours and all day Saturday.

It was only recently that Clayton, who was at Miller, S. D., for a time buying and selling, took a trip by plane to Midland, Texas, on a buying expedition, shipping several hundred head of cattle into different parts of South Dakota.

The boys are the sons of Mr. and Mrs. Charles Jennings of this place, and nephews of Orin Jennings of the Jennings Livestock Commission company of Chicago.

Stock Dealers enroute to Texas

Clayton Jennings left here on February 3rd for western Texas in the interests of the Jennings Bros. livestock business. The main attraction is the stock cattle for the coming pasture season. If suitable conditions prevail the Jennings Bros. may handle 2500 Texas cattle during the months of April and May. Most of the cattle will be shipped into the range country of western So. Dakota and No. Dakota, where the Jennings Bros. bought several thousand head during the drought of 1934 and 1936.

Because of feed conditions, ranchers and cattle companies in those territories have sold cattle down to so close that the percentage of cattle now on hand is the smallest in many years. Last summer and fall the Jennings Bros. bought and shipped into northwest Iowa and terminal market centers approximately 7200 cattle from this territory, with Ted on the selling end here at Livermore and Clayton buying and shipping them in. A good per cent of the ranchers sold their entire herds last fall and must have replacement stock to be in the cattle business.

All this territory received late fall rains and now have snow ranging from 6 to 10 inches deep which will be sufficient moisture to start early grass. With a very bright outlook ahead for the cattle industry, ranchers are confident of a good grass crop and are anxious to stock up.

Clayton spent several days in So. Dakota in December contacting ranchers and dealers, and he has since received numerous inquiries and orders for May delivery.

a good steak and we looked forward to next year. I bought about the same ranchers' cattle for a number of years and I can't recall any instance in these cattle deals that either side was dissatisfied.

I was able to buy nearly all these ranchers' cattle so that I had a fair margin of profit. As a courtesy to them, I bought each rancher their choice of a Stetson hat or a pair of Justin boots from the Fischer Brothers Merchandise Store in Fort Pierre.

I bought a lot of cattle around the Mission Ridge area, which was about fifty miles northwest of Fort Pierre. This is the area where the Tibbs family homesteaded and raised their family. Among the Tibbs' boys was Casey, future World Champion Saddle Bronc rider. He was about ten or twelve when I met him and he participated in all the drives. He would gather up the unbroke horses and make the drive on a green two or three-year-old horse. He would have this green horse well broke by the time the trail drive got to town. He would then sell him to someone in the Fort Pierre area. After the first drive, I sent Casey down to Fischer Brothers Merchandise Store in Fort Pierre to pick out either a good Stetson hat or a pair of Justin boots. He picked a hat, which was the first he had ever owned. He swelled up like a toad and said the hat made him feel like a million dollars. The next year I bought him a pair of good boots, and he was overjoyed. Casey became a personal friend of mine over the years. Following Casey's many accomplishments on the rodeo circuit over the years was an inspiration.

Chapter 14

Brown Hotel

During the late 1930's, the Brown Hotel in Miller, South Dakota, was my home for several years. I made a deal with Frank Brown, the owner, for a monthy rate. I had a room at the back of the hotel where there was a door for easy access. It made no difference how dirty I might be from working livestock, I could come in the back door and not offend anyone. I had a telephone put in the room, so it was as handy as any place could be. It was my home and office.

My back room entrance was very convenient for customers who came to talk business. Of course, I had a great admiration for good looking gals, and they also enjoyed the convenience of my back room!

The Brown Hotel, Miller, South Dakota, Clayton's home when he first came to central South Dakota.

I met Jeanette, a girl a couple of years younger than I. She was a good looking girl in every respect with a blazing personality. She went with me quite often when I drove to the country, or sometimes we went to a movie together. Anyway, we became very fond of each other and shared most of our spare time.

One evening when we were driving around, we pulled up to the rear of the hotel and went to my room. After that it was quite regular that she would come to the back of the hotel. If the lights were on in my room, she would scratch on the screen and I would let her in without hesitation, as I knew who it was. In the fall, she left for college and I lost track of her.

Frank Brown kept a card table set up in the lobby at all times. Nearly every night some of the guys who stayed at the hotel would play cards. Most of the time we played Pitch. I became very well acquainted with one of the fellows. In fact we became very good friends. His name was Millard Scott, and he was working for the Rural Credit and was the salesman for all the land that had been turned back.

Millard was a very talented man, and I liked him. Off and on during the day, we would see each other, and he would tell me about the land he was trying to sell. Every day he would mention he would like to have me take a ride with him to show me some of the land that was for sale. I told him I didn't think I wanted to buy any land in South Dakota, but I would go with him all day or any part of a day, whatever fit his schedule. In a couple days we took the ride. All the while he told me that this was probably the greatest opportunity that anyone could have.

We drove about twenty miles south and five miles west of Miller. We came to a place called the Dolliver Ranch. Most of the fences were down flat, and the buildings hadn't been painted in years. The only good things about it were the well and the grass. I wasn't shocked, but it was hard to fathom the condition of the fences and buildings.

Millard explained everything as we went along. The potential was there, and anyone with an ounce of courage should buy it. The Federal Land Bank would finance it, and there would be no problem as far as any amount of money.

There were 1,200 acres, 840 acres of it was farmland. The price he would take was $4.00 per acre or $4,800.00, 20% down and equal payments for the next 20 years at 4% interest.

We drove through the middle of the ranch and on to the adjoining place, called the Erb Ranch. The fences and buildings were just as bad as the Dolliver Ranch, but the grass was good. The buildings were an old dilapidated house and one old sheepshed. This was a section (640 acres) and he could sell it for $3,000.00, or $4.68 an acre.

We kept talking as we drove along. Millard didn't put any pressure on me, but he felt that these ranches were an opportunity of a lifetime and never before had this kind of land sold for these prices since the pioneer days. The people who lost these ranches had been subjected to the most severe drought in the history of the state. They were victims of unprecedented circumstances.

There were two more sections of land that had gone back to Hand County — all really good grass, no farmland. He said it could be bought for $2.75 an acre.

We visited all the way home, and Millard completely convinced me that any or all of the land he had showed me was a buy that only happens in several lifetimes! He felt the drought would surrender, the grasshoppers would die off, and feed and crops would be bountiful once again. The value of the land would increase tenfold!

This was a startling experience for me. We had dinner together, and I thanked him for his kindness and consideration. We agreed to talk again the next day.

The Federal Land Bank had an office in Miller, and I went there the next morning. This was the first time I had met Charlie Gardner. Charlie verified the financial loan on the land and volunteered to loan me the money on the terms that Millard had quoted. Ted and I had made good money on cattle and pigs that we had bought and resold. I knew Ted was "game as hell" when it came to buying livestock. I called him in Livermore that evening and told him what I had run into. I described in detail each piece and that this land was all blocked together, but we could buy any or all of the three plots of land. I explained about the run-down condition of the buildings and fences. They looked like hell, but the soil and grass were very good. I went into detail about the financing and told him that it wouldn't take peanuts of our cash. We could borrow 80% with payments spread over 20 years at 4% interest, or could repay at any time. I told him it was an unbelievable circumstance.

Ted listened as long as I could talk. When it was his turn, he said, "There's not a hell of a lot to lose. Just buy it all. We have plenty of cash on hand in the bank so go ahead."

I saw Millard the next morning. It was very early, and he asked me to have breakfast with him. After breakfast, we went to his office in the Brown Hotel. We went over the deal, and it was exactly as I remembered it. I told him "We're going to buy it all." I'm sure he was shocked, as it took him several moments to get back his normal smile. That's the deal on our first land purchase in South Dakota.

God bless Charlie Gardner and the Rural Credit! It did start raining, and the grasshoppers died!

The year 1937 was the beginning of the Jennings Brothers' land purchases and sales in South Dakota.

Chapter 15

My Sheep Story

Now we needed a South Dakota banker to finance our ranch operation. We needed to hire a good ranch hand. Good ranch hands were easy to find in those days. Good men were looking for jobs.

I sat down with the president of the First National Bank of Miller, Art Cahalan. He recognized me, as I had bought a lot of livestock from his customers in the area. Otherwise, we were complete strangers. Art invited me into his sweatbox, as I called it, and he was very congenial. He knew that Ted and I had bought this land, and I told him we would like to finance some cattle and sheep to stock the ranch. He made a quick property statement and said he could finance me up to $50,000.00 at 6%. This loan could be for either cattle or sheep or both.

We got some second-hand machinery and equipment at a real bargain price. Nobody was buying machinery. Some were just walking off and leaving it behind.

That spring we planted a section (640 acres) to sooner milo, and 200 acres to spring wheat. It started raining soon after we had planted these crops. They grew into beautiful crops, as we had timely rains. The grasshoppers did come into the wheat fields just as we were ready to harvest, and they cut off 50% of the wheat heads. The wheat still averaged 18 bushels per acre. The grasshoppers didn't seem to bother the sooner milo, and it looked as good as any I had seen at any place or any time. I'm sure it would have made 100 bushels per acre. In September we received a heavy rain with lots of wind that broke the stocks off almost 100%, laying the milo on the ground. There was no way we could harvest it, except with some sheep.

I had a friend in San Angelo, Texas. I contacted him and told him what I thought we needed to have to feed up this field of milo. He knew where there were lots of sheep for sale and told me of a band of good white faced ewes, three and four-years-old, that he could buy for me. I had him verify a price on them, delivered to Miller, South Dakota, by rail. This fellow was an expert sheepman. He was completely honorable, and I was willing to have him ship them to me sight unseen.

Within two hours he called me back. He had a price on the 1,750 short but sharp-toothed ewes at $3.35 per head, laid into Miller. He could get them loaded within a week.

The sheep seemed priced under the money, but I was not one bit skeptical of the quality and condition of the ewes because he was representing them. I told him to ship them as soon as he could. They arrived in Miller about ten days later. We took them to the ranch and put them in a small pasture so they would get located. A few days later we turned them into the milo field and just hoped they would do really well on this heavy green milo. They located even better than we had hoped. We had an open winter, and the sheep did exceptionally well feeding entirely on the sooner milo and a little salt and mineral.

We bought a bunch of black-faced bucks (about 40) and turned them in with the ewes so we would lamb about the first of April. The bucks did their job of breeding and looked better when they came out of the breeding pen than when they went in. With this good feed all the sheep, grew an abnormal amount of wool. We contracted the wool for .28 cents per pound to be paid at shearing time.

To hold our risk down, we purchased 300 medium quality, light weight steer calves. They averaged 350 pounds, and the cost was a modest .08 cents a pound. We took these calves to the ranch about the first of October and turned them into the 200 acre wheat field that we had harvested. It had rained and the wheat, cut off by the grasshoppers, had germinated and grown a lush six inches tall. It was as thick as the hair on a dog's back! It afforded feed for these calves that was second to none. They were able to graze without supplement until the middle of December. Then we finished wintering them

Ewes with lambs at side.

on prairie hay, oats, salt and mineral, and they gained to the maximum.

When spring came and the grass greened up, the calves and the sheep were turned out to graze all summer. We had practically no death loss with the calves. We sold them around the first of September. They weighed 760 pounds and brought .09 cents a pound.

We took a gamble with the sheep. We lambed them all on the prairie. They had good, big, strong lambs, many twins and triplets, about 140% lamb crop. The weather was absolutely ideal, and we had practically no loss in winter or during lambing time.

Up to now, let's say, you don't have to be smart if you are lucky enough. We could have had the biggest shipwreck ever among the sheep men, if there had been a wet spring. It was a beautiful sight to see 1,750 ewes with 2,450 lambs at side.

By June it was getting late to shear and the sheep were getting maggots. A good sheep man saw them and told me we needed to get them sheared now!

I started looking for sheep shearers and a crew to castrate and dock (cut tails off short) the lambs. Our facilities to shear were about as lacking as you could find, as all we had was the old sheepshed that the shearers could work in. We did get organized in a couple of days. We made several make-shift pens out of tall woven wire and snow fence so we could sort the lambs from the ewes. We gathered the ewes and lambs and brought them to the make-shift pens. We sorted all the lambs off and corralled the ewes near the shearing shed. The crew knew they could castrate and dock all the lambs in one day. The shearers figured it would take a couple of days to get all the shearing done.

We planned an early start the next morning. We did get all the lambs castrated and docked by late afternoon. We had eight to ten helpers, who caught the lambs and set them up on the assembly line. One man docked the lambs and one castrated the males. We hired Bud Palon to do the castrating. He was an artist and a professional. One of the helpers would bring him a lamb, lay it on the castrating bench and Bud would cut off the bottom of the testicle sack, squeeze the two

Lambs sorted off and ready to be worked by the crew in the picture.

testicles out, grab them both with his teeth and pull them out. He was swift and precise.

About 5 o'clock that afternoon the weather changed. A big black cloud formed in the west, and it got cold. It started raining sheets of cold rain and continued until we decided we had only one choice. We had to turn all the ewes and lambs out on the prairie where they could stay clean and where they would dry out sooner after the rains stopped. We could then finish the shearing. Otherwise, if we left them in, the loss would be unbelievable. The ewes would trample the lambs in the mud.

It rained for several days, and the cold temperatures and rainfall were a record for that time of year. Each day we hoped it would quit so the ewes would dry off, and we could finish shearing.

We rode horseback through them during the day and into the night to keep them from piling up. The sheared ewes quickly started showing the effects of the cold and rain. They were suffering and standing humped up. They started dying off in bunches each day. As we rode through the sheep, we could hear the baby lambs bleat. It was the most pitiful sound ever. If you have ever heard a lamb bleat that was accidently or intentionally separated from its mama, you have experienced

Baa

the ultimate in the most pitiful sound ever. If you have an ounce of compassion you soon have tears and feel more humble than ever before. That bleat is something you can't get used to. The ewe has a somewhat similar blat but more businesslike and normal. Can you imagine me riding or walking through this mess of sheep? Everywhere I looked there were bleating lambs and blatting ewes. They scattered over two sections of prairie. It was more than I could handle so I talked with my foreman Jim McKown. I told him he would have to finish this fiasco. This all had humbled me so much that I was of no value or help to the crew. Waves of depression swept over me. I had never before experienced such a bewildering and helpless feeling. I cared not whether the world or I survived!

Jim McKown and the crew took over and completed this mess to the best possible conclusion. When it came to loyalty

I doubt if I have ever had a better hired hand. He was willing to work any kind of hours and in any kind of weather. Just being in his presence made you feel comfortable.

The bum lambs (ones whose mothers had died) either died or we gave them to the neighbors. We got the word out for anyone to come and get as many bum lambs as they could handle. We gave away hundreds! The balance of the ewes that hadn't been sheared and their lambs came through it all right.

After the rain, we drove by the north side of the sheep pasture. I said "I didn't know there were so damn many rocks in this pasture." Upon closer inspection, we found the white rocks to be dead sheep, both ewes and lambs. The prairie looked like white rocks showing after a prairie fire. Eventually, every sheared ewe (about eight hundred) died. We had two men with a team of horses and a hayrack picking up all the dead sheep every day. They piled them in a low slough area!

Had we started shearing a day earlier, we would have lost every ewe and every lamb. This sheep wipe-out would have been in the Guinness Book of World Records!

After the live sheep dried off, we finished shearing. We managed to have the wool off the 1,750 ewes (none of the unsheared sheep died) and it averaged nearly ten pounds per head at .28 cents per pound, which brought us $4,900.00.

Shearing crew in old barn on Erb Ranch.

After this escapade, we decided to get out of the sheep business. I found a fellow named Herman Steinlitner who wanted to buy some sheep. He was willing to buy them all at $6.00 per ewe and $6.00 per lamb, we sold him the 950 ewes and 1,750 lambs we had left, giving us a total of $16,700.00. The market had gone up and this was another bit of luck that helped this sheep deal!

We bought 1,750 sheep, we lost 1,750 sheep, owned them less than 8 months, and still made damn good money!!

The sheep and the calves were gone. I went in and paid off the First National Bank of Miller and had a good visit with Art Cahalan. He was amazed and pleased to see how well we had done, in spite of the near catastrophe we had with the death loss on the sheep.

Then I went to pay off the Federal Land Bank. Charlie Gardner seemed glad to see me. I told him that I wanted to pay off the land loan that I had with him. He said "Well, you don't have to pay the loan off this soon. You have nearly 18 years of term left." I could see he was trying to persuade me not to pay off the loan. I said, "Well, Charlie, I've just sold a bunch of sheep and cattle off the land, and my brother and I think we should pay it off." He said, "You have the privilege of paying it all off, if you wish to do so." He figured the amount due plus interest, and I wrote him a check on the First National Bank of Miller.

I remember his closing remarks to me as he said, "If you ever want to borrow more money on land, come see me." I told him I sure would as this deal had been very pleasant for me!

These calves and sheep made enough profit to more than pay for the land, twice over!

Chapter 16

Another Sheep Story

In 1938 Art Cahalan was president of the First National Bank of Miller and we started doing considerable business with him on our South Dakota ventures.

One day when I was in his office sweatbox, he said that he wanted to buy some yearling, coming two-year-old ewes for some of his customers. Each customer could handle from two hundred to five hundred to keep the weeds down on their premises and in the fields after harvest. The sheep had a potential of making them good money. He said he would furnish all the money if I would go buy them for him. He would pay me a nice commission. He said he would place them, but if I placed them it would be on an extra commission basis for

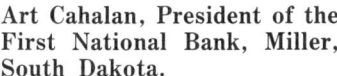

Art Cahalan, President of the First National Bank, Miller, South Dakota.

me. I knew there were a lot of sheep for sale in Montana and Wyoming. We agreed on the details and he gave me an envelope full of drafts to be drawn on the bank for the ewes I might buy. I agreed that I would call him every evening or during the day if necessary. I went home and packed my suitcase and headed for Wyoming, where I knew of several big sheep men.

I first went to Lander, Wyoming. I went into the bank and inquired about sheepmen who had ewes for sale. The banker was very cooperative as he had customers with sheep to sell. By going to the bank I avoided a finders fee, which amounts up in volume deals like this. The banker lined me up with a rancher who had two bands of yearling ewes. The rancher came to town and picked me up. He took me to his ranch and showed me some of the ewes, as many of them were still in the mountains, but I saw enough to satisfy myself. After considerable negotiation of price, I wound up buying the two bands of 1,000 ewes each for $9.00 per head to take in early October and delivered to the nearest railroad station. I issued him a draft on the First National Bank of Miller for $1.00 per head down payment with the balance due on delivery. He then took me back to Lander. I went north to Riverton and pulled in for the night. That evening I called my boss Art Cahalan to tell him what I had done. Art was always quick on the trigger. He said "That looks awful good. Try to find some more!"

The next morning I went through the same procedure, going to the bank and finding some ranchers with ewes for sale. These were better than the ones I had bought the day before. They had about 2,500 ewes that I could use, but they were sitting on $10.00 per head. I told them I had bought some yesterday, similar to theirs for $9.00. These people were really and truly top sheepmen and I knew I couldn't outsmart them, but I ran a little bluff as I was getting ready to leave. I told them I would split the difference which would figure $9.50 per head. They didn't come easy, but I sweat them and tried them in ever manner and finally they sold them to me at $9.50 with the same delivery instructions. They didn't know it but I would have given them $10.00 per head if they had set tight a little longer, as they had good sheep. I issued them a draft for $1.00 per head on the Miller bank. I then drove on up to Thermopolis, Wyoming, to stay all night. I called Art and told him what I had done. He was really pleased and said, "Find some more and get them bought. I can sure use more."

I used the same procedure with the same results the next day. I found two ranchers who ran together and each had 1,000 yearlings for sale. It was another tough negotiation as they were asking $10.00 and I didn't want to pay it. But finally we wound up at $9.50 with $1.00 per head down. I went on to Worland, Wyoming, to stay all night and give Art a call. I gave him all the information and he was really pleased, but I told him I doubted if I could buy any more of these yearlings for $9.00 or $9.50, because the trend of the sheep market was up and the ranchers were going to set on them if they didn't get $10.00 or more. Art told me to go ahead at $10.00 if the ewes were really good.

Again the same procedure the next morning, banker-to-rancher-to-me. I went out with a really nice rancher and bought 1,200 at $10.00. I had tried him at $9.75 but he gracefully thanked me as he turned me down. I went on to Sheridan, Wyoming, to stay the night and call Art. I told him of the 1,200 I had bought that day, and that I had one more ranch to stop at. Then I was heading home. I knew a superb sheepman who lived in Billings, Montana, but his ranch was at Ingomar, Montana. He was rated by all other men in the territory as a super deluxe sheepman. His name was Sonny Mogelson and I agreed to meet him at Hardin, Montana, at the Stockman's Cafe for breakfast the next morning.

When I arrived at the cafe, Sonny was already there. We had some breakfast and then took his vehicle to the sheep camp. He had a band of 2,500 Columbia sheep. These sheep are noted for their rapid growing lambs, heavy fleeces of medium wool, good size and vigor. They were the biggest and best sheep I had seen anywhere. He also had some ewes of a different breed like I had been buying, but I fell in love with these Columbia sheep. I wanted to buy this band of 2,500 in the worst way before I headed home. When I got into the price on them, he asked $12.00 per head. I told him I had bought several thousand good ewes in Wyoming for $9.00 or

$10.00 per head. He said, "Yes, I know, but those sheep couldn't carry water to mine!" We did a lot of looking and a lot of dickering. He was a really nice fellow, highly experienced in the sheep business, knowing it inside and out, having been a sheepman all his life. I tried every bit of psychology that I knew and so did he. We finally agreed on $11.00 per head. I knew it was time to head home, but especially so when he got me back to my car in Hardin and I counted up the sheep I had bought and they totaled 10,200 head. I knew it was time to get back to Miller. I didn't call Art that night, as I was afraid I had overbought.

The next morning before the bank opened Art let me in and we went into his sweatbox. This session is real fresh in my mind today. He got out a big yellow tablet and told me to read off the ranchers and numbers. I also recall he held a long yellow pencil with an eraser on one end. I gave him the names of the ranchers, numbers of ewes, price per head and the amount of down payments. It seemed like an everlasting time as I watched the sweatbeads come out on his forehead. The sweatbeads broke and ran down his cheeks. He used his big white handerchief to soak up the perspiration. He said not a word until he totaled up the sheep and down payments. He laid his pencil down and looked me in the eye and said, "Boy, did you need to buy all the sheep in Wyoming and Montana?" I had a hunch I had overshot the runway! But no complaint did he say. He did commission me to help sell some of the sheep. I agreed, but I would not accept any commission until we had the sheep all cleaned up.

I went to my room in the Brown Hotel and changed into my working clothes and started calling customers. The first customers to come see the sheep were Ray and Reg Baloun, two brothers living 25 miles north of Highmore. They liked the sheep when they saw them. I was aware they were tough buyers and they tried me in every way to take off from the asking price which was $15.00 per head. They finally agreed to my price and bought 500 ewes. They picked them out of 1,500 head, but there was no need to sort them as they were one like the other. We helped them put them through the chute to mouth, vaccinate and worm them.

Art called several of his farm clients and had them get in touch with me about the sheep and they did. I sold sheep every day and sometimes several times a day in large and small groups and all at our asking price of $15.00. It took us about thirty days to liquidate these sheep and it was smooth and pleasant. They made plenty of money and when it was all over Art gave me a commission check for $20,000.00. I had my own expenses on the buying trip of travel, room and meals. I don't know or do I want to know if Art got the net profit. I do know that his clients had a bonanza and made nothing but good money on these sheep. They were the best volume string of sheep to ever come into South Dakota.

I can say that Art Cahalan, for my money, was the quickest and gamest banker I ever worked with. He had a way of inspiring me to accomplish whatever the challenge might be.

Chapter 17

Restocking the Drought Areas

It was 1938 and the exodus of the livestock from the dry areas of the Dakotas and Wyoming had finally reversed. Suitable conditions prevailed. All this territory received late fall rains and winter snows, so there would be sufficient moisture for grass. There was considerable demand for cattle.

Because of the drought and feed conditions, many ranchers had sold their entire herds. Now they were in need of replacement stock to stay in the cattle business.

When I first came to Miller, South Dakota, on a cattle trip I met George Wermersen and his son Kenneth. George was an experienced and high-rated livestock man. He gave me much time and knowledge about South Dakota. He was easy to like and most sincere. We had a partnership that was a growing experience for me.

George and I decided to go to Alberta, Canada. We had heard there were large bunches of two and three-year-old steers for sale, weighing from 1,000 to 1,500 pounds. Our first stop was on the Milk River in Alberta. We bought a trainload of these steers to be driven to Browning, Montana, which was the port of entry and the railroad. Everything went well in all segments of this deal, until we had to pay the import costs which included an additional $1.50 per hundred to be placed in escrow in case the quota was full. We had very little chance of getting it back after time and red tape had dealt with us. Well we didn't get anything back. We had to pay the price.

We shipped these cattle to Hawarden, Iowa, and sold them right off the railroad cars to the feeders with very little negotiation. It afforded us a quick turnover and a neat profit in spite of the extra charge at the Canadian border.

We purchased thousands of cattle in Utah, Canada and Montana, but mostly from West Texas, around the Midland

LIVERMORE MEN CLOSE DEAL WITH THE FEDERAL GOV.

(Republican-Independent News Service)

LIVERMORE— Jennings brothers of this place have closed a deal with the federal government by selling them 500 head of yearling heifers to re-stock the Cheyenne Indian reservation.

Jennings brothers own more than a thousand head of cattle in the state of South Dakota at the present time.

Clayton Jennings, youngest member of the firm, chartered a plane at Miller, South Dakota, and flew to Midland, Texas, to buy the consignment that was sold to the government. They were shipped to Miller for distribution.

Jennings brothers are the sons of Mr. and Mrs. Charles Jennings of Livermore, and nephews of W. O. Jennings of the Jennings commission company of Chicago.

GO TO UTAH TO BUY CATTLE

Clayton Jennings returned home last Friday from a business trip in the Northwest. He was accompanied by G. W. Wermerson of Miller, South Dakota. They drove something over 5000 miles in Montana and Canada, buying a train load of cattle. The cattle were high quality feeders and were sold upon arrival in western Iowa.

Mr. Wermerson and Clayton Jennings left yesterday for Utah where they have made arrangements to meet several cattlemen and ranchers.

Cattle Return To Hyde County Ranges

MILLER, May 2—(Special)—Jenning Brothers of Livermore, Ia., are engaged in the movement of some 800 head of cattle into the pasture lands of Hand County.

The exodus of livestock during the dry seasons of 1932-34-36 has now been reversed and banks in this locality find financing profitable livestock operations an important part of their business and with the abundance of feed assured this year herds will be replenished.

Buffalo grass pastures in this vicinity produce approximately 10,000 pounds of beef per quarter section of land yearly with favorable moisture conditions.

Forty-Seven Cars.

Jennings brothers of this place who have been buying cattle in Texas are having a train load of forty-seven cars shipped to various points, including Livermore, Titonka, Swea City, Garner, Lakota and Miller, S. D. Eight cars reached Livermore Tuesday and will be sold to farmers desiring feeders.

Steer Yearling Shipments Begin Early Next Week

From 3,000 to 4,000 head of steer yearlings will be shipped from Midland and nearby points around May 1, recent purchases have indicated, although the number is much smaller due to the fact that most calves sold last fall were moved directly to Corn Belt and Panhandle feed pens.

Clayton Jennings of Miller, S. D., here for his third season, had bought up to today 550 head of steer yearlings from Mabee & Pyle, 400 from Roy Parks, 250 from Frank Cowden, 100 from Buck Kelton and 50 from Sherwood Foster, also approximately 1,000 head from ranchmen of the Big Spring and Sterling City areas. Part will shipped to pastures near Miller, S. D., and part to feed lots at Livermore, Iowa.

A. R. McIlray of Phillip, S. D., west of the river near the Black Hills region, has bought from 500 to 600 head of steer yearlings from the McElroy Ranch Co. He runs big steers, up to three year olds, on his pastures where there is strong grass for beef animals.

Clayton Jennings and C. W. Wermerson of South Dakota returned a few days ago from a 5,000-mile trip through Canada and Montana, where they had been on another stock buying trip. They shipped a train load of high grade feeders into western Iowa and found they sold so easily that they left Livermore again Wednesday for Utah to meet ranchers with intention of buying more cattle. Clayton is a member of the Jennings brothers firm here. Ted, the older member, left Livermore Thursday for Texas, where he will buy several thousand head of cattle to fill fall orders. Jennings brothers are outstanding buyers in the state of Iowa and have during the past few years shipped thousands of head of cattle in and out of the Dakotas. They are now reaching into many other states.

—Clayton Jennings left Livermore Monday for Pierre, S. Dakota, where he will meet and accompany three other young men on a trip to the west coast. They plan to combine business and pleasure. Jennings has business interests in Huron and Pierre, S. Dakota, and in Denver, Colorado; and plans to stop enroute. The boys plan to take in the Rose Bowl football game in Pasadena on Jan 2nd. They will return by the southern route and stop a few days in west Texas, where Jennings will contact several cattlemen and ranchers, and line up stockers and feeders for spring delivery.

Midland Yearlings Bought By Iowans

MIDLAND, Feb. 19.—(AC)—Several loads of steer yearlings were bought here this week for early spring delivery by Wermersen and Jennings, cattle firm with ranches in Iowa and South Dakota.

They bought 1,500 head from Proctor and Faskin, 100 head from C. P. Bennett, 150 head from Pete Wheeler of Odessa, 150 head from Jack and C. W. Edwards of Monahans, and 50 head of two-year-old steers from Ratliff and Hurt of Odessa. The steers will be divided equally between their Iowa and South Dakota pastures.

Sell Cattle.

Clayton Jennings and Thomas Johnson returned Monday from South Dakota where they have been selling and distributing cattle purchased earlier in the season in Texas.

The 1700 head that Jennings brothers pastured here during the summer have now been sold.

Jennings and Johnson have been gone about six weeks. They expect to return to the Dakotas for a short time to finish some sales and then will return here for the winter months.

Clayton Jennings was accompanied by his brother-in-law Paul Robinson when the two drove to Miller, S. D., in the interest of cattle buying recently. Jennings went by plane from Miller to Midland, Texas, on another stock buying expedition.

Wemersen & Jennings, members of a cattle firm of Miller, S. D., and Livermore, Ia., are here today looking for more cattle as result of heavy rains in that section. They recently shipped from Midland and vicinity 53 cars of cattle, mostly steer yearlings, which they had bought from various ranchmen.

Jennings brothers, stock shippers, have begun their hauling of cattle into western Iowa and South Dakota by truck, with six trucks leaving Livermore the first of the week. The firm have brought cattle in large numbers in Texas to replace the drouth stricken area in South Dakota and Iowa.

Mr. and Mrs. Charles Jennings who have been wintering in the south and California have returned to their home here having spent an enjoyable time.

Clayton Jennings of Livermore, Iowa, bought to be shipped to South Dakota pastures about May 1, the following: 250 steer and heifer calves from Frank Cowden, Midland; 558 steer calves from Mabee & Pyle, Midland; 385 steer and heifer calves from Coahoma ranchers, and 100 head of steer and heifer calves from Buck Kelton, Crane.

Clayton Jennings, younger member of the Jennings brothers stock firm here, will return this week from Texas, where he is in the interest of shipping cattle into South Dakota and western Iowa. Different members of the firm have made several trips into Texas during the past few months and have purchased more than 3,000 head of cattle. Leonard Tuttle, who accompanied them, has also returned to his home here.

area. These ranchers had good cattle. With lots of money from oil, they up-graded their cattle each year by buying the best bulls on the market.

One particular deal Ted and I had was with the federal government. We were to furnish 500 head of yearling Hereford heifers to restock the Cheyenne Indians herd on the Wind River Reservation in Wyoming.

I chartered a plane at Miller and flew to Midland, Texas, and bought choice and of one brand, the best set of Hereford heifers ever shipped into Wyoming for the Cheyenne Indians. They were good and they were big. They proved their worth by becoming one of the best sets of producing cows in the state of Wyoming!

Chapter 18

Miller Livestock Auction Company

In early 1939 the City of Miller realized the need for a livestock sales pavilion to bring buyers and sellers together. Sellers were going to Redfield and Huron as they already had sales pavilions. This was to be a community project. The city donated the land and some money was raised by subscription. The old sales pavilion at St. Lawrence was purchased and moved to Miller.

In July 1939, J. M. Magness and I presented a proposal to the committee to buy the pavilion, which was not ready for a sale yet. Jim was a professional auctioneer and he and I were good friends. The committee accepted our proposal and we were in business. Times were tough, real tough, but we felt this was a great opportunity.

Miller Livestock Auction Company 1939.

We held the first sale on Wednesday, July 20, 1939, at the Miller Livestock Auction Company. The initial sale was a boomer with 1,000 cattle, 1,000 sheep, 300 hogs and a carload of horses. It was a $50,000 sale.

We could see that this salebarn had a chance to be one of the best ever. We needed more pens for the livestock we knew were headed our way. We immediately hauled many loads of pitch pine posts (10 and 12 feet) and many two inch planks from the Black Hills. We continued each week to build more pens.

We were operating on a shoestring from sale to sale and it was necessary for us to have accounts in two banks—probably you would call it "check kiting" but we skimmed by somehow. I'm sure both banks gave us the benefit of the doubt and helped us all they could. I recall Magness and I had a mutual friend in Miles City, Montana who was well healed and on several occasions he would mail us a check and we would send him one right back after the sale. Our bookkeeper, Bud Palon, was a genius in moving money. The sale prospered each week and finally this tight money situation eased.

The Chicago and Northwestern Railroad made available fast freight service for the movement of livestock on Thursdays.

Bud Palon—bookkeeper and utility man for livestock operations.

Miller Livestock Auction Company
Miller, South Dakota

Phone 110

Date: Sept. 13, 1939

Owner: G. L. Dennis

Sale Every Wednesday

Pen No.	No. Head	Weight	Price	Total
10	3 blk cows	850	6.55	55.68
21	16 Red N.F. strs	10825	8.20	887.65
21	5 Red N.F. strs	3960	8.00	300.80
34	1 red spot str	720	7.10	51.12
34	1 red spot hfr	700	7.65	53.55
34	3 hol. hfrs	1735	6.80	117.98
34	5 Red N.F. strs	3010	7.95	239.30
34	1 red str	670	7.45	49.92
34	1 red spot hfr	700	7.10	49.70
34	1 Red N.F. hfr	610	7.10	43.31
34	2 Red N.F. hfrs	1430	6.65	95.10
	3 hogs	25,010		1944.11
	36 cattle	Less Exp.		51.03
				.08

Commission ... 34.02

Total ... 1893

Freight ... ✓
Feed ✓ yd ... 10.80
Inspection ... 1.86
Ins. ... .75
Brand Insp ... 3.60
_____
51.03

September 13, 1939 Account of Sales.

25010
860
2616

Connections with the train were to be made at Huron on each Thursday afternoon, this would speed the movement of livestock to the cornbelt.

This salebarn was acknowledged by the livestock industry as the newest and best in the state of South Dakota. The sale barn was first in volume in the state and among the top ten in volume in the nation for many years.

During 1942, 34,000 cattle, 779 horses, 13,400 hogs and 33,400 sheep went under the auctioneer's hammer in this ring. During that year it did a $3,178,000.00 business. In 1941, the gross business amounted to $2,075,000.00 and in 1940 $1,200,000.00.

About 70 per cent of the livestock brought into the sale barn was made up of locally grown sheep, hogs, horses and cattle. It was estimated that about 30 per cent of the feeder and stocker animals went back to local farms.

In 1941 Ted moved his family to Miller from Iowa. He took my place in the sale barn business and the ranching operation while I was in the Navy.

My sister Nadine and her family also moved to Miller. Nadine worked in the sale barn office and very faithfully kept me informed about what was happening in the livestock business by sending me a recap of every sale. She also sent me all the other news of the area. I looked forward to her letters at each mail call.

When I returned from the service, Ted and I bought considerable more land. The sale barn continued to flourish and consumed all of our time. We had the desire to put more time into our ranching operation, so we sold our interest in the sale barn to Kenneth and Pete Knapp for a nice profit.

The facilities have been greatly improved and expanded over the years. It has been a successful livestock auction and is still rated among the good sales of the area. It has changed hands several times. The present owner is Jay Anderberg.

Chapter 19

Frazier Vs. Jennings

Charlie Frazier was a tall, dark, handsome man about fifty years old. He stood six feet with a stocky build and weighed no less than 250 pounds. He had an admirable physique, except for a quite prominent midriff. His belly protruded to a complete hangover of his over-sized belt buckle. Charlie was a highly successful cattleman, who owned and operated two ranches in the Fort Pierre area where he raised choice quality Hereford cattle. He was acknowledged as a high-powered salesman of his cattle. It was not unusual for him to sell them for a premium price and higher than any other rancher with the same quality of cattle. He also raised a lot of really good horses, both quarter horses and Belgian draft horses.

Charlie had the respect of many for being a highly successful cattleman but others detested his boldness and disregard for a deal made with a handshake, which on several occasions was questionable and doubtful, and yet he was a big name in the territory.

Charlie possessed a commanding personality and no one could call him cheap. He was a booster and contributor of the area rodeos. He was a big spender in the bars and was known to buy rounds of drinks for the house. He also was a heavy drinker, which led to numerous fist fights in the past. He would create a fight over nothing. He just liked to fight. He was known as a bully. Many feared him and avoided him. Without a doubt, he was one tough hombre!

Late one summer afternoon in 1938, Earl Sonnenschein and I drifted into the Hop Scotch Bar in Fort Pierre to check the atmosphere. Soon Charlie Frazier came in and stood next to me at the bar. We had a pleasant conversation. He asked me if I would buy 700 three-year-old Hereford steers with delivery in about a month, which would be around September 1st. I told him I would buy them if the price was right. He priced the steers higher than I could pay, but after another drink, I bid him $10 per head less than his asking price. We negotiated terms of delivery and sort back, and I thought I had bought them. But quickly and firmly he said he was not going to sell them to me. So that was it, no handshake, no deal what-so-ever.

The next week the cattle market went down severely every day, and I was happy that Charlie did not sell these 700 steers to me. With the down market they would have been at least $20.00 per head too high for a loss of about $14,000.00.

Charlie found me about a week after our first negotiation on his steers. He said he would sell me the steers at the price I had offered him. I told him it was a week later and a new deal, and besides the market was down at least $2.00 per hundred weight or about $24.00 per head. If he wanted to start a new deal on today's market, I was ready. He became loud and boisterous and said he thought my word was good and that I was backing out on the cattle deal. Enough was said, and we parted with severe ill feelings.

Saturday night after the bars had closed, everyone congregated at the Tumble Inn, a popular hangout to eat and meet people after hours. This place had a row of booths on each side (about ten booths each holding four people). There was an open space in the center of the room of about twenty by thirty feet. I was seated in a center booth with my friends, Earl Sonnenschein and his girl friend Bertha and my girl friend Lorene. Earl and I were seated on the outside seats of the booth. The place was full.

Charlie Frazier and two of his ranch hands came in and strolled to a far corner of the open room. My adrenalin started to flow immediately. I could see that Charlie had been drinking heavily. I sensed that I was going to have some kind of trouble with him. I was never known as a fighter, but I had been called "a lover." I didn't want to fight anyone unless I had to defend myself against Frazier. I knew that the only advantage I had was the quickness of my hands and feet. I was in near perfect condition and had lots of wind. I knew I didn't dare let him hit me squarely on the head or the show would be over. If I allowed him to get hold of me, he would twist me around until I looked like a pretzel. If he got my feet off the ground he would have walked out the door and dragged me through the gutter. Frazier weighed 250 and Jennings 135, a complete miss-match.

I watched him come across the floor toward me. I could see he meant business and my adrenalin struck me full force. He came directly to me, and I shall always remember his words. Loud and clear he said, "You are just like an old sow, you piss out behind." As soon as he said these words, he grabbed me by the neck. Instinctively I jerked loose from his grasp and jumped up and got my feet on the seat of the booth and threw a right hand that caught him on the temple or eye. It staggered him backwards a step or two. Then I jumped up on the top of the table and leaped out on the floor keeping my feet under me. The fight was on! I seemed to have no fear, why I don't know. I was aware that I had to duck his punches and dance him to death in a manner like Cassius Clay (Mohammed Ali) did to so many so called fighters. I could see that he had a little trickle of blood dripping from his temple and eye from the first punch. Frazier came after me. I threw a left and a right and caught him squarely on the head. I could see that I could easily hit him, but I knew that I dare not let him hit me solidly. I started my dancing and went to both sides, and when I caught him open, I would throw two-handed right and left and seldom missed his head. He was really easy to hit. Blood started and with lots of rights and lefts he soon was a massive mess of blood all over his face and shirt. I remained cautious and kept respect for his punches. He kept coming after me and delivered numerous wild swings and punches that I ducked or side danced. Then I remembered his prominent midriff or belly. I decided to work on that as it was easy to hit. Maybe I could eliminate his wind by punching his belly. I gave him the one-two punch many times and it felt like I was punching a giant marshmallow. My rights and lefts beat a rapid tattoo to his belly. It appeared that he couldn't see because of the massive amount of blood. He would try to wipe it off with his sleeve or arm. He kept coming forward, and my punches in the belly were telling on him. He was losing his stamina and wind.

All of a sudden the two hired hands who had come with Frazier walked out on the floor and each took an arm and led him out the front door without resistance. Word had it that he didn't come out of his house for a week because of his eyes.

All the people in the Tumble Inn had a ringside view as good as any seats in Madison Square Garden. I ended up with skinned up hands from punches to his fancy engraved belt buckle. This episode was all pure luck for me. Had not Charlie been drinking so heavily, he would have eaten me alive in short order!

Chapter 20

Diamond A Cattle Company

In the summer of 1940 I was in the territory around Faith and Eagle Butte, South Dakota, buying cattle. I usually stayed in Faith at the West Hotel. I'll always remember the unusual wooden plank sidewalk around the hotel. One evening while in the hotel bar I ran into Nels Babcock. Nels had just been made foreman of the Diamond A Cattle Company at Eagle Butte. The Diamond A Cattle Company was owned by Captain C. A. Mossman of Wagon Mound, New Mexico, and Eagle Butte, South Dakota. I had bought cattle off the ranches all around their holdings of 500,000 acres on the Cheyenne River Indian Reservation. They ran so many cattle that there were too many to count! When the drought of the 30's hit they had over 14,000 cattle on the ranch. I had a deep desire to find someone who would sell me some of the Diamond A cattle. That brand alone was probably recognized and known foremost in the cattle business.

Nels Babcock and I got to visiting about the cattle business, and what and when they were going to sell. He told me they

Nels Babcock showing off his new chaps he got for Christmas.

wanted to sell the steer and heifer calves off the three-year-old heifers, so the heifers could get back into shape for the winter. I told him I was interested in looking at them. He said he would pick me up first thing the next morning. We would use his pickup to look at the cattle as there are very few rocks on the prairie in that part of the country. It would take most of the day to have a good look. I liked this Nels Babcock almost as soon as I met him. I knew from visiting with him that I was with a high-class gentleman, no sign of an hombre in him. I also felt he was sharp and knew the cattle business.

The next morning early we had breakfast together, with each trying to analyze the other. We started out even and had a shot at each other when we looked at the cattle. By the time we got to the area where the three-year-old heifers were I had opened no less than ten gates. The heifers and their calves were scattered over a vast area. We had a good look at them because they were not bunched. The heifers and their calves were absolutely beautiful. As we rode along I kept telling myself I was going to buy these calves, if he was anywhere near my figure. The calves were so uniform in size and quality that I would not have needed to see them all, but we did. We had probably seen about half the calves when we started to talk about delivery time, sort and price. I knew I had to use some real psychology to make this deal and stay on the right side of the ledger. He mentioned he wanted to sell these calves by the head and he would drive them to the Mossman Yards, which were at the north end of the ranch near the small town of Parade, where I would receive and load the calves out on the Milwaukee Railroad.

I felt the time was right and I said to Nels "We've talked over all the details of this cattle deal and we have agreed on that. Now I need to know how many dollars per head you want!" All along I kept making favorable comments about the calves and heifers and each time he gave me a little smile. In a firm voice he said, "Clayton, I want $40.00 a head for the calves with a good down payment." I took about three breaths before I answered him. I told Nels he was in my ballpark and I would like to look at the rest of his cattle. He seemed pleased that I said that. We rode and rode and rode some more and I'm sure we didn't see them all, but we saw most of them. When we were headed back to Faith and I had opened and closed the last gate, I asked him how much down payment he wanted. He told me he would like $5.00 a head and I said "Nels, we've made a deal!" When we got back to Faith we negotiated details, made a contract and set a date for delivery for October 1st. I gave him a check for $3,700.00 as he thought there would be around 740 steer and heifer calves. I felt that I had bought a great bunch of calves at a favorable price as Ted and I already had buyers for all the calves in this bunch.

Nels talked with Cap Mossman and told him he had sold the steer and heifer calves off the three-year-old heifers to Clayton Jennings of Miller, South Dakota. Cap Mossman immediately asked where the calves would be going and Nels told him that I had said some would be going to Miller and the balance to Iowa. Cap Mossman said he wanted his brand to go out of state. They telegraphed back and forth several times (there was almost no phone service in that part of the state). Nels advised me of a meeting in Pierre. I said I would be there. The meeting consisted of Nels, his attorney Mr. Martin, his banker and me. They had the contract there. We sat around a table and the attorney expressed Cap Mossman's wish and the banker verified it and Nels said "There's the contract." After we had all talked about this deal and the contract, the banker counted out $3,700.00 cash for me to cancel the contract and asked if that was okay with me! The banker and the attorney were working for Cap Mossman's interest and I'm sure that Nels Babcock was working for what he thought was fair and right. In my deal through Nels nothing was ever mentioned in the contract or verbally about the brand on the calves going out of state. I took a good breath and said that I had bought these calves in good faith. I had them sold and customers were depending on me, so there was no way I could justify releasing these calves and I was going to stand my ground.

The three of them wanted a short recess and left me sitting all alone. They came back within five minutes and said the contract would be honored. The banker picked up the $3,700.00 and as they left there was not a frown or an insult.

Mossman Yards—1993.

In fact they each had a small smile on their faces. Nels and I had a really good down to earth visit and he indicated he was really proud of me for standing my ground!

Nels and I were both ready to ship on the contract date. He delivered the calves to the Mossman Yards as I knew he would. They were driven in without being spooked. We sorted the calves from the heifers slow and easy. When we got through we wound up with 746 head and they were immaculate. Before we loaded the calves on the railroad cars we weighed some of them on the scale at the Mossman Yards. They weighed 427 pounds and at $40.00 per head that made them cost $9.36 cwt, which puts this deal among my financial best of my cattle deals to date.

Chapter 21

Against the Wall

During the early 1940s Ted and I were contracting yearling cattle around the Midland, Odessa, Monahan and Big Springs, Texas areas. We had contracted two trainloads of these cattle weighing around six hundred pounds with delivery of them within thirty days. The market went on a sharp down, and nobody wanted to buy cattle as they feared the market would continue to go down. For the first time in our dealings we could not find any buyers. We were borrowed heavy at the bank, about to the limit. What were we going to do?

In our business Ted had certain customers who preferred to deal with him and others preferred to deal with me. Louis Dinklage of Wisner, Nebraska, was one of these customers. Ted had sold him many truckloads and trainloads of cattle the past few years. He was among the very best cattle feeders

Loius Dinklage

in the business. It was not unusual for him to have 50,000 cattle on feed at one time. During the 50's and 60's he was thought to be the biggest cattle feeder in the country. He was a legend in his business and will be remembered forever in that territory. He was always civic-minded and founded the Wisner Improvement Corporation to help the people of his home town of Wisner. He was the kind of fellow whose word was gold. He either believed in you totally or he wouldn't have anything to do with you. I enjoyed meeting Louis every year for ten to fifteen years at the National Western Stock Show in Denver. We both stayed at the Cosmopolitan Hotel and I think we both looked forward to a good visit.

Ted always did business with Louis over the phone, and it was as good as any handshake. They usually talked twice a week. Louis had the uncanny ability to know the future trend of the market and he was right most of the time. He said he wasn't afraid of this down market. He could use some thousand pound steers, just like the ones Ted had sent him recently from the Ft. Pierre area. Ted opened up then and told Louis about the two trainloads of six hundred pound yearlings that we had contracted in Texas. Ted told him we were going to be in a financial pinch until we could get some of these cattle sold. Louis took over the conversation. He had the picture in his mind. "How much do you need, Ted?" he said. Ted said, "Until I get some more cattle sold, it will take about a million dollars." Louis said he would have the check in the mail the next morning.

Louis told Ted he would prefer not to have yearling cattle, but to help us out he would take one trainload of the yearlings we had contracted. Later we could get him enough thousand pound cattle for the balance of the money. This got us out of a potential financial disaster and he seemed pleased that he could help us out.

The market turned around somewhat and there was some activity on the yearling cattle. We got over a trainload of them sold. We shipped Louis the balance of the yearlings and a string of thousand pound steers to amount to $1,000,000.00. Let me say that it was a distinct honor to know a man of his calibre. Ted and I will always be grateful for a friend like Louis Dinklage!

Chapter 22

Navy Days

The world situation was becoming highly volatile. Japan had joined forces with Germany and Italy. The United States had moved from neutrality to a state of preparation by expanding our armed forces, building defense plants, and giving aid to European Allies. In September 1940, we had enacted the Selective Service Act and the armed forces began building for the inevitable. The Pacific Fleet (San Deigo, San Francisco & Seattle) were moved to Pearl Harbor.

Clayton Jennings—1942.

It was quite evident that I would be drafted into the service. In March 1941 we decided that Ted would move his family from Livermore to Miller to take over my interest in the Miller Sale Barn and my ranching interests.

Then the inevitable happened. The Japanese bombed Pearl Harbor on December 7, 1941. The next day the United States declared war on Japan.

It was April 1942, and instead of waiting to be drafted, several of my friends and I decided to enlist in the Navy. We were all accepted and left from Miller on the train. We arrived in Omaha, Nebraska, where we were inducted into the Navy. From Omaha we took another train to San Diego, California. We arrived in San Diego and were taken to the naval air station, where we would go through an indoctrination period (boot camp) for about six weeks. They put us through the standard procedure for all new recruits. We all got G. I. haircuts. Our heads were practically shaved. It was real shocking to go back to our barracks and look at ourselves in the mirror. It seemed as though the way we were treated the first ten days, they were intentionally trying to humiliate and embarrass us. They sure as hell did!

Every day we had roll call, which was a must to attend, plus other meetings that had been listed on the bulletin board. After the first ten days, we started a routine of marching in unison for miles. Then we went to the firing range to practice all calibre small arms. They made it quite clear we had better practice because where most of us were going, we would have to defend ourselves. That didn't scare any of us, because we wanted to get out where something was going on!

At boot camp an annual contest was held for all naval personnel. It was a "hand-over-hand" tight rope over and down a twenty-foot solid plank bulkhead. There was a strong rope, similar to a hay rope, that hung down from both sides and fastened on top. You were timed from the time you had hands on the rope until you scaled the wall and went down the other side to the ground. You could hand-over-hand all the way or use your feet against the plank. It so happened that I won the contest in San Diego with the best time, including all other naval camps in America! My best time was 8½ seconds. The next closest was 11 seconds, and some couldn't make it at all.

I only weighed 135 pounds and had extra bi-cep and shoulder muscles that I give credit to my days in Iowa when I was working on construction crews in the summers.

After boot camp, several from my company put a preference in for aviation ordinance school in Seattle. We were given a series of aptitude tests, and if our qualifications were high enough, we could go to a school. There were only six out of our company that got this school, and I was one of the lucky ones. They expected me to come out of this school of four months as a specialist in all phases of naval aviation ordinance. This included rifles, machine guns, bombs and torpedoes.

I arrived at the beautiful Seattle Naval Air Station on May 23, 1942. The accommodations were adequate. School started the next day. The ordinance instructors were very professional, and the study consisted strictly of aircraft armament including machine guns, torpedoes, bombs, depth charges, small arms and ammunition and accessories in connection with them. This was truly an inspiring experience and time went by fast. One of our specialities was the 50 calibre machine gun, and believe me when I say there were a lot of parts

New Paris Inn, San Diego, California. L to r: Hoot Moncur, ?, ?, Kay, Clayton Jennings, Clyde Helspar and Mac Jones—during boot camp at San Diego.

Ted and Polly Jennings, Mom and Dad Jennings, Duff and Margaret Howard, Paul and Nadine Robinson. Mary Margaret and Dean Robinson. Clayton Jennings holding Ronnie Jennings and Jerry Howard, when Clayton was home on leave from Seattle, 1942. Last time Clayton saw his Dad alive.

in that gun! We had to be able to name each part by sight and know its purpose and function. On the first day our instructor brought out one of those guns and laid it on the table. He told us what he expected from everyone of us, when we had completed this class. We would have to be able to take it down and put it back together again—blind-folded. And we did!

We went through a real test of bombs and detonators. We went through the torpedoes and lesser explosives. I passed the test and became a specialist in August 1942 and was transferred to Port Hueneme, California shipping docks. We were to participate in the loading of a freighter and then ride overseas on this freighter to the war zone, the Solomon Islands in the South Pacific.

At Port Hueneme, we went to work with the ship's crew. We could immediately see what would be on the ship—bombs of various sizes and aviation gasoline! We loaded all the lower deck compartments with bombs, torpedoes and aviation gasoline to within a foot of the top deck. Within two days, we had the ship fully loaded, and we took off for the Solomon Islands.

We got about five to eight miles out to sea when we ran into swells. The ship listed from one side to the other and the front to back. It rolled and tossed much more because of the heavy load it was carrying. It seemed that all of us amateurs, who had never been on a ship before, got seasick, and that is a sickness that you can never forget. It is a sickness that will make you want to die, but you can't quite do it.

I was on the upper deck when I felt this horrible sickness, and I started vomiting profusely. I headed for the latrine. It was a big area. The floor was nearly covered with sick sailors, lying flat on their backs or on their stomachs, vomiting and groaning and moaning. The floor was saturated with vomit, and it was a sight the likes of which I had never seen. The odor was indescribable—it was terrible, bad, horrible! I wasn't as sick as I thought after seeing this mess. I returned to the top deck and vomited what little I had left into the Pacific Ocean.

We had very little work on this ship, so we spent our time looking at the ocean on all sides. We didn't see land for 28 days. Let me say, this was the most monotonous con-

Chris Williams and Clayton Jennings on bombs on the island of New Georgia.

Clayton Jennings the third from the right—standing in front of the crane used to load the bombs on the plane on the island of New Georgia.

Chris Williams of Houston, Texas and Clayton Jennings in front of one of the bombers on the island of New Georgia.

tinuation of seeing nothing but water that I can recall. Finally we saw land. Everyone started smiling, laughing and making jokes. This was New Caledonia, an island in the South Pacific. We stopped to refuel, and after a day and a night we pulled out and headed for Guadalcanal. We never did get to go ashore.

We arrived at Guadalcanal under the cover of darkness. We had four kamikaze planes on suicide missions attack us. Our machine guns and 90 millimeter guns crippled them before they could reach us as a target. They all dropped into the Pacific Ocean. I happened to be a gunner on a 90 millimeter gun, and I would like to think that I shot one of them down — but there was no way of telling "who hit what!"

At this time Guadalcanal was about the hottest spot in the war zone and our ship was unloaded there. We were going to stage a new front on the island of New Georgia, a small island were the only occupants were natives and coconut trees. We were to leave at dusk and arrive there before daylight. We rode in LSTs (landing ship tanks) along the shoreline of several islands so the Japanese couldn't detect us as we made our way to New Georgia.

We took a battalion of Marines on the front, followed closely with a battalion of Seabees, then our Navy cooks and Naval aviation personnel. The Marines were to land and take control of the island and the Seabees were to immediately build an airstrip. It meant tearing down all the trees in the strip area, and dozing off and leveling and packing the coral, which made one of the best air strips known to man. The Seabees worked twenty-four hours a day and built the finest aircraft runways that I know of. They had a multitude of dozers, scrapers and packers. When the strip was ready, the operational planes would fly in, and everybody was in business.

I was in charge of one crew, and we immediately serviced their planes with machine guns or bombs or both. The weather permitting, they made at least one flight, and sometimes two, to find and destroy the enemy. Everything seemed to fall into place, and our pilots were getting a good many kills on the enemy and our losses were small in comparison.

One sad day I can well remember and visualize was when we sent out one wing of four planes and only one plane returned. The returning pilot told us as best he could what had happened. Our planes ran into a hornets nest of Japanese fighters and were over-matched in numbers and the three went down in the ocean.

While on New Georgia we became short of some aviation ordinance supplies and I volunteered to fly down to Guadalcanal to get them. As I was going down the muddy strip headed for the supply base, I saw someone coming my way who looked familiar. I couldn't believe my eyes, it was Bob Gard from Miller, South Dakota. We were both real happy to see someone from home. We spent a couple short hours visiting before I had to fly back to New Georgia.

We had been issued tents for crews of six men per tent. We were told to dig foxholes in the jungle, large enough for the six men. They had to be deep enough to cover the top with at least two feet of dirt and the men still be able to sit on the seats fashioned on the side of the foxhole. We could be in the foxholes from one to three hours. Everyone had been issued a good sharp spade and shovel. We religiously dug the foxholes.

Starting that first night, the Japs raided us with planes that sounded like an old gas washing machine. From the very start, we nick-named them "Washing Machine Charlie."

Nearly every night for the next month or two, the Japs raided us at 2 o'clock. You could set your watch by it.

We also endured a few heavy daytime raids. Everybody headed for the foxhole when the alarm went off. We usually had time—sometimes just barely. They would start stringing the bombs about a mile away. The next one would be closer, and you felt that the next one would be right on target. That would be total destruction to the foxhole and everyone in it! But it missed and fell on the other side of us. Then we gave a sigh of relief as they had missed us again!

The Navy sent more planes to us, and we were able to overcome the Japanese until we had our island under control. Then the Navy staged another landing on the little island of Emirau. Most of our crews went in LSTs, and we went through the same procedure as on New Georgia.

Following is a letter that I wrote home from the South Pacific:

Dear Folks:

Well, the evening sun has gone down, so we are all clustered around in groups doing various things. Each day that goes by is a slight consolation that we are one day closer to the end of the war and back to the United States, and friends and the ones we love. We'll have a much better and finer conception of life's appreciation for the American way of life and all privileges and comforts that are ours. This has been and will be an experience far beyond my previous imagination, and to those with whom fate is not too unkind it will be well worth the price paid. I am writing this letter by the light of a coconut lamp, which we fashioned from a coconut with the husks on. We cut the bottom off so it will set level on a bench; then cut the top off level, until we contact the shell of the coconut proper; then we drill holes in the shell and let the milk out, fill the coconut with fuel oil and insert a piece of clothes line rope in the hole, light it, and we have primitive and crude lamps, but it does work. We have two or three such lamps in our tent.

> Somewhere in the South Pacific
> Where the sun is like a curse
> And each long day is followed
> By another slightly worse.
>
> Where the coral dust swishes
> Sharper than the sifting sand,
> And a man dreams and wishes
> For a far greener, fairer land.
>
> Somewhere in the South Pacific
> Where the mail is always late,
> And Christmas cards in April
> Is considered up to date.
>
> Where we never have a pay-day
> And never get a cent,
> But we never miss the money,
> 'Cause we'd never get it spent.

Somewhere in the South Pacific
Where ants and lizards play,
and a hundred fresh mosquitoes
Replace everyone you slay.

Where Tojo's nightly droning bats
Robs man of blessed sleep,
And those hissing, blasting bombs,
Pierce with terror, the heart so deep.

So take me back to the U. S. A.
Let me hear a peaceful bell;
For this God-Forsaken outpost
Is a substitute for hell.

Love, Clayton July 22, 1943

Originally, when we left the States, we were informed that our stay in the South Pacific would be no longer than six months because of the adverse conditions. It was all jungle — hot and humid and lots of mosquitoes. We had been there nearly a year and nothing was said or heard of when we would be going home. All this time we were issued atabrine to control malaria fever caused by the mosquitoes.

Finally, in July 1944, we got the word that we were going home. All the way we were telling each other that we would go out and get the biggest and best dinner we could buy. Not one of us could eat over half of our meal as our stomachs had shrunk from being on C and K rations for sixteen months. Also, we all wanted some sex. We found out later that we were nearly all impotent. We had the desire but could not perform. It took us a month or two to get back to normal!

I had a thirty-day leave. I stayed with my sister and brother-in-law, Nadine and Paul Robinson, in Miller. I thoroughly enjoyed seeing my family. It was just like heaven is said to be. I had been home about two weeks and had neglected taking my atabrine. I came down with a severe case of malaria and spent a week or more in bed under a doctor's care. I wired my commanding officer and explained my situation, and he graciously granted me a thirty-day extension on my leave, which really meant so much to me. That is one big reason why I respect the Navy so much.

Following my leave, I reported to Treasure Island, San Francisco for re-assignment. My stay there was, without a doubt, the most pleasant part of my tour of duty in the Navy with more fun and fantasy than I had experienced before. I was assigned to the U.S.S. Cabot, an aircraft carrier. I knew that I was going back overseas. The Navy notified me that I might be in San Francisco for two or three months, and if I liked, they would put me on shore patrol. My duties would be night or day, whichever I liked. I was generally assigned to a different part of San Francisco each night. I wore my uniform plus leggings and carried a billy club. The shore patrol was to keep surveillance over all naval personnel and prevent any rowdiness on the streets or in the bars. It was an unwritten law in San Francisco that the bar owners give the shore patrol access to liquor. I would say that every bar in San Francisco had a little back room where the shore patrol would find a table that had most any kind of the best liquor. This was a courtesy to the shore patrol.

One morning about 3 a.m., my three buddies and I had just finished patrol duty and were headed back to Treasure Island. We were waiting for a trolley at the far end of Market Street, a big wide sprawling street that handles lots of traffic. It is just like a bumble bees' nest and is known the world over for all its hustle and bustle.

While we were waiting for the next trolley, three sailors and their girlfriends were also waiting for a trolley about thirty feet from us. We had had a few drinks in the backroom of several bars while we were on duty. We were classic examples of the brashness and cockiness associated with sailors. We all agreed that the girls were very attractive. We all made smart aleck remarks about the girls which they all must have heard. I made a completely out-of-line remark that was unforgivable. I said, "Look at those boobies on that girl in the blue dress. She's something else!" Evidently enough was enough, as the sailor that was with the girl in blue came over to us. He said nothing but punched me square on the chin, and I went down on my knees. The fight was on. I became aware that he was a tough kid. We exchanged punches for some

Clayton Jennings, Betty Hoover, Paul Robinson, Ted Jennings and Cliff Spenser in a bar in San Francisco, California.

Shore Patrol—Clayton Jennings on left.

time and finally I landed a head blow that sent him down. He jumped right up and before he got square on his feet, I hit him again on the head. He went down but got back up again very quickly. I was getting out of wind, and I knew if I didn't get him soon, I would be exhausted and whipped. I hit him a left and a right to his ribs and that left him open to the chin. I followed up quickly with a blow square on his chin. He went down and was flat on his back. I went down on his chest and put a hammer lock on him so he could hardly wiggle. Then I grabbed him by the hair with my right hand and beat his head up and down on the concrete several times. Then I'd stop to see if he'd had enough! It took two or three treatments like that, and he finally said he'd had enough!

This was an unnecessary fight, and I was to blame 100% and deserved to get whipped. The remark I made was unforgivable and about as common as a human can get. I have

Chief Petty Officer
Clayton Jennings—1944.

lived with this shame ever since and have vowed that never ever would I belittle any female again. This nasty episode happened fifty-one years ago and is as clear in my mind as if it were yesterday!

One day in July 1945, I got my orders to report to the U.S.S. Cabot. No one knew our destination, but we were all sure that we were headed out to meet the fleet and make an invasion of Japan. We had been out to sea a couple of weeks when we found out by radio that the Japanese had surrendered. The war was over!

The next day we heard all about the surrender over the speaker system. We would be put ashore on the coast of Okinawa until a ship could pick us up and return us to the States. We arrived and unloaded on the shore. We lived in tents for about two weeks. Then the battleship U.S.S. California picked us up. We slept on the decks, but that didn't matter because we were on our way home. We arrived on the west coast. Then we were sent to Minneapolis where we were finally discharged in October 1945.

Then as fast as I could, I headed for South Dakota, the state that I loved!

Chapter 23

Letter to Mother

This is the letter I wrote to my mother after learning of my father's death a month earlier.

March 15 - '44.

My Wonderful Mother,

Last evening I came in from duty to find a good many letters, the first mail received since we have been on this island. My Dad passing along was a terrific shock and by far the toughest blow thus far in my life. Mother, words fail this occasion simply because words are insufficient to express my sentiment to you. My desire is that these lines somehow will bring some comfort & consolation to your heart & give you at least a little more peace of mind. I do regret that circumstances prevented the sad word to reach me until last evening. I realize that my letters are but a wee bit toward alleviating this sorrowful situation, and the fact that I cannot at the present do anything materially, makes me feel tremendously sad and disgustfully helpless. I'll be home again in a few months, possibly sooner than

I have previously written. Naturally, home can't possibly be exactly the same without Dad but we will keep it the grand home it has always been.
I can't realize coming home and not having him there.
Now, I will attempt to give you an idea of the heartfelt sorrow since the sad news came. The many letters dated from March 12th to March 30th so you can see that I had a complete story of everything in detail. When I found the letters on my cot I segregated it as usual and arranged in order as to the various addresses and post marks, and of course as always started reading the older post marked ones first so as to keep the trend of thought straight. As it so happened I started reading Nadine's letters first. It was really inspiring to read that Dad was improving so well

and was feeling so good and that his spirit was so keen and that he was making plans to get out of bed and among his friends again. Next came the letter written from Livermore and saying Dad wasn't with us anymore. That was all I could read for a couple hours. Then with the consoling efforts of a couple of my good buddies, I read & reread every letter from Ted, Margaret, Nadine & then yours and Dads — then came Uncle Arens, Aunt Graces & many more letters of sympathy. It was all difficult for me to understand at first and I couldn't believe or realize. After the boys finally went to bed I wandered out and sit on a pile of coral and saw the moon come up and saw it go down. Many & various were the visions that passed through my mind — uncountable were the thoughts and inspirations. Finally everything cleared.

up and I'm feeling much better about it now. When I thought back to the time Dad was critically ill & when all doctors give him but little time to live it give me a different slant on this sad event. It is evident that he was spared at that time because we asked in prayer that he would get well & he did. In this 14 years it has been all of our enjoyment and a whole lot of it too. Then too, I think Dad's achievements in life were fullfilled in seeing his daughters & sons attain an honorable & successful life. His grand children were his pride & joy as I know they are also your pride & joy. His son-in-laws & daughter-in-law were very dear to him as they are to you. Probably I hadn't attained all that he had hoped I would but I do know that he believed in me & had unlimited confidence in me.

Both yours & Dad's belief & confidence in me has been an inspiration for me all through life & has certainly been the major factor in my achievements thus far. When there were temptations for me that might bring dishonor I would think of Mother & Dad and say, "nothing doing - not for anything in the world." When I have been in contests of games or business it has always been Mother & Dad I thought of & through my mind would go this thought "Wouldn't Mother & Dad feel proud if I win. I will win." Not every one has been so fortunate as to have a Mother & Dad that inspired them to achieve.

 Even though this irrepareable loss to me has cause much grief & sorrow it has also been a wonderful satisfaction know that such grand tribute was paid to him. Everyone who has written to me, have emphasized the fact that Dad's was the most impressive funeral services, the largest crowd of tribute payers, & the most & nicest flowers ever at a funeral in Livermore. This was a great consolation for me but the many little details about respect & admiration from young to old meant even more to me. All in all, I have always been tremendously proud of both of you but at this time I am even prouder if that is possible.

Mother, you really have a lot of admirers — people wrote so many nice things about you that it made me feel swell. I will send you some of the more valued ones & wish you would save them for me.

Mother, now is the test of courage so let us determine to continue on in life as you know Dad wants us to. Everyone has to part with their loved ones sometime so let us not be selfish & resentful. There is much in life for us to do yet. When I get home we will all spend the time together. The first place I will come will be home to you. We will make lots of plans. Maybe I'll bring "Peaches" home if that is possible.

Now please don't worry about me as everything is fine here. My health is good, chow is good, there is no danger & soon I'll be on my way home — perhaps Sept. — maybe a little sooner or a little later.

God bless you   All My Love
                          Clayton

Charles and Mary Jennings, 1942.

Chapter 24

Buying and Developing the Hyland Angus Ranch

The land buys in South Dakota looked so good to Ted and me that we decided to buy more land and start a big purebred Angus herd. We were now very desirous of buying land with a good location. It was highly important to buyers to be accessible at all times preferably on or near a hard surface road. There was more land for sale than I think had ever been for sale before, so the opportunity was there.

In 1946 we had the opportunity to sell our first two ranches that we had bought in the 30's. We could sell them to Marvin Fernow and Orville Rose of Marion, Iowa, for $15.00 an acre, approximately four times what we had paid for them. This land had more than paid for itself in its operation each year that we owned it.

Happy to have sold our first two ranches to Fernow and Rose, we went to work and bought a lot more land between 1945 and 1960. We were very fortunate to be able to buy land that blocked out solidly. We had quite a little of this land on the north and south sides of Highway 14 between Highmore and Ree Heights, South Dakota. It was an ideal location for a purebred herd. We selected the name Hyland Angus Ranch because our town of Highmore was the highest point on the Chicago and Northwestern Railroad between Chicago and the Black Hills. We changed it to Hy and added land. So it became the Hyland Angus Ranch. We liked that!

We kept putting ranches together. We'd sell or trade if we found one we liked better or one that fit our program better. When we paid $40.00 an acre for one ranch, everyone said we would never make it!!!

SOUTH RANCH

These ranches were in the area east of the Stephan, South Dakota, corner.

1945 O. C. Nicolls Ranch – 2,340 acres @ $5.00 an acre. This ranch impressed me as probably the best ranch land we had bought. It had relatively good buildings, decent fences and fresh water during the summer from the numerous springs all along the creek that ran kitty corner through the ranch.

1947 Caryl Enger Ranch – 800 acres @ $12.50 an acre. This land joined the Nicolls Ranch and was a valuable asset. The buildings were moved to other locations.

1947 John Trammell Ranch – 160 acres at $12.00 an acre. The buildings were either moved to another ranch or demolished.

1947 Harold Nedved Ranch—160 acres at $15.00 an acre. The buildings were either moved to another ranch or demolished.

1948 Theodore Grosz Ranch—1,200 acres at $12.00 an acre. We made improvements on the buildings and corrals. This ranch then became the home of Jimmy Krick and his family. They have lived there continuously over the years. Jimmy said he has been bought and sold at least five times. Each time the ranch changed hands, he went with the deal.

1952 Charles McBride Ranch—160 acres at $15.00 an acre. The buildings were either moved to another ranch or demolished.

1952 Isburg and McIntosh Ranch—160 acres at $15.00 an acre. The buildings were either moved to another ranch or demolished.

1952 Frank Lingscheit Ranch—1,500 acres at $20.00 an acre. We kept the buildings and improved on them and the ranch.

NORTH RANCH

These ranches were on both sides of Highway 14, between Highmore and Ree Heights.

1946 Wes Newell Ranch—3,040 acres @ $15.32 an acre. This included three sets of buildings. Wes had sold all his cattle, so we bought the balance of his feed, machinery, six horses and harnesses and his brand, the Bar Bolster. Wes used this brand on his ranch for 47 years, and we continued on the same. We purchased all six locations for the brand, both shoulders, both hips and both sets of ribs. Our use of this brand made it internationally known. It is still used by Ted and Ron Jennings. Wes and I discussed the details and terms of the land deal. We parted with a handshake, agreeing that we would draw up the papers the next day. Wes died that night, but his family desired to go right on with the deal as agreed. We sold 320 acres of this ranch to Lyman Hanson, a neighbor, for $25.00 an acre, to square up his deal. This was to be our headquarters for all the ranches and was my home for eighteen years.

1946 Otto Sandcamp Ranch—1,460 acres at $17.00 an acre. We kept the buildings, but improved on them and the corrals. This was the home of Junior Suhn and his family until we purchased the Buck Steers ranch. Jim Blair came to work

Headquarters Ranch before the buildings were painted white. (Wes Newell Ranch)

Home of Jim Blair and his family for many years. (Sandcamp Ranch)

for us in 1955. He and his family lived on this ranch until he retired in 1989.

1947 J. M. Prostrollo Ranch – 160 acres at $15.00 an acre. There were no buildings.

1949 Ed Fawcett – 40 acres @ $20.00 an acre. There were no buildings.

1950 Buck Steers Ranch – 2,700 acres at $40.00 an acre. There was a good set of buildings that we remodeled. This ranch became the home of the Junior Suhn family. Junior had come to work for us in the fall of 1946. Junior was our ranch foreman for many years.

1951 Roger Paine Ranch – 1,880 acres ′ $20.00 an acre. We remodeled the buildings. This ranch became known as the "Bull Ranch," and was the home of Bud Hahn and his family for many years.

1951 A. B. Cahalan Ranch – 1,280 acres @ $20.00 an acre. We traded this 1,280 acres to Roger Paine for 1,280 acres that he owned next to the 1,880 acres we had just purchased from him.

1954 John Manning Ranch – 320 acres at $20.00 an acres. We moved the buildings off.

1954 Healey & Lackey Ranch – 680 acres @ $20.00 an acre. There were no buildings.

1954 J. M. Prostrollo Ranch – 440 acres @ $20.00 an acre. There were no buildings.

1955 Harry Robinson Ranch – 800 acres @ $35.00 an acre. We improved the buildings and we sold 240 acres to Fred Dittman to square up his ranch.

1958 Leo Tompkins Ranch – 640 acres @ $35.00 an acre. The house was moved to the bull ranch and remodeled. There were no other buildings.

1958 John Bietz Ranch – 380 acres at $35.00 an acre. All the buildings were moved off or demolished.

1959 Dale Robinson Ranch – 800 acres at $35.00 an acre. All buildings and corrals were remodeled.

1960 John Renner Ranch – 228 acres @ $25.00 an acre. All the buildings were moved off.

We applied major overhaul jobs on all the buildings and fences on all the ranches which took several years. We used the scheme of white buildings with green asphalt shingled roofs

Bull Ranch, home of Bud Hahn and his family for many years. (Paine Ranch)

Another set of excellent improvements. (Dale Robinson Ranch)

and white corrals with black posts on all the ranches. This scheme became the trademark of the Jennings Brothers ranches. We hired special crews of three to five men to do this work during the summers, and it was seldom that we didn't have a crew working on one part of the ranch or another. We completely renovated all the corrals, so we had good working facilities on each ranch. Emphasis on feed was very important on our ranches. One survives in raising good cattle by first being able to keep them fed. We didn't plan or try to plant cash crops, but all our farm land was planted to a feed crop, with emphasis on oats and alfalfa hay. Harvesting an abundance of hay, silage, oats, cane and corn was just part of a good job of being prepared. When we purchased the headquarters ranch, there were about 600 acres of farmland that we decided to convert to alfalfa for hay. It would give us more rough feed for winter every year. I went to see the Fawcett Brothers at Ree Heights, who were rated as the best for getting a stand of alfalfa. They advised me to be sure and work the ground well, and then seed in five or six pounds of alfalfa per acre. They also suggested seeding about ten pounds of flax as a shade crop for the alfalfa. They told me not to plan on a flax crop. It was merely for protection of the new alfalfa. We got the field ready and planted double the seed necessary. We figured if so much was good, then twice as much would be better. In normal years it probably would have been a flop, but we had an abundance of rain giving us a thick field of alfalfa and flax. When we harvested the flax it made ninteen bushels per acre. We sold it to Hawkinson & Quirk in Highmore for $6.05 per bushel. We averaged $114.35 per acre from the flax on land that we had paid $15.32 an acre. This was on a crop that we had not planned on. We also had a beautiful stand of alfalfa for feed.

 The Hyland Angus Ranch was the first outfit to artificially inseminate beef cattle, by the volume, in South Dakota. We started in 1955. A. I. gave us the benefit of a tighter calf crop, (71% were on the ground within three weeks), better prices because of uniformity and quality, and the savings of bull costs. Rand VanDervoort was our first A. I. technician and continued every year as long as we had the Hyland Angus Ranch.

The Jennings Brothers' trademark wasn't just white buildings with green roofs, but good clean places with nothing strewn about, hard working people who respected each other and good Angus cattle. We were fully aware of the fact that a cattle ranch operation is relative to the men and women who work for it. We gave our men an extra incentive by making them feel a part of the Hyland Angus Ranch. We paid a good wage with bonuses being optional to us in accordance with the financial status of the ranch. Each family was furnished with a modern home with the operator being responsible for the upkeep of their place. We furnished each family with prime beef the year around by maintaining a small feed yard at one of the ranches for the development of fat cattle for slaughter. They had no need to tell us when they needed beef. They could just go and get one for slaughter either on the place or take it to a locker plant in town. We also offered them any sized garden they were willing to tend with the use of our equipment at no cost to them. Everyone was eligible for a few days off at a time but it would be arranged when there was no real important cattle situation planned. Our ranch hands always worked for our interest and were loyal in all respects. They never kept track of their hours and many days

Sign for Hyland Angus Ranch

were long and hard, especially during haying season and calving season. Our ranch was like a salt mine, toil and sweat. The women also held up their part of the deal by cooking for the whole crew whenever necessary. We always found jobs for any of the families who had boys old enough to work. From this "on-the-job" experience, these boys turned out to be men, and good ones! We felt we were giving our hands an opportunity and many of them did stay with us for twenty, thirty and even up to forty-five years. I doubt if anyone ever had a better working crew than we had all through the history of the Hyland Angus Ranch.

Visitors were always welcome which added to our future business. We had many visitors over the years and they came from almost every state, Canada, Mexico, Ireland, France, England, Australia, South America, and Scotland.

My brother Ted and I had always been very close, even as children. We became partners while still following in our dad's footsteps. The Jennings Brothers was a fascinating partnership that was pleasant from the very beginning. We stood together on all decisions. I truly believe no one ever had a better partner than I had in Ted Jennings.

In 1962 both of our families had children of or near college age, and we decided for all concerned that it would be a good time to divide our partnership. We were in excellent financial

A friendly wave from Clayton Jennings.

shape. We divided all the land, cattle and equipment to both our satisfaction. We had real estate in both Hand County and Hyde County We split our real estate holdings at the Hand-Hyde line. Ted received all our land in Hand County. I received all our land in Hyde County.

We had just finished all the legal work necessary to divide our partnership at our laywer's office and I jokingly told Ted I was going on a trip to see the world. Ted said, "Well, I'm going out and buy another ranch!!

Chapter 25

Hyland Angus Ranch Crew

A RANCH IS NO MORE OR NO LESS THAN THE MEN WHO WORK FOR IT.

We made a three-year-lease for JACK COOK's place and paid him a wage, plus he had the privilege of keeping 30 cows of his own. We had about 200 cows there when on May 5, 1950, we had an unusual rain and snow storm that drifted these cows and calves into a big dam. The cows swam on through but the calves were unable to get all the way across the dam. When the storm was over we rode horseback into the dam trying to get the calves out, but most were dead by then. We lost about 65 calves by drowning. They were about a month to 6 weeks old. Jack lost about the same percentage of the calves he had on his 30 cows. It was an unusual storm for that time of year, but there's always a new first in the cattle business and in South Dakota.

Jack Cook

James Krick—1993

Ernest Suhn, Jr.

Ernest "Bud" Hahn

JAMES KRICK was one of the first men to work for us starting in 1945 and staying to the end. He was a utility man deluxe. He was equally as good with cattle as with farming. He could make any kind of machinery work and keep working. When Ted and I divided our partnership in 1962 he went with Ted.

ERNEST "JUNIOR" SUHN was foreman of the north ranch commercial cattle. He had a knack of knowing every cow in the herd and always got them bred and calved out as good as any man. LORETTA SUHN had much to do with the commercial cattle records. They came to work for us in 1946 and worked for us continuously until Ted and I divided our partnership in 1962. They went with Ted.

ERNEST "BUD" HAHN was foreman of the range bulls. He knew every bull and knew how to handle them. ELINOR HAHN did a lot of caretaking of my children. They always lived on the bull ranch and stayed with me after Ted and I divided our partnership in 1962.

James Blair

JAMES BLAIR was foreman of the haying and feed crop operation and a utility man. He was highly important on our overall operation. He came to work for us in 1955 and stayed with us continuously until Ted and I divided our partnership in 1962. He went with Ted.

HAROLD PARLIN was foreman of the registered cattle. He could sell bulls as well as I could. He was very well liked by all of our customers. PHYLLS PARLIN kept the registered cattle records. They came to work for us in 1956 and stayed. When I sold the ranch to Ankony in 1964 they continued to work for them.

The Hyland Angus Ranch crew as a whole was the most capable and loyal as any crew ever to work on a ranch. These men and women were professionals in their line of work and never once could I question their decisions. Their sincerity and honesty made it possible for the Hyland Angus Ranch to be prominent in the Angus cattle business for many years.

Harold and Phyllis Parlin in the western sunroom at the Headquarters Ranch.

1950's—James Krick, Bill Pender, Ernest Suhn, Jr, James and Bill McKown.

1955—Charlie Jennings on Thunder. Argyl Conner, Jim Hupp, Jack Cordell, Ernest Suhn, Jr, Jim Blair, Harold Wulf, Bob Fratzke, Keith DeRouchey and Jack Engle.

1964—Melvin Fischer, Allen Hanson, Ernest "Bud" Hahn, Harold Parlin, James Palon and Dean Hensen.

Chapter 26

Dorothy—My First Wife

I met my first wife Dorothy Fish in Miller, South Dakota before I went to the service. We became very fond of each other. I thought she was the most beautiful girl I had ever met. She was of purebred Irish descent with beautiful coal black hair. She had a lovely personality and the Irish wit and brogue that made her a standout!

Clayton Jennings and Dorothy Fish on their wedding day in 1946.

Dorothy followed me to Seattle, Washington where I was attending naval aviation ordnance school. She got a job and elected to stay in Seattle as long as I was overseas.

Following my discharge from the service in 1945 and my return to Miller, she also returned. We renewed our romance and were married October 5, 1946.

We lived in Miller a couple of years where our son Charles Clayton (Charlie) was born January 12, 1948. We moved to the Hyland Angus Ranch headquarters in June 1948.

I made sure that Dorothy always had good wheels. The first car I bought her was the best Buick available. I traded every other year and she always had the best Buick. I drove a standard Chevrolet. I put many many miles on my car, so I traded every year.

I traveled extensively in the cattle business. Dorothy was unable to travel with me as often as she would have liked because of our baby. Our relationship deteriorated and finally we divorced.

Dorothy holding Gloria, Clayton and Charlie Jennings in front of their ranch home—1954.

Dorothy missed our son Charlie. She came back for a visit and decided to stay. She wanted to get married again. I demanded that we have at least one more child if we were to get married again, and she very reluctantly agreed. I loved that little Charlie and was getting so much enjoyment from him that I just had to have more children. While on a cattle buying trip to Michigan, Dorothy and I re-married.

Our daughter Gloria Jean was born April 10, 1953. I thought she was the most precious little baby ever born on this earth.

Dorothy was highly interested in the ranch operation and contributed greatly in its promotion.

Our marriage was somewhat like a roller coaster. Our good times were fantastic, but after a few years the roller coaster derailed! We finally divorced again in 1956. We mutually decided and agreed that the children would stay on the ranch with me.

I have always had high respect for Dorothy. I believe Dorothy's brother Gene said it like it was when it came to Dorothy and I. He said, "You can't put two thoroughbreds in the same stall!"

Chapter 27

Artesian Well

One of the most valuable assets on any ranch is the water. With the help of the federal government, we installed an unusual water system on our ranch.

In the mid 1950's ranchers could participate in a program in which the government would pay 60% or more of the cost of an artesian well. We dug our artesian well on the head-

Jim Leachman, Les Leachman and Clayton Jennings examining the artesian well.

These young herd bulls are taking their ease at one of the many livestock dams that serve as a reserve water source.

quarters ranch. Our well rose to the surface from the depth of more than 2,100 feet with a natural pressure of more than 100 pounds. We participated further in the program and laid more than six miles of 1½ inch plastic pipe to every corner of the ranch south of Highway 14. We used a road maintainer to dig a ditch 18 inches deep to lay the pipe (a government requirement). Water was circulated through the pipes by the natural pressure and at a temperature that never froze in winter and was always fresh in summer for as many livestock as we had.

This was without question the best money we ever spent on remodeling or rebuilding on any of our ranches.

It has been thirty-five years since installation and it is still flowing strong today. It is a sight to behold!

Stock dams are another water source on most ranches. Many of the dams have been in since the 1930's in WPA days when they were built with teams of horses and scrapers. The Works Project Administration was a government program that guaranteed work for the farmers during the depression. These dams are filled with run-off of winter snows and heavy spring rains. The overflow from the artesian well also drained into various dams and kept them full.

Chapter 28

Cattle Business in Old Mexico

During the 1950's I had the good luck to meet Bill Adams of El Paso, Texas, and Teofilo Borunda of Chihuahua, Mexico. They were long term friends and both owned vast cattle ranches in Mexico. They were both rated among the top cattlemen on the entire continent and they were financially fixed in the top echelon. Bill Adams operated in Chihuahua a lifetime and owned one of the most highly rated ranches in all of Mexico. He was one of the best judges of cattle and best operators ever in that territory. He used the handshake the same way as I was taught in the Pierre area. Teofila Borunda was also one of the all time big men in Mexico, later becoming governor of Chihuahua.

I had flown into El Paso on business. The gentleman I was meeting with told me of these two Mexicans who were interested in improving their cattle herds. He thought I was just the man to do that. He made me acquainted with Adams and Borunda.

Bill Adams invited me and my pilot Cecil Ice and Mr. Borunda out to his home in El Paso. He insisted on us coming out now! We went!! I will never forget that he had Jack Daniels liquor. He put the bottle out on the kitchen table with four highball glasses and four shot glasses. They liked their whiskey by the shot, mix your own or straight from the shot glass. He gave us the privilege to mix ours, which we did. We had a drink or two and got better acquainted. Bill spoke pretty decent English. I could understand him easily. Teofilo could not speak English, but he could understand everything I said. Bill translated his responses to me. We decided that we would fly out the next morning to look over both their ranches.

The next morning we flew to Chihauhua, which was about 300 miles from El Paso. We flew the outside of both ranches, which adjoined each other. We flew at a low level and we could see the oceans of grass, trees, rivers and lots of cattle from the top side. We flew to the center of the Borunda ranch where he had his home. We circled his house. I couldn't believe it was a home. From the air it reminded me of an extra large motel with lead-offs sprawling in all directions. I thought "This is a house of fantasy!" It was a Spanish style home of block and brick.

We got back to El Paso in the later afternoon. All the time we were talking about cattle and land. Each of them told me about the size of their operations, and the size of their cowherds and ranches. I remember the cattle were very mediocre in quality and size and showed the distinct signs of the longhorns, but were crossbreds of many kinds. Their cowherds were multicolored. I visualized on the trip back to El Paso that there was a big opportunity for both these gentlemen and for Ted and me.

Upon arriving in El Paso we wound up in the Adams' home where we were the day before, at the same table in the kitchen. Bill again set the Jack Daniels and the four highball and four shot glasses out on the middle of the table. He went to the refrigerator and brought out two large plates of cold meats. Then he grabbed the boxes of crackers, similar to our saltines, and said, "Let's get at it boys. Help yourself!" That tasted about as good as any lunch I remember. The lunch plus a couple shots of Jack Daniels and they were feeling in a glorius mood. They didn't know it but they opened their own gate for me!

Adams did most of the talking, but not all. Borunda was a good listener and I could see his expressions and his eye on me. He was fascinated with me. Bill said "Now, Clayton, we have told you and showed you everything we have, and several top men have told us that you have the best Angus cattle in the business and in volume."

I was dreaming and had lots of visions of what could be beneficial to them and me. I wanted to tell them the truth without exaggeration and that's not easy for me! I had heard that Adams had killed two men or maybe more, so I wasn't about to add myself to that list. I tried to stay humble as long as I could, but by nature and another shot of Jack Daniels I exploded. I condensed my explanation of our operation so it would be more effective. I told them we had more and better commercial-type Angus bulls than anyone else in the business and we sold from one to two thousand Angus bulls every year. We sell them into Canada and all over America. I looked one in the eye then the other, then back again. I tapped my hand on the table and said in slow words, "They are exactly what you need for your ranches." Neither of them wanted me to quit talking, but I decided I had said enough. I saw Adams and Borunda exchange eye glances. They were proud people. Maybe I had said the wrong thing!

They looked at each other and Bill said, "Would you consider sending one load down to us and if they suit us, we might buy a lot of bulls." It didn't take me long to say that I'd send them a load of bulls and guarantee them to suit them. If not they could turn around and send them back to me. They both smiled but I had an alternative plan. I said "I am here and you have been exceptionally nice in showing me everything. Now I would like to have both of you come to see me." That's the way it turned out. Adams had his own twin engine plane equipped with everything and they came and landed at Miller, South Dakota. I picked them up and it was late evening when we arrived at my home on the Hyland Angus Ranch.

The next morning we went out to see as many of the cattle as we could. To save time I had gotten my men organized to be on a schedule to open the gates for us. I told them not to be late, be early, and that they were. There was a man at each gate when we arrived even if we were late.

I tried to remain humble and I hoped they would keep asking questions. Their smiles and expressions let me know they were highly impressed. We had over ten pastures of purebred cattle to look at and we saw every one of them thoroughly. We had time enough to show them the commercial cows with five month old calves at side. I made some remark that if they had straight black cattle on their ranches I would be willing to buy all their steers. Borumda paid special attention to the heifer calves each time we stopped.

We went back to my ranch home to rest and eat. We were seated in my beautiful and unusual western style sunporch. I followed Adams manner of entertaining. Take what you want and fix it the way you want it! I set out several kinds of bourbon and blend, vodka and gin. I was trying to be gracious and I missed the boat! I had learned already that Bill was commanding and meant whatever he said. I recall Bill looking over the bottles and saying, "Clayton, where's your Jack Daniels!" I said "Bill, we aren't in the habit of drinking that, so I don't have any, but I can get some right soon." He smiled and said he surely would like that as he never drank anything else. I called my head man and told him to get two bottles and get it quickly and that he did!

My wife Dorothy fixed an excellent meal and everyone ate heartily. After dinner we went back to my western sunroom and started visiting and they took the lead. They liked our cattle and would be interested in three hundred of the bull calves that they had seen, to be delivered at weaning time. They desired this age (six or seven months) so they could get acclimated to the weather in Mexico for nearly a year before they used them. I could understand that theory well. Mr. Borunda indicated through Bill that he would like to buy six hundred of the heifer calves. He wanted them delivered in October or November and I could sort them as the calves were uniform in kind and size. Mr. Borunda wanted these heifers for a new foundation herd and he said he would be happy to sell me his steer calves. I would have the first chance each year. I priced the bulls and heifers to them and they did not even attempt to negotiate or bargain, which usually goes with every deal of volume. I did try to price them right, but had they known they could have bought them at a somewhat lesser figure. We delivered them to El Paso where they arrived in fine condition. Adams and Borunda accepted them and then took them on in to Mexico. This first deal was very satisfactory. From then on we did lots of bull business every year for fifteen or more consecutive years. We also purchased lots of steers from them for numerous years. I never returned to Mexico and they never returned to South Dakota. Everything was done over the phone.

These men made a lasting impression on me the minute I saw them. I feel that I learned much from them. They were high-class gentlemen and they looked the part. They wore black Stetson hats and alligator boots, handsomely tailored pants and elegant white shirts with engraved silver tips on the collars. Never had I been so impressed by two more elegantly dressed men. Why can't I dress like these guys?

I had a vision and it came true the next time I got to Denver. I started on this project. First I went to the Stockman's Store and bought myself a black Stetson hat, almost no one wore black hats, so they didn't keep many in stock, but they did have one that fit me. Then I saw a display of belts and buckles. I bought a black belt with a fancy silver buckle with gold engraving. I also ordered a custom-made pair of boots. They were to be black leather with silver capped toes and green and gold uppers. What a gorgeous pair of boots they would be! Then I inquired about a shirt store. They directed me to a store that had more shirts on the shelves than I had ever seen. They also had a little department that tailor made shirts. I talked with the tailor and told him what I would like. He said he could make me any color and any style, but I would have to bring him the material. He measured me and directed me to Mays Department Store. It was about a half mile so I walked. I bought velveteen for ten western-styled shirts with two large pockets on the chest. I bought enough material of each of these colors for a shirt: light blue, royal blue, red, black, green, olive, gold, turquoise, beige and white. The white shirt had black snap buttons and all the rest had white snap buttons. After I completed the deal with the tailor, I told him not to mail them to me when they were ready, but just let me know and I would come to Denver and get them. I next caught a cab to Gross Tailors where I intented to buy two pair of nifty trousers to go with my hat and shirts. I was lucky to have two very capable young man waiting on me and I ended up buying two tailor-made western suits, one navy blue and one light blue, but identical in design. I thought I could just use the trousers or I could use the full suits for church and cattlemen's conventions. Again I told them not to mail them but I would come and get them.

Chapter 29

Winter of 1951/52

In the fall of 1951 we were able to put up an enormous amount of feed: alfalfa hay, oats hay, lots of orange cane, and prairie hay. The prairie grass was also in good shape for

Kusser trucks loaded and ready to go.

winter grazing. We hired Simon Kusser and his haying crew to mow, rake, bale and haul the hay on the Schaub Ranch at Burkmire, South Dakota. His crew consisted of Phil Kusser, Dale Wurts, Ben Heenan, Frank Snell, LeRoy Ruark and Eddie Kusser. When the job was completed they had baled 28,723 round bales weighing 50# each with one Allis Chalmers baler. They used trucks to haul the bales to the ranches. Half of the hay was hauled 90 miles to the south ranch and the other half to the north ranch of the Hyland Angus Ranch. The snow was flying by the time they finished.

We had our ranches stocked with a normal amount of cattle. We were prepared to handle almost any kind of weather, as we had teams of horses and bobsleds with hayracks to feed the cattle on each of our six ranches. We had spare horses on each ranch in the event of an exceptionally tough winter.

It started snowing in October, but the heavy snow started in late November and continued all winter. It seemed like there was a new blizzard or ground blizzard every day constantly keeping the roads blocked. We thought it would never end. In order to keep the roads open for necessary ranch operations, we hired Melvin Grable of Highmore with a caterpillar tractor to open the roads. He did an excellent job until in late December when it became impossible as there was too

Melvin Grable moving the snow with his caterpillar.

much snow and no place to put it. The drifts were so hard we could go over the top or around them with a team of horses and bobsled. A heavy vehicle would break through and drop out of sight in the deep snow.

Many farms and ranches were isolated most of the winter. The wind continued to blow, keeping the snow constantly moving and swirling around. Most side roads were blocked. County road crews worked constantly to keep county roads open. The drifts were so high they looked like tunnels after the dozers broke through. Planes were hired by the county to drop groceries and mail to farmers and ranchers isolated by the continuous storms.

Clayton Jennings standing on the road in one of the many tunnels of snow after the plows cut through.

Our only practical means of transportation was our great team of horses, Pat and Mike, and a bobsled. In order to get to Highmore for supplies, we would travel across the pasture the three miles north to Highway 14 near the Mosher place where we left the team and sled. We would prearrange by phone for someone to meet us there and take us into Highmore. After we conducted our business, someone would bring us back to the team and bobsled for the ride back home over the prairie to the ranch.

We had good equipment to load and haul the feed to our cattle. We kept our cattle well fed, and they looked good. This is why Ted and I came up with a plan to buy more cattle and put our excess feed into cash. Because of the snow and cold many ranchers needed to sell part of their herds in order to have enough feed for the balance of their cattle. The cattle were shrunk down and froze out because of the severe weather which made for a real buy. We decided this was the proper time to buy as many cattle as we could. We had the necessary feed, without buying any more, and the circumstances proved worthy of buying cattle.

We would have to borrow more money to buy more cattle, but when we talked with our local bank, the First National Bank at Miller, S.D., they quickly told us that it was over their limit, but they would recommend us to the First National Bank of Denver, Colorado in care of F. M. Peterson. He was the head of the agricultural department of the Denver bank,

Moving a stack of hay with a caterpillar before the snow got too deep.

and he handled most of the large livestock loans. We were ready to get something done, so the Miller bank called F. M. Peterson and made arrangements for him to come and inspect our loan.

The snow was deep and the weather terrible but Ted, who lived in Miller, arranged to pick up F. M. Peterson at the airport in Pierre and bring him to the point on Highway 14 three miles north of the ranch. We used Pat and Mike and the bobsled to inspect our cattle and feed. This team could go where cars, pickups or tractors could not go.

We had cattle at six of our ranches. We felt it would take two days to properly inspect our cattle. We would inspect three ranches one day and the balance of them the next day. I was to keep in touch with Ted in Miller to let him know how things were progressing.

F. M. Peterson was the man to accept or turn down our loan. He was a unique person. As we drove through the cattle on each ranch, he showed no expression to give me an idea of what he thought of their condition. He didn't give any negative opinions about our operation. In fact, they were relatively positive. A little before dark, we pulled into the headquarters ranch where I lived. We unloaded his gear and showed him his room. My wife Dorothy had prepared an excellent meal which we enjoyed after a highball or two.

We planned to start early the next morning. After a hearty breakfast, our team, Pat and Mike, and driver were waiting for us. They were the most loyal team I have ever experienced in the ranch operation. They would not hesitate to go over the ten to twelve foot snow drifts. They traveled all day to the three ranches that we had to inspect and were still going strong when we came in that evening.

Mr. Peterson had made some favorable remarks during the day about the cattle and operation that made me feel good that we could get a good sized loan. Ted and I were shooting for as much money as we could get as we felt the cattle were one of those unusual buys. I feared I might ask more than he would loan us and that I did not want!

The cattle were represented well by the men who worked for us and the two day exhibit of our cattle and ranches made me truly proud.

Moving a stack of hay across the prairie.

That evening when we came to the house and had our little highball, Mr. Peterson volunteered to ask me. "How much money do you want?" I emphasized that we wanted to buy as many cattle as we could. I knew I was in a big gamble, but I had to say something. I said "Well, we would like to

Horses standing on the snow looking over the corrals at the bulls. The snow had been removed from the bull yard.

Charlie Volek riding his pony to school through the deep snow.

The school children built a snow man on top of the snow bank. On the right the outdoor toilet can be seen between the children's legs.

have a million dollars!" He said "There's no reason I can't let you have a million dollars in accordance with your plan." A firm handshake sealed the deal. We had a couple more highballs plus a good dinner, and everyone went to bed happy.

The next morning F. M. Peterson was ready to go back to Denver. I had Pat and Mike hitched to the bobsled, and I took him the three miles to Highway 14 where Ted met us and took him back to the plane at Pierre.

There is but a fine line between being a nice guy and a damn fool!

F. M. Peterson came to South Dakota to make us a loan and all he saw in the three days he was here were snowbanks, haystacks and cattle that were already mortgaged at the First National Bank of Miller. It so happens we paid the First National Bank of Denver one hundred cents on the dollar plus interest the next fall. F. M. Peterson made it possible for us to enhance our present operation and to capitalize on the circumstances of the long hard winter, making him a damn nice guy!

Chapter 30

Champions

We decided that in order for the Hyland Angus Ranch to establish a reputation as top breeders of Angus cattle we had to prove it by competing and winning at the major beef cattle shows and fairs in America.

We had exceptionally good luck in the competitions and it created more and better sales for us each year. We also made many connections through and during these shows and fairs that greatly enhanced our bull business, which developed into a great bonanza.

The first eight pictures in the group are of Champions bred, fed and shown by the Jennings Brothers Hyland Angus Ranch, Highmore, South Dakota. The balance of the Champions were bred by us but fed and shown by other individuals.

1953—Clayton and Dorothy Jennings holding the Champion and Reserve Champion at the Red River Valley Fair, Fargo, North Dakota.

1953—Clayton and Dorothy Jennings, Russell Bucks and Phil Hazard with the First Prize Load of Junior Bull Calves at the National Western Stock Show in Denver, Colorado. They were sold to K. T. Cattle Co., Marysville, California. Last July 1952 K. T. Cattle Co. purchased 350 Hyland Angus Ranch yearling bred heifers. To complete their program they purchased this carload of Champions.

1955- ?, Ernest Suhn, Joe Pekarek, Marvin Fernow, Jim Hupp holding the First Prize Load and Reserve Champion Angus Bull Calves at the National Western Stockshow in Denver, Colorado.

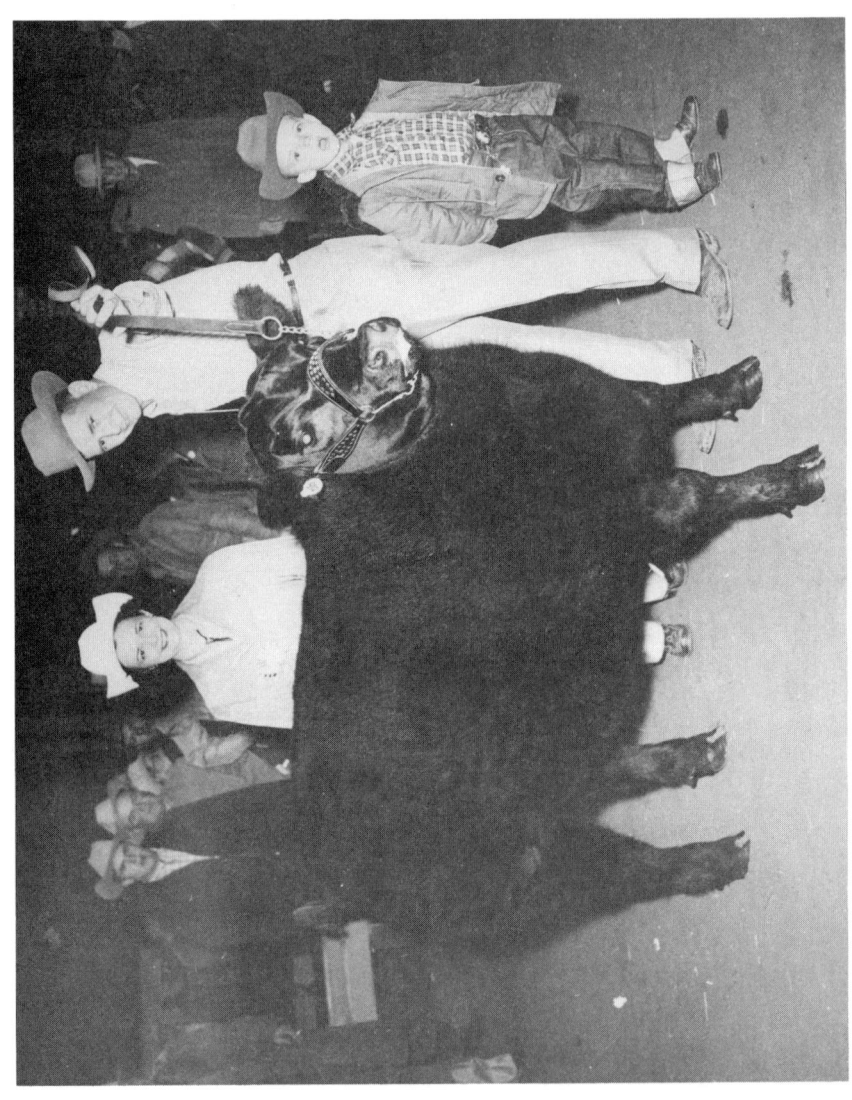

Dorothy Jennings, Argyl Conner and Charlie Jennings with Hyland BlackJack, Reserve Grand Champion over all Breeds and Champion Angus Steer, National Western Stockshow, Denver, Colorado.

1955—Hyland BlackJack, Reserve Grand Champion Steer and Champion Angus Steer, National Western Stock Show, Denver. Also: Grand Champion Steer, 1954 Red River Valley Fair, Fargo, North Dakota; Grand Champion Steer 1954 South Dakota State Fair, Huron, South Dakota, Reserve Champion Angus Steer 1954 International, Chicago, Illinois.

1955—First Premium and Reserve Champion Junior Bull Calves. National Western Stock Show, Denver.

1956—Grand Champion Junior Bull Calves. Argyl Conner, ?, Clayton Jennings, Ross Van Valen, Jap Gadd, Gordon E. Gadd, at the National Western Stock Show, Denver.

1956—Grand Champion Junior Bull Calves. Clayton Jennings, Jap Gadd, Ross VanBalen, Argyl Conner on fence at National Western Stock Show, Denver.

1951—Kansas City Royal, Grand Champion Angus Steers. Bred by Jennings Brothers Hyland Angus Ranch; Fed and shown by Russell Bucks, Davenport, Iowa. ? , Clayton Jennings, Dorothy Jennings, Russell Bucks, ? .

1953—Great Western Livestock Show, Los Angeles, California. Grand Champion Carload Fat Steers. Bred by Jennings Brothers Hyland Angus Ranch and fed and shown by Karl and Jack Hoffman and Vern Joy, Ida Grove, Iowa.

1953—Chicago International, Chicago, Illinois. Reserve Champions of the Show and Champion Angus of the Show. Bred by Jennings Brothers Hyland Angus Ranch and fed and shown by Karl and Jack Hoffman and Vern Joy, Ida Grove, Iowa.

1954—Chicago International, Chicago, Illinois. Grand Champions of the Show. Bred by Jennings Brothers Hyland Angus Ranch and fed and shown by Karl and Jack Hoffman, Ida Grove, Iowa.

1953—Eloise Jennings, Karl Hoffman, Clayton Jennings, Doc Cropsey with Grand Champion Angus Steers, National Western Stock Show, Denver. Bred by Jennings Brothers Hyland Angus Ranch and fed and shown by Karl and Jack Hoffman, Ida Grove, Iowa.

1957—Reserve Grand Champion Fat Steers, National Western Stock Show, Denver. Bred by Jennings Brothers Hyland Angus Ranch and fed and shown by Karl and Jack Hoffman, Ida Grove, Iowa.

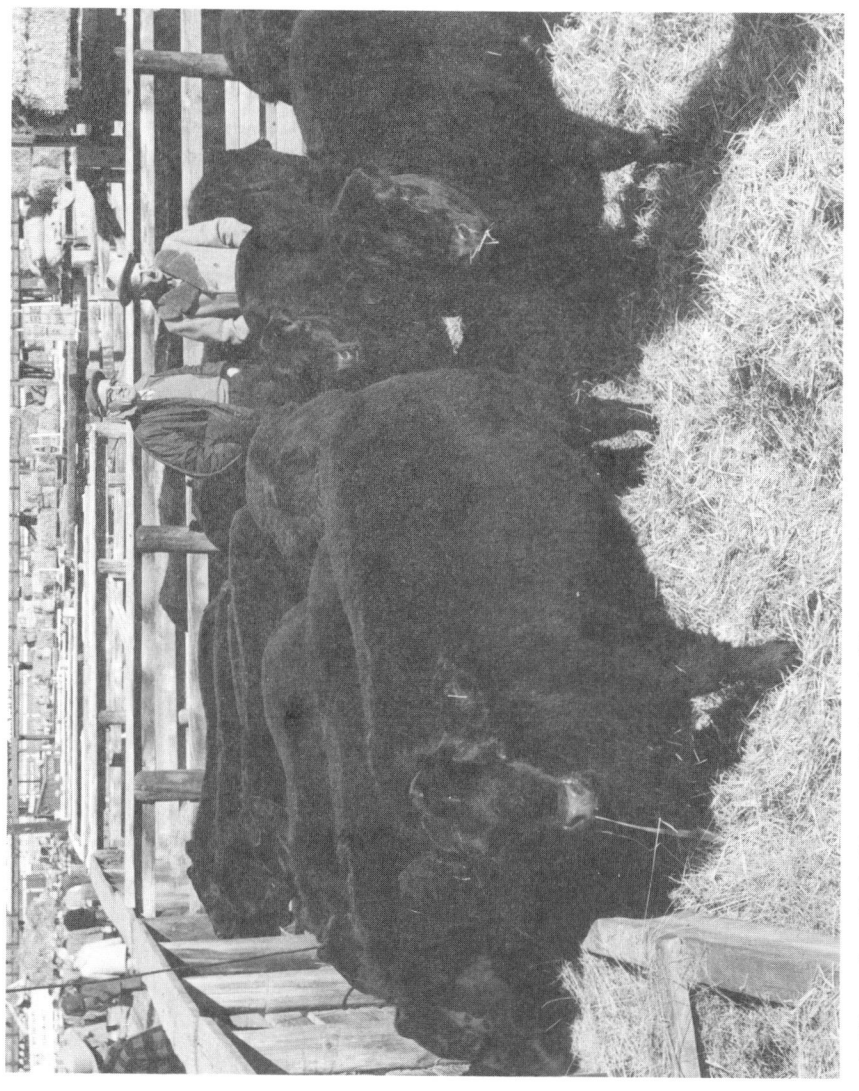

1958—Grand Champion Fat Steers, National Western Stock Show, Denver. Karl Hoffman and Ted Jennings.

1959—Grand Champion Angus Fat Steers at the National Western Stock Show, Denver. Bred by Jennings Brothers Hyland Angus Ranch and fed and shown by Karl and Jack Hoffman, Ida Grove, IA. Karl Hoffman, Clayton Jennings, and Jack Hoffman.

1963—Karl Hoffman with Grand Champion Angus Fat Steers at the National Western Stock Show, Denver. Bred by Jennings Brothers and fed and shown by Karl and Jack Hoffman, Ida Grove, Iowa.

Chapter 31

Denver Bars and Girls

I have found that throughout my life and experiences in my line of business that most men — not all — thoroughly enjoy a drink and show a deep appreciation for a nice looking girl with a good personality, and I am definitely one of those kind of people. I enjoy the atmosphere of a good bar, and all that goes with it. To this day, I still have my favorite bars in each area into which I frequent. I love the hospitality of the people who come and go and are of my kind. I can sincerely say, in these bars over the years, I have created a lot of business in the livestock industry. I'm sure it would be difficult for you to believe me, the amount of business I have created in

Rod Kusser, Karen Hemminger-bartender, Richard and Karen Kusser at the bar at Kusser's Branding Iron Bar, Highmore, South Dakota.

a bar. There is something about a social drink or two with a complete stranger that allows you to become good friends, and opens the doors for everyone involved.

I have a favorite little bar right here in Highmore, called The Branding Iron Bar. I frequent it whenever I have the opportunity, which is almost every evening. These days, I only stay a short time, but if the crowd is good, I have been known to close the place. I want to say I have a great appreciation for a good drink and the atmosphere of mixtures of personalities. It is the quickest way I know to make friends out of strangers. The last things I want to give up in my life are my friends, male and female, and a good drink.

I'm not trying to tell you that I have, over my lifetime, frequented more bars and dated more girls, than any other living man, but I have frequented more bars and dated more girls, in my lifetime, than most men!

Starting in the early fifties, and for the next thirty years, I spent a week to ten days, every year, at the National Western Stock Show in Denver, Colorado. I stayed at the Cosmopolitan Hotel, which became the gathering point of many of the top cattlemen in America. I made many lasting friendships and business associates, which I still cherish today. I made numerous deals that were financially lucrative to all parties involved.

One evening, upon my arrival in Denver, I went down to the stockyards to find our exhibits and show cattle and I happened to run into four of my friends from Texas. They were all staying at the Cosmopolitan Hotel. We decided to get a cab and go together to the hotel. On the way I happened to suggest that we stop at Nora's Bar and Lounge and have a social drink. I had frequented this bar from the first time I was in Denver. Nora was the lady proprietor and it was rated the hottest bar in Denver. Nora was a genius in developing a thriving business.

Nora seated us and personally took our order and delivered it to our booth. She sat with us and immediately enjoyed the company of my friends. There were numerous girls that came in and they were fancy – good looking and had personalities to burn. They were entertainers and could sing and play small musical instruments. We stayed a couple of hours and during this period, Nora volunteered to get these girls to sing and play for us that night. These fellows were excited. We arranged to have them come to a three room suite that I had at the Cosmopolitan. We asked that Nora come along, if she could get away. We told them to check with the head bellboy at 10 o'clock and he would escort them up to my suite, which was on the 10th floor. Everyone was enthused about this get-together.

At 10 o'clock the girls arrived, and Nora was with them. They were all beautifully dressed and had personality and smiles second to none. They had brought their own music with them. I don't pretend to be a musician, but their music was an inspiration. They took turns and did special numbers and were glad to dance with me and my friends.

They danced and sang for about two hours. Then we gave Nora some money for their time. Nora and the girls were impressed with my friends. Nora told us that anytime we wanted to have a little music and dance, she could arrange it with any number of girls of the same calibre, which was tops. Before they left, the boys decided they wanted a bigger party, so they could invite their friends. I arranged for a small ballroom at the Cosmopolitan on Sunday night. We told Nora there would probably be around one hundred men. and she would need to arrange for twenty or more girls to be there to sing, play music and dance.

The word got scattered around that there was going to be a big party Sunday night at ten o'clock at the Cosmopolitan Hotel. No one really knew what kind of a party this was to be, but cattlemen are always anxious to find out what's going on. They are always willing to smile and laugh and have a good time.

The Cosmopolitan Hotel set up a bar in the ballroom and they allowed us their security guard to handle the rowdies and misfits, if any. The arrangements were made with Nora to have someone at the door to take up a collection from each one attending, which was for the ballroom, liquor, the girls, and a tip for the security guard. They all gave liberally, as they knew they were going to have the time of their lives!

Men began swarming in by ten o'clock and everything was in full swing shortly thereafter. There were twenty or more girls of the same calibre as the girls at the first party. When the girls filed in, they were so beautiful that they reminded me of the Miss America Beauty Pageant. They brought their own music including some combos. The contents of the show was similar to the first party, only more of it, and people were smiling and laughing and joking. There also was a lot of dancing. I think everyone, and I mean everyone, had an enjoyable time. They came with a smile and left with an even bigger smile.

This show was so highly successful for everyone, without rowdiness or trouble, what-so-ever and the request was so great for another show, that we decided to have one each year on the Sunday evening of the Denver stock show. It was real evident to us that these parties would become bigger each time, as Nora told us that every capable and quality girl in Denver wanted to come to the party.

I talked with the management of the Hotel and told them we would like to reserve a big room for next year at ten o'clock on Sunday evening of the stock show. They suggested that we book the big ballroom on the 15th floor, where the music and noise would not interfere with the hotel customers. They volunteered to tell us that the hotel security guard would be available, and they would set up a bar at each end of the ballroom. We had the full cooperation from the entire hotel management.

The word must have gotten around from different men who were there before, as it seems everybody wanted to come to this party. Sunday night at ten o'clock, people were flowing up to the ballroom on the 15th floor. Nora had come with thirty or more girls of the same calibre. By two a.m. everyone had left the ballroom. We knew from the comments from the men that they thoroughly enjoyed this entertainment and were looking forward to next year's party.

The next year we were ready. We had made the same arrangements with the Cosmopolitan Hotel for the ballroom on the 15th floor. We also made a deal with the Radisson Hotel, which was within walking distance of the Cosmopolitan Hotel, for a similar ballroom with a bar to serve liquor. We also made arrangements for a security guard. A donation would be taken at the door to cover expenses.

By ten o'clock both the Cosmopolitan and Radisson ballrooms were filling up, and both places were packed within a few minutes. The music had already started. There were combos playing on each end of the ballrooms, and it was the most gala affair I had ever seen. The smiles made it apparent that all were enjoying themselves. I personally walked from one hotel to the other to see that everything and everybody was in line and that all was going along as hoped. There were no rowdy or doubtful characters in the crowd, and everything went along as smooth as possible all evening long. It was an unbelievable sight of entertainment of super class people.

We tried to close both places at one o'clock, but it seemed as though everyone wanted to stay forever, and the girls seemed to be in no hurry to go home. The men had all contributed liberally at the door, and this made for an excellent bonus for Nora and all the girls. They were very grateful and appreciative of this opportunity. The men, to this day, tell me how well they remember these parties. Many permanent personal friendships were established through these get-togethers that are still meaningful today. Many romances came about and numerous marriages resulted. I didn't keep track of the divorces! What they did when they left the ballrooms was none of my business. In reality it was nobody's business but their own.

Organizing these get-to-gethers took a lot of time and consuming work, and a big risk of accidents, so I told myself this was getting too big — and this was my last year of trying to make people happy in this manner! Enough is enough!

There is but a thin line between being a nice guy and a damn fool!!

At a later date when we were in Denver, Nora called Eloise and told her she wanted to see her for a few minutes. She wanted Eloise to go with her to a jewelry store, as she was having a bolo tie made up that she wanted to give to me, from her and the girls, to show their appreciation. It was especially from Nora because I had helped her build a flourishing business.

Eloise went with Nora to the jewelry store to get the bolo tie, and she couldn't believe how beautiful it was. It's a black string tie with a silver heart-shaped neckpiece with a large zircon set in gold in the center. Around the edge of the heart are twelve small rubies and emeralds which are alternated. Eloise stood right beside Nora as she wrote the check for $2,500.00. I think it's a beauty! I still have it after more than thirty years, and it still shines just like new! This is one of my most cherished possessions now and will be for the rest of my life!

Chapter 32

Judging Major Shows

I have judged numerous Angus shows and fairs, one or more times each, during a 20 year period from 1950 to 1970 over much of the United States and Canada.

I have judged shows in Sacramento, California; Alberta, Canada; Edmonton, Canada; Denver, Colorado; Bismarck, North Dakota; Bozeman and Great Falls, Montana; Ft. Worth, Texas; Roanoke, Virginia.

I have judged state fairs in Minnesota, Wisconsin, Iowa, Illinois, South Dakota, Nebraska, Michigan, Montana, North Dakota, Missouri, and Mississippi.

Judging gave me the privilege of meeting all the Angus breeders who had consigned to each show or fair. To personally meet all the consignors created a situation that gave me a "short cut" to buying cattle from them or selling some of our own cattle to them. Many deals were made over a long period through my affiliation with these registered Angus breeders.

I remember one especially interesting experience I had while judging a big Angus show in Greensboro, Mississippi. There were between 300 and 400 entries. One lady, a doctor's wife, had entered every class (10 or 12). She had big cattle and

Western States Angus Ass'n "Bonanza" in Las Vegas, 1962. Dr. and Mrs. R. M. Taylor, owners of the bull, Clayton Jennings was the judge of this show. Do not know the man holding the bull.

Clayton Jennings alighting from a plane.

they didn't fit in those days. She stood last in every class. I tried but just couldn't place her any higher. She was a good sport and showed me no ill feelings. After the show she looked me up, took my hand and said, "Well at least you are consistent in your placing!!"

The shows were sometimes on one coast or the other or in Canada so I flew much of the time. Flying in those days was extremely reasonable and my time was valuable. I flew commercial or had Cecil Ice Flying Service of Pierre, South Dakota, or Ralph Myers of Highmore, South Dakota, fly me to my destination and back.

In those days, hedgehopping and flying interstate fit my purpose better than trying to drive. Today, I couldn't justify much interstate flying because of the bad connections the commercial lines provide and the high cost of charter planes. With their insurance so high, it's impractical.

Flights Ralph Myers flew for Clayton Jennings

Date	Route	Time
11-30-66	Home - Faith SD	3:10
12-5-66	Home - San Angelo, Texas	6:50
12-7-66	San Angelo - North Platte, Nebr.	4:10
12-8-66	North Platte - Home	2:00
12-12-66	Home - Hastings, Nebr.	4:00
2-3-67	Home - Sioux Falls SD	3:00
2-23 & 28-67	Home - Hastings Nebr.	5:00
3-19-67	Home - Sioux Falls, SD	2:30
5-16-67	Home - North Platte, Nebr	4:00
8-16-67	Home - Rapid City	1:50
8-17-67	Rapid City - Steamboat Springs	2:30
8-19-67	Steamboat Springs - local	1:00
8-20-67	Steamboat - Denver - Home	4:30
8-22-67	Home - Sioux Falls, SD.	2:40
9-10-67	Home - Mason, North Dak.	4:10
3-26 & 27-68	Home - Hastings Nebr. - Home	5:15
3-29-68	Home - Sioux Falls - Home	2:30
6-7-68	Home - Bismarck - Highmore - Huron - Home	4:20
10-4-68	Home - Spencer Iowa - Home	3:30
10-28-68	Home - Highmore - Eagle Butte - Highmore - Home	1:45
10-30-68	Home - Highmore - Mobridge - Highmore - Home	1:50
11-3-68	Home - Highmore - Spencer - Home	4:00
11-3-68	Home - Denver - Home	5:30
11-5-68	Home - Pierre - Highmore - Home	1:30
11-8-68	Home - Scottsbluff	2:15
11-9-68	Scottsbluff - Hastings - Scottsbluff	3:45
11-10-68	Scottsbluff - Home	3:10
11-20-68	Myers - Spencer - Myers	2:45
11-21-68	Home - Carrington ND. Home	3:40
12-9-68	Home - Pierre - Spencer - Highmore - Home	4:15
12-10,11,12,13-68	Home - Hastings - LaMars, ND - Home	7:20
12-23, 24-68	Home - Bozeman Mt. - Home	9:00
12-29-68	Home - Platte - Home	1:45
1-5-69	Home - Omaha, Nebr - Quincy Ill - Jackson Fla.	11:00

Hours Flying Time - 352:15
Days away from Home - 110 days
app. miles flown - 52,825

Page of Clayton Jennings' trips from Ralph Myers' log book.

Chapter 33

Purebred Herds

Between 1952 and 1954 we purchased several registered Angus herds—in tact.

A total of 320 purebred cattle were purchased from Jewett Angus Farms of Michigan. We purchased the complete dispersal of the Kemp Angus Farms herd of Marion, Iowa. They were wanting to retire, so we purchased their entire dispersal of 200 cows with 185 calves at side, 80 yearling and two-year-old bulls, and 50 yearling heifers. They were of the very popular Bell Boy breeding. We also purchased the Bell Fontaine Angus Farms herd of Michigan in its entirety, which was about 240 head.

We also purchased the Raona Angus Farms herd of Lansing, Michigan, over 300 total numbers. This was one of the highest rated herds in the purebred Angus in all of America. We had been buying a number of bulls from them every year for several years and bringing them to South Dakota to use and to sell. They had always performed well and were very popular.

We had developed a tremendous bull trade with the commercial cattlemen in several states. We had been selling over 1,000 bulls per year, with the demand growing more every year. With the herds we purchased, we would be able to raise the bulls ourselves and take care of our customers both in and out of state.

THE RAONA HERD

As some of our friends and customers already know, we bought the entire Raona breeding herd of registered Angus cattle earlier this year. For the progressive and practical trade area, served by our purebred operations, the Raona breeding herd was considered the most worthy possible addition to our present herd. We have been intimately acquainted with this breeding herd for many years as Raona-bred bulls have been a dominant factor in the improvement of our purebred and commercial herds. The addition of this herd to our present registered Angus operations will enable us to produce about 500 registered calves each year. The Raona cattle are being moved to our ranch this spring.

We realize the practical advantages of Angus cattle in the range country and the growing popularity of top Angus cattle with feeders in the corn belt. With this foremost in our minds, we are pleased to be able to bring to this area one of the nation's top Angus herds.

As an Angus breeder or Commercial cattleman, you will always be most welcome at HYLAND ANGUS RANCH. Your friendship, your counsel, or your needs will be of genuine concern to us.

With humble pride and great determination we intend to go forward with our sole ambition—to produce "Quality Angus in Quantity", at prices practical cattlemen in this area can well afford.

JENNINGS BROTHERS

The Raona Herd comments by the Jennings Brothers in the May 10, 1954 bull sale catalog.

BLACK BARDOLIER
"THE GENESIS OF THE BARDOLIERS"

Grand River Stock Farm
Registered
Aberdeen Angus Cattle
J. J. Hendren, Owner
Webberville, Michigan

February 15, 1954

Clayton Jennings
Highmore, South Dakota

Dear Clayton:

    The 1954 Michigan-South Dakota Trail will soon be open for business. This season with the moving of three hundred head of cattle, (cows, calves and bulls) a distance of twelve hundred miles will really be a big event. With me such an undertaking would seem impossible, but with you and your "know how" and having watched you move cattle, you probably look upon this event just as another job that has to be done. Anyway, I wish you the best of luck.

    When you acquired the Raona herd, you gave us a real shock. I realized that you were a cattleman but I did not know that we had cattlemen buying fine bred herds of the calibre and numbers like the Raona herd. I do want to congratulate you and I do want you to know that, in my opinion, you bought one of the very top herds of cattle in the land and that I wish you luck in your breeding program. You certainly have a great foundation.

    How is Black Bardolier G. R.? You know he is the second youngest son of Black Bardolier and the last son to be dropped at Grand River. Black Bardolier of White Gates 3d is the youngest and he was dropped five days after the Grand River Dissolution Sale. It might be of interest for you to know that he was calved on the Pennsylvania Turnpike when the dam was being moved to White Gates Farm in New Jersey. The trucker took the calf out of the truck and put him in the cab and went on his way. During the time I used Black Bardolier I never used his entire name in registering his calves. I always expected to get a better one and when Black Bardolier G. R. was calved, I was sure that he was the best bull calf that I had ever seen, so I named him Black Bardolier G.R. When I purchased Black Bardolier G.R., then two months old, and his dam in our dissolution sale, I had to pay $10,000 in order to acquire the pair. When he was fourteen months old I refused $25,000 for him, but never put a price on him. His blood is certainly carrying on well here. A number of top producing females are his daughters. They are really breeding true. I know you will have a big demand for his get. He breeds great headed cattle with lots of quality so don't sell yourself short. Remember, he is one of the last two or three sons of Black Bardolier living.

    When you come to Michigan be sure to come and see me. I always enjoy visiting with you and look back on our bull transactions with satisfaction and pleasure.

    With kindest personal regards to you and Mrs. Jennings, I am,

Very cordially yours,

J. J. Hendren, M. D.

JJH/wh

"The Home of the Phenomenal Bardoliers"

Letter from J. J. Hendren, M.D. after our purchase of the entire Raona Herd.

Chapter 34

Bulls—Montana Bound

In the late 1930's and early 1940's when George Wermersen and I had bought lots of cattle in the state of Montana we observed that this vast cattle country had a lot of top ranches with practically all Hereford cows and bulls. There are a lot of top ranches in these two states.

When Ted and I started in the purebred Angus business the opportunity was still there. Most all of the cattle in Montana were still Hereford. Occasionally there was a small herd of black Angus. There was a lot of room for a lot of Angus bulls and I wanted to be part of this opportunity. I vowed to myself that I would somehow "paint Montana black" with the use of our Angus bulls.

I was asked to judge the 1954 Angus cattle show at the Montana State Fair at Great Falls and that opened the door for me. I judged the show and had the privilege of meeting all the fair board members, plus a multitude of breeders. Buck Moore, an aggressive young banker in Great Falls, was on the fair board, as was Sam Dawson, owner of the Hidden Valley Ranch at Belt, Montana. Buck told me that there were quite a number of ranchers who were looking for a source of Angus bulls to put on their cows and heifers. Most of the ranchers were his customers at the bank. He volunteered to tell me that he would request that several of these ranchers come to my ranch in South Dakota and buy some good Angus bulls. He hoped that the price would be feasible to commercial cattle people. I told him that without question I could sell them the best bulls at the best price anywhere in the U. S. Buck and I created a lasting friendship from that day on.

I went through Great Falls several times the next summer and stopped at the bank and furthered our desire to put black Angus bulls in volume to his customers.

Sam Dawson, Belt, Montana.   Floyd Dawson, Belt, Montana.

Buck called sometime in late September in regard to when I would be available and I told him that I would guarantee that I would be available on the ranch any time he called.

Sam and Floyd Dawson, (father and son) Johnny Marn, manager of the Willow Creek Ranch and Buck Moore made the first trip to the ranch in late October 1954. I put them up at my home on the ranch. After supper we had a few highballs and got a poker game going until the wee hours of the morning. I invited my neighbor and good friend down for the game. He was a great poker player and the life of the party. We all got better acquainted than we could have in any other circumstance. I studied the banker as best I could and he was exceptionally likeable and yet really business minded.

The next morning after a hearty breakfast we all loaded into my best pickup and headed up to the bull ranch, which was about 4 miles northeast. We had the bulls sorted into several pastures and we took our time having a good look at each bull. These were coming two-year-old bulls. They were very gentle and we could walk among them easily. Feeling my way as we went along looking at the bulls, I knew they were interested in a volume deal. I felt real confident that they would like our bulls and their smiles and expressions gave them away.

They were all busy people and they were anxious to head back to Montana. We went back to the ranch and sat around an octagon table in my western designed sunroom. They asked what I wanted for the bulls. I said "Fellas, it amounts to this first. How many bulls do you want to buy and do you want to buy your choice out of all the pastures or just one pasture?" They looked at each other and said that they were so much alike they would take one potload (50 to 55 head) out of one pasture. I volunteered, "Well, that way I'll let you pick them." Because of the future potential I priced them about $100 less than I would sell them for in singles or small groups. I wanted to get a toe-hold in that country. They really liked the bulls but said they were priced higher than a lot of bulls in Montana. We negotiated on the delivery and all the other details. Then Sam Dawson cut in and said, "Clayton, we will give you $700.00 per head." This was $50.00 a head less than I had priced them. He didn't know it right then, but he had already bought the bulls. I stalled a little and changed the conversation somewhat because I didn't want to seem too eager to sell bulls. I wanted to see them sweat a while and then I said, "Fellas, in the first place I like you and it's a pleasure and an honor to send a set of bulls like you are getting to Montana, because I know you will be back for more bulls next year. When your neighbors see these bulls and the calves they sire, they will try to beat you here for bulls!" Everyone of them expressed a sigh of relief. They were pleased and whereas I had sold a bunch of bulls a little under the money I was betting on the come and come they did!

The next year they bought twice as many bulls, plus many other Montana ranchers came, making Montana the best state, except South Dakota for Angus bull sales for a long period. Their money was always good on the bulls we sent as many of them were banked by Buck Moore, one of the most aggressive and knowledgeable bankers in the livestock business and my friend. Buck believed in our cattle and he was instrumental in many of these ranchers coming to buy our bulls. He often used the phrase "Faith Well Placed."

I sent potload after potload after potload of bulls every fall, winter and spring "painting Montana black!"

Chapter 35

First Sale at the Hyland Angus Ranch

Ted and I held our first sale at the Hyland Angus Ranch on May 9th, 1955. This was a two-day affair which included meals, entertainment and refreshments as well as the sale. This was our third annual bull sale. The other two were held at the Miller salebarn. We had just completed a new salebarn on the ranch. It was 36' by 144' with a 64' section forming the sale ring "T" at the east end of the building. To the west of the salebarn we had cattle pens and corrals extending for one half mile, with a capacity of two thousand head.

Sale time was at 12:00 noon. The sale started off with a bulging salebarn of standing room only and although the crowd changed several times during the selling, there was still standing room only at the conclusion of the sale. There were four hundred cars and trucks from twenty-three states and Canada with an estimated two thousand one hundred people in attendance.

At this first sale on the ranch we sold 155 Angus bulls that averaged $711.00 and 100 commercial heifers that averaged $129.00. Arnold Martinmaas of Faulkton, South Dakota, paid the top price of $2,500.00 for a January 1954 bull calf sired by O Bardoliermire 2nd. Another yearling Hyland Bardalier 151, a definite herd bull prospect, sold for $2,300.00 to George Becker of Sheldon, North Dakota. Two bulls going for $525.00 and $550.00 were purchased by the Davenport

Hyland Angus Ranch Salebarn completed in 1955 just before the first sale. It had not been painted yet.

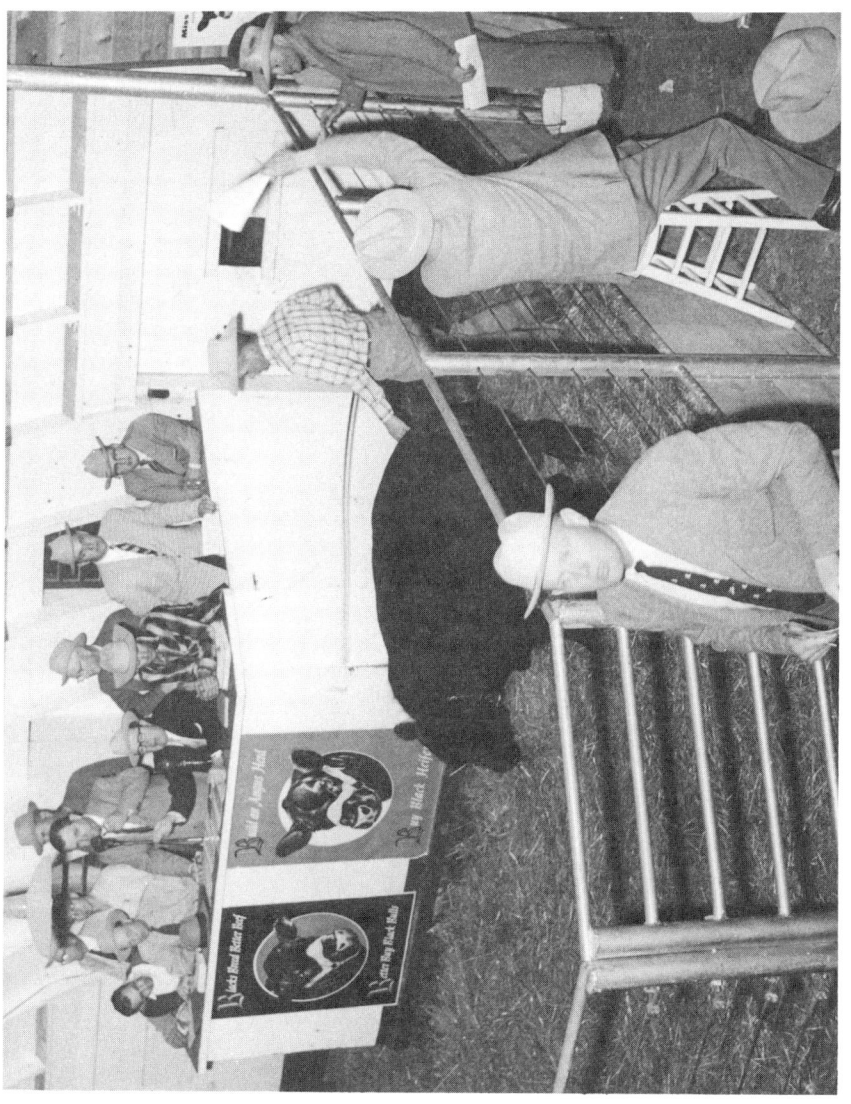

The sale-ring—Hamilton James, auctioneer standing at microphone; J. B. McCorkle, sitting at microphone; Clayton Jennings in stripped shirt; J. M. Magness, auctioneer behind Clayton; Pat Goggins in front of ring; Argyl Conner in ring; Frank Bosler of Wyoming farthest right.

Perspective buyers looking over the bulls before the Hyland Angus Ranch sale—1955.

Aerial view of the cars and trucks at the first sale—1955.

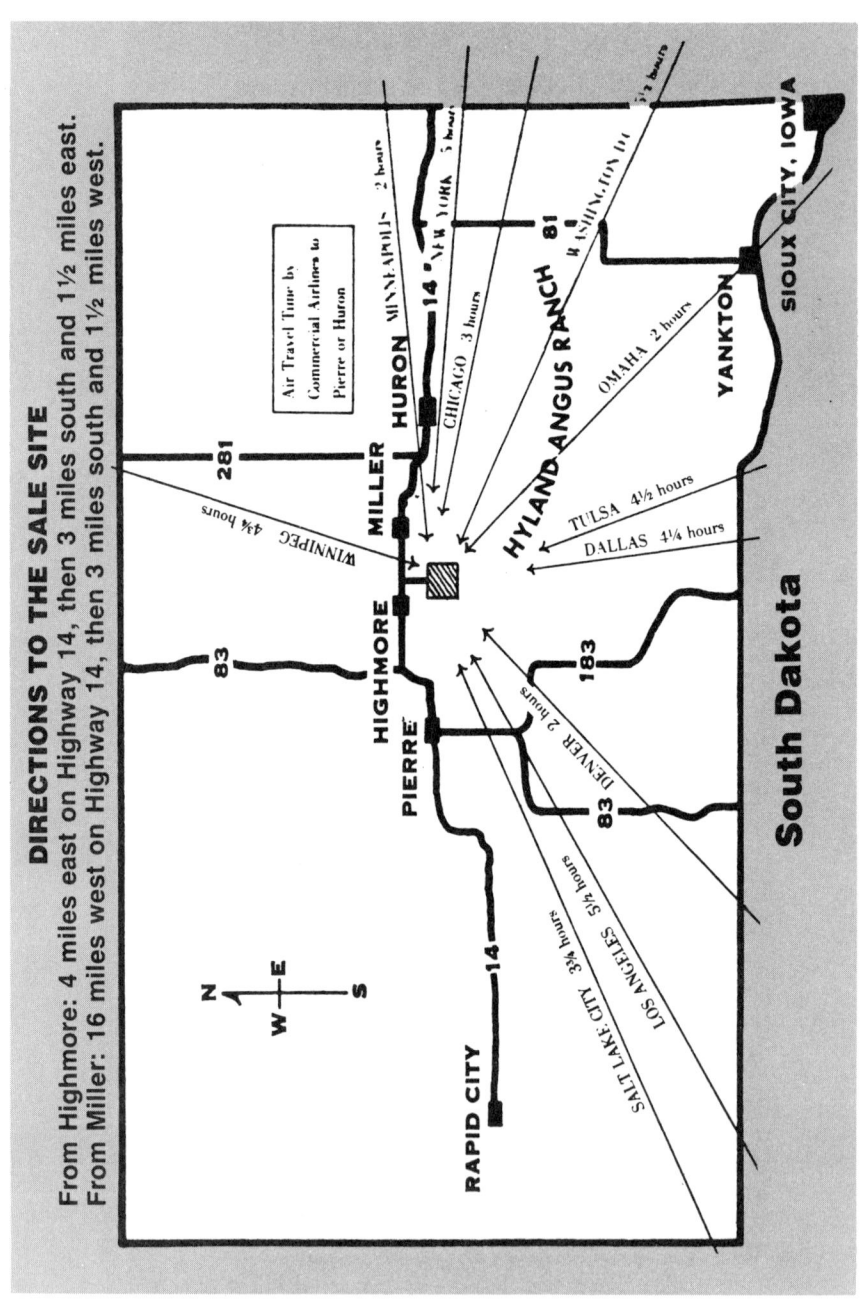

All roads and flyways lead to Hyland Angus Ranch, Highmore, South Dakota.

Angus Ranch of Goldendale, Washington, giving them the distinction of being purchasers of bulls going the farthest distance from the sale. The sale's volume bull buyer was Bruce Orcutt of Miles City, Montana, who bought twenty-one bulls in the $400 to $800 price range for a total of $12,760.00. Orcutt runs commercial cattle, both Hereford and Angus.

The top selling set of commercial heifers sold to Faye Quinn of Cody, Nebraska. He took twelve head at $152.00 a round. The largest buyer of heifers was James Langley of Wolsey, South Dakota, with twenty-six head.

This first sale was most active and most successful and was just the beginning of many more sales to be held at the Hyland Angus Ranch.

We knew the demand for Angus cattle and the expansion of Angus cattle had just begun. We knew that ours was but a small part in this great crusade but we were greatly enthused by the challenge. We were determined to make available as many of the right kinds of bulls in the right kind of condition as our operation would support.

Chapter 36

Copenhagen

One day in 1956, I stopped at Fred Dittman's ranch to sell him 240 acres of the Harry Robinson Ranch, as it bordered on his pasture. I thought he could use it to a real advantage, and I was willing to sell it to him for $35.00 an acre, which was my cost the previous year. I thought it would make our good relations even better.

Fred and his eight year old son, Jim, were standing in the yard, when I drove in. I got out of my car. I was wearing a fancy Stetson hat, a blue velveteen shirt with white snap buttons, Levi's and black boots with silver caps on the toes. Jim thought, "Wow, this guy is impressive I wonder what he does for a living?"

I pulled my Copenhagen out of my pocket, tapped the can, opened it, and took a chew. I then handed Jim the can, he tapped it and took a good chew for a kid of eight. Within a few minutes, Jim disappeared. We saw him running toward the barn. Fred and I visited about the land deal, but he needed to talk to his father-in-law, Bert Bawdon. Then he would let me know in a day or two.

I stopped by a few days later. Fred had decided to buy the land, which made our friendship even more friendly. He told me then that Jim had gotten really sick from the chew of Copenhagen. That's why we saw him headed for the barn so fast. He vomited until he was almost dehydrated! Jim's second chew was much later in life, but it was also from me, and he has been chewing Copenhagen ever since—over thirty years!

Clayton Jennings and Jim Dittman—A chew in 1993.

Chapter 37

Discipline

The government had a program which gave the farmers and ranchers an incentive to plant trees to create shelterbelts and windbreaks. They paid enough to make it worthwhile plus adding much to the value and beauty of the operation. We signed up for trees for a large horseshoe shaped shelterbelt on the Jim Blair Ranch that we had just recently purchased. The horseshoe shape was so the cattle could have shelter from storms from any direction. Each year we were paid to keep the trees clear of weeds. If we did not keep them clean there was no government payment!

We prepared the land by plowing it and keeping it black for one year. Then in the spring of 1956 a crew came out and planted the trees. We had six rows of trees, each being 1.3 miles long, for a total of 7.8 miles of trees. We planted three rows of Chinese elm and one row of Russian olive. The trees were planted about ten feet apart. We planted honeysuckle in the north row with the bushes five feet apart and thorny green barberry bushes in the south row with the bushes four feet apart making a grand total of 5,148 trees.

We had a tracter with a sharp disc to keep the shelterbelt clean, but we needed ten or twelve kids to hoe and pull the weeds in the tree rows. The creeping jenny was the biggest problem. It was a vine that would entwine the small sapling and eventually kill it. The jenny had to be unwrapped from the sapling and then pulled out of the ground. It was impossible to kill, but it could be controlled. We made a deal with some of our ranch kids and some kids from Miller who were eager for a job. We would pick them up each morning about eight, except the weekends, and take them back home at five. I paid them on Friday evening of each week. We issued each child a new hoe and a pair of canvas gloves. The first day out, I sat the kids down in the back of the pickup and told them exactly what I expected of them. I talked at length to them in regards to their work and why it was important to do it this way. Then we went out to the trees and I showed them personally how I wanted it done between the trees. I told them that they could either hoe or pull the weeds. It didn't matter just as long as the ground was black and contained no weeds. Then I said, "Do you all understand?" and they all nodded their heads affirmatively.

I put two kids on the start and then two more down the line and so on down the rows, so we had no more than two working close together. After I got them all placed I told each pair I would be back at noon with something for them to eat and drink. So long till noon!

Dorothy and I decided on a menu for the kids. She made them roast beef sandwiches, cake and cookies, fresh lemonade or iced tea. We had some really large thermoses and throw away cups with everything in abundance. We fed them right in the tree claim and boy did they eat! The lemonade was the favorite I couldn't count how many cups they drank, always finishing it first. We let them rest for an hour, and then back to work.

I came back about 4 o'clock and could see that the kids were really tired, so I took them back to town. This went on most of the summer. The kids were doing a really nice job and they were having fun. There were a couple spots that didn't suit me, so I took a couple kids over to clean that up, without embarrassing those who were a little slack in their work. Everyone of them developed into top-notch pullers and hoers. We used this same procedure with some of the same kids for three consecutive summers. There were some tomboy girls among the crews who did as well as any of the boys.

Two of the crew were my nephews Ronnie and Gary Jennings, Ted's boys. Gary had a few defugalties with Ronnie, I don't know about what, but one day Gary had had enough. In the middle of the afternoon he walked the three miles to Highway 14 and hitch-hiked a ride back to Miller.

He wasn't there when I paid the kids on Friday night, so he didn't get anything for his work. He should have remembered that payday was on Friday night, but he wasn't there! * * * * *

At the time of this tree claim deal I had two boys, Alfred Meyer known to all as "Rawhide" and John Gerlach of Miller putting in treated posts for a corral fence at my headquarters ranch.

I had the boys get a dirt auger, shovel, spades and a couple five gallon buckets. I sat down with both of them and told them how and what I wanted. I wanted the posts set even on the inside of the corral where we would attach the plank. I told them to always sight down the posts so they could only see one post—they were to be in line. I wanted the post tamped really heavy so the wind or cattle would not push the posts or plank out of shape. They were to dig all the post holes by hand and if the ground was too hard they could use the five gallon buckets to carry water to soak it. I told them they could go to the house for dinner. I left and did not get back in time to have dinner with them.

I came back shortly after noon and went to check on the boys. Their project looked good upon approaching it, but I sighted down from one end where we were going to hang a gate and then I went to the other end and sighted back (100 yards) and found that the one post that they started from was about five or six inches out of line. I told them, "Sight down there boys. Then go to the other end and sight back and tell me what you see." They did and saw the post out of line and one of them said, "What can we do about that?" I said, "That's simple boys. You just dig that post up, clean out the hole and put it in where it belongs." This was an eight inch post about twelve feet long with about four feet in the ground. It would be a job digging it out by hand but I wanted it done right. I was paying them by the day so it didn't cost them anything, but it did cost me a little extra.

I left them in a bewildered state of mind, but when I returned that evening they had just finished that job and had done it well. From then on these boys were on our fencing crew and could fence with the best of them.

* * * * *

I love kids and have always enjoyed them, especially the bratty and ornery ones. There's something about these kids that contest you that I like and I can handle them.

My theory of handling kids I learned from four years in the Navy. The Navy way is the best I have ever been affiliated with in my lifetime. If you fail to fulfill your assignment in the Navy, they simply make you wish you had. They will assign you duty that will make you think and wish you had not defied the orders. This Navy discipline has stayed with me. I have never whipped or spanked any kids, but when they need discipline I merely demand their attention and that's all I have ever needed with them.

* * * * *

These next two stories on discipline were written by my daughter, Gloria Jennings Holdman.

THUNDER'S LAST BUCK

Little girls (and big girls) are always trying to win the love and approval of their fathers. I was no exception. I always liked to have a "surprise" waiting for Dad when he got home at night. On this particular day, I was the one who got surprised.

I was about five years old and had a black and white spotted pony named "Thunder." As is true with a lot of ponies, Thunder could get pretty ornery. Dad had left before I got up that morning and I decided to learn a trick on Thunder to show him when he got home that night. My trick was going to be making Thunder lope (or canter). Well, Thunder and I practiced the trick on the grassy area in front of the house all day long. By the time Dad got home at dusk, Thunder was beginning to get cranky.

When I saw Dad's car turn the corner, I jumped off Thunder and raced on foot to meet him. He could barely get the car turned off before I was dragging him out to take a seat on the fence to watch my performance. I jumped on Thunder and took off full force. Thunder had had enough. He kicked up his back feet, and I went flying through the air and landed on the ground in front of him. Well, little ranch girls don't cry. I got up, dusted myself off, and heard Dad yell, "You get right back up there and show him who's boss." I jumped back into the saddle, took off again, and Thunder bucked me off for a second time. I was getting up a little slower when Dad came over and said, "You get right back up there and show him who's boss."

After Thunder bucked me off a third time, while still on the ground and still no tears, I peeked under my arm to see if Dad was going to be crazy enough to make me get back on that blasted pony. He wasn't, but he was mad. The pony's bridle had long reins that reached his entire length. Dad came over, took those reins in hand, and whipped that pony for what seemed like forever. Dad then turned to me and said, "Get back up there now." Thunder performed like an angel, and although he bucked with every other kid on the ranch, he never bucked with me again. It was the only time I had ever seen my dad strike an animal, other than a sorting stick in a pen. He made Thunder a believer, and me, too.

NONSENSE

Growing up on a cattle ranch can be hazardous for kids. There are potentially dangerous situations with livestock and machinery. Dad and our ranch foreman Harold Parlin were constantly warning us kids about the things to not do or stay away from. Of course, the temptation for mischief was always present for us.

Dad never spanked me when I was growing up. There are some people who say that is what's wrong with me now, and I can remember Dad saying on more than one occassion that I was "uncoachable." Some things never change.

My brother Charlie was five years older than I, and my brother Jim was eight years younger. Charlie and I were a couple of outlaws, constantly fighting and bickering. Dad had a fear-inspiring word he used when we were, in his assessment, "acting the fool." That word was NONSENSE. What power that word had for us!

Dad used NONSENSE in a lot of different ways: "This NONSENSE has got to stop!" – "I'm not going to take any more of this NONSENSE." – and, of course, his short and to-the-point favorite "This is NONSENSE!" Charlie, Jim and I always knew if Dad used the word NONSENSE, we had better quit what we were doing immediately and never even consider doing it again! Dad has always had a great sense of humor, and we got by with a lot. But there was always something about the tone of his voice and manner when he used the word NONSENSE that told us we had better straighten up and fly right or else. Don't guess we ever did find out what the "or else" was. We just took him on his word.

Chapter 38

Eloise—My Second Wife

I met Eloise Dwyer in Denver through a mutual friend. We dated regularly. She had a tantalizing personality that no one could forget. No matter where we went, she always stole the show. All eyes turned to her. She was always dressed to the hilt with never one of her red hairs out of place. She

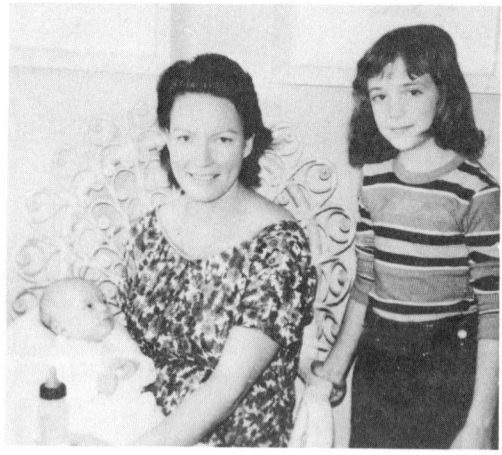

November 1961. Eloise and Gloria Jennings and baby Jim.

March 1, 1959, Clayton Jennings and Eloise Dwyer wedding at Denver, Colorado. Johnnie Turner and Calvin Gadd attendents.

Clayton and Eloise Jennings with children Charlie, Gloria and Jim—1965.

was an accomplished singer and an excellent guitarist. "You name it and she could play it."

We were married in Denver, March 1, 1959. We made our home on the Hyland Angus Ranch headquarters. She contributed greatly to the promotion of our livestock operation.

Our son, James Ted, was born November 21, 1961. I was immensely happy to have another son.

I made sure Eloise had a good car. The first car I got her was the finest Cadillac I could find. She drove Cadillacs for several years. Then I got her a Lincoln Mark IV. When it came time to trade again Eloise said she would not trade for any other car as she loved the Mark IV too much. I was still driving a standard Chevrolet.

Our life together was good, until we got on a roller coaster and couldn't get off. We were divorced in 1979.

Chapter 39

Rocks Galore

Rocks have always been a menace to every agriculturally oriented industry in this country. They are the cause of a lot of grief when farming and when driving around with vehicles. The actual damages done to vehicles and equipment is unbelievable. That is why the rocks are picked and either piled in the fields or in the fencelines with hopes of moving them out all-together some day. It is seldom that a rancher can move any amount of all the rocks he has.

We observed in the aftermath of the great fire in 1944 the many rocks on the charcoal blackened prairie. Rocks could

Rock pile on one of the ranches.

Rip-rap along the Big Bend Dam at Ft. Thompson, South Dakota.

be seen clear across this vast land. It was unbelievable how many rocks there were in semi-rock country.

After purchasing our ranches, we spent some time each year picking and piling rocks in piles and in fencelines. It was a never ending job.

George Niederauer of Miller talked to me one day in the fall of 1960 about removing all the rocks from our ranches. He had the equipment, dozers, front-end loaders and trucks. He also had a sub-contract with Western Contracting to furnish all the rocks to the government for the rip-rap on the Big Bend Dam that was being built across the Missouri River at Fort Thompson, thirty miles south of Highmore. He would pick up all the piles of rocks and the rocks off the fields and pastures and he would guarantee to get all visible rocks on the entire ranch. He would deliver the truckloads of rocks to the damsite each day. Then Western Contracting would use them to rip-rap the dam. He would not charge a thing for the rocks removal. We helped him with some of the fencelines and piles. He worked parts of four years on this project and gave us a rock-free ranch.

You don't have to be smart if you're lucky as this increased the value of the land by no less than $25.00 an acre!

Chapter 40

Sugar Loaf Scot 913

I had been asked to judge the Great Atlantic Bull Show and Sale in Richmond, Virginia, in May 1961. I had judged this show twice previously and found it a very enjoyable show and sale of Purebred Angus bulls. There were about 500 yearling and two-year-old bulls in this sale, not highly fitted, but a really good honest set of bulls. I needed some additional bulls for my bull trade that year, so I bought a potload of these young bulls to come to South Dakota for development and sale.

When the load of bulls arrived at my ranch and were unloaded, my herdsman, Lefty Kluge, spotted an exceptional bull. We decided this bull would make a great show bull. Lefty wanted to put him in the show string immediately, so we could get him started. We watched him closely, and he developed exceptionally well all summer and fall.

We took him to the National Western Stock Show in Denver in January 1962. We entered him in the Angus show and the bull sale afterwards. He was an impressive young bull, and we gained confidence in him, as we could see he was a big-time bull. On show day he stood Reserve Grand Champion bull and was Champion Sale bull.

There was a big interest shown in this bull all through the week at Denver. We could see there would be a lot of interest in the sale.

Voldseth Bros. of Lennep, Montana, talked with me about this bull. They were interested in buying him to use, either naturally or artificially, on their Angus herd in Montana.

The bidding was fast and furious and the Voldseth Bros. had the final bid on him for $12,200.00, which set a new high for a bull in Denver's National Western Angus sale. Their bid, sent to Montana Jenning's Bros. Sugar Loaf Scot 913, Reserve Senior Champion bull of the National Western. A bull that had cost us $550.00, less than eight months earlier.

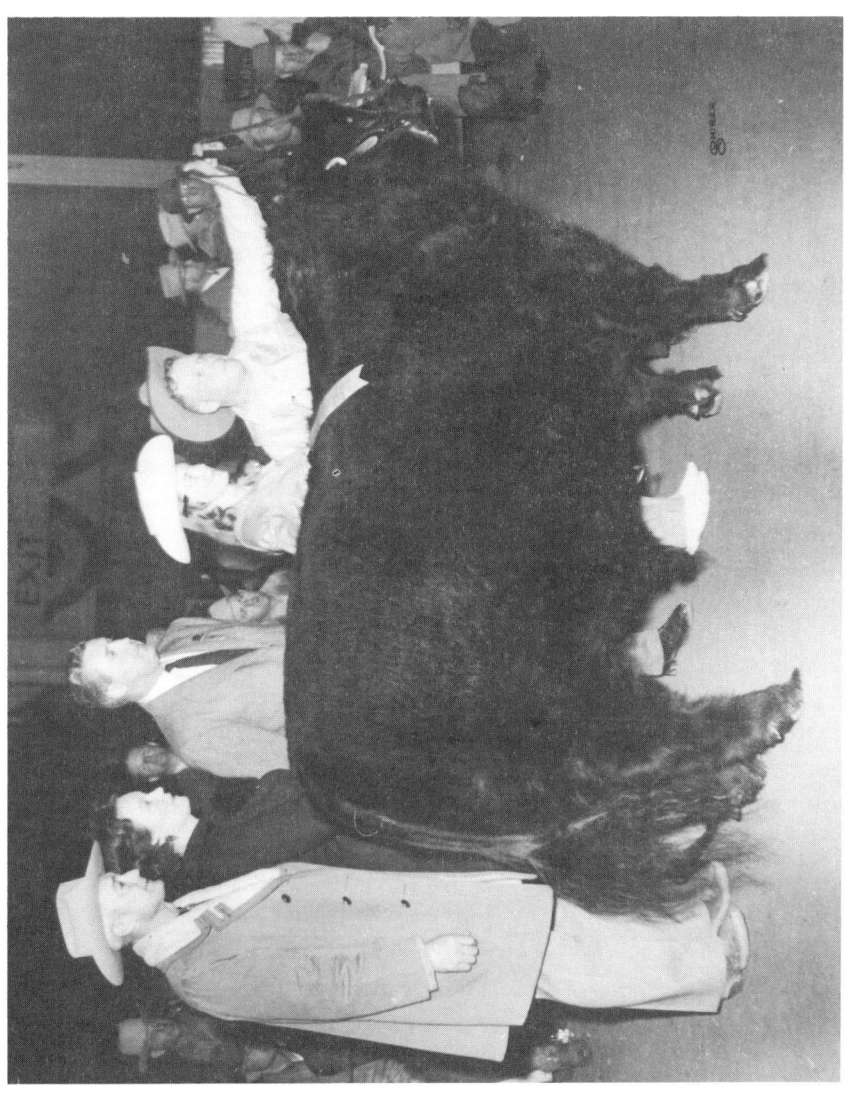

1962 National Western Stock Show, Denver, Colorado. L to r: Clayton Jennings, Eloise Jennings, Lee Leachman, Judge, the Angus Queen, Lefty Kluge holding Sugar Loaf Scot 913.

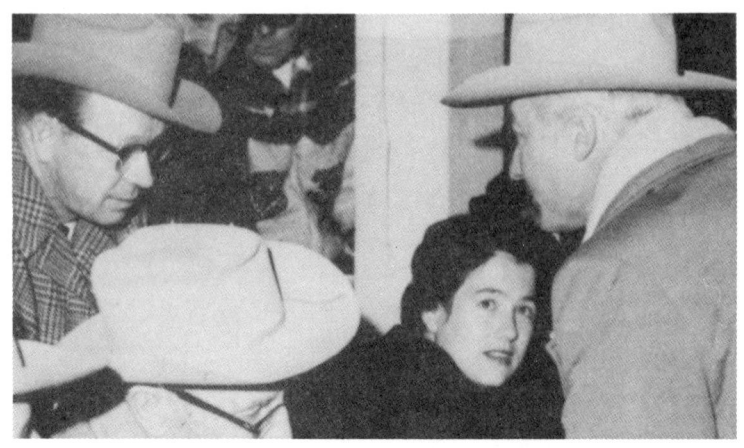

Moments later an Angus record

George Voldseth, Lennep, Mont., (top left) nodded after this short eye-to-eye consultation with Clayton Jennings, Hyland Angus Ranch, Highmore, S. D. That $12,200 nod set a new high for a bull in Denver's National Western Angus Sale. It sent to Montana, Jennings Bros.' Sugar Loaf Scot 913, reserve senior champion of the '62 National Western.

Chapter 41

The Big Move

I was aware that I had about the nicest life anyone could ask for, living right on the Hyland Angus Ranch for 18 years. There was absolutely nothing that my family and I lacked in material things for our needs and desires. My family was

Our home on the Hyland Angus Ranch.

basically happy and the children loved every minute of every day. They had their ponies to ride wherever they liked around the ranch and over to the neighbors to play with their children. They had their own bedrooms and were independent to come and go from all the facilities on the ranch. They rode their ponies to country school and back every day, if the weather was fit. The children were given a white German Shepherd dog by Frances and Stanley Johnston, so naturally they called her Frances. This pup and the children grew up together. She was with them every minute of the day or night that they were outside of the house. She was a constant companion to the children and protected them in many ways. She would allow no one to scuffle or wrestle with the children. This was the most loyalty from a dog I had ever experienced. She died when she was about ten-years-old. That was a sad day for all of our family. We gave her an honorable burial under the shade of a large cedar tree. Frances has been gone for twenty-five-years and to this day when the children and I are together, there is always a conversation about Frances. Jim was just a baby, so he hadn't enjoyed the luxuries the other two had.

All my life, I had enjoyed working long, hard hours but there were times when I had more stress than I could handle. Also I had a mental stress that went along with a lot of land purchases, cattle dealings and general operation of our ranches.

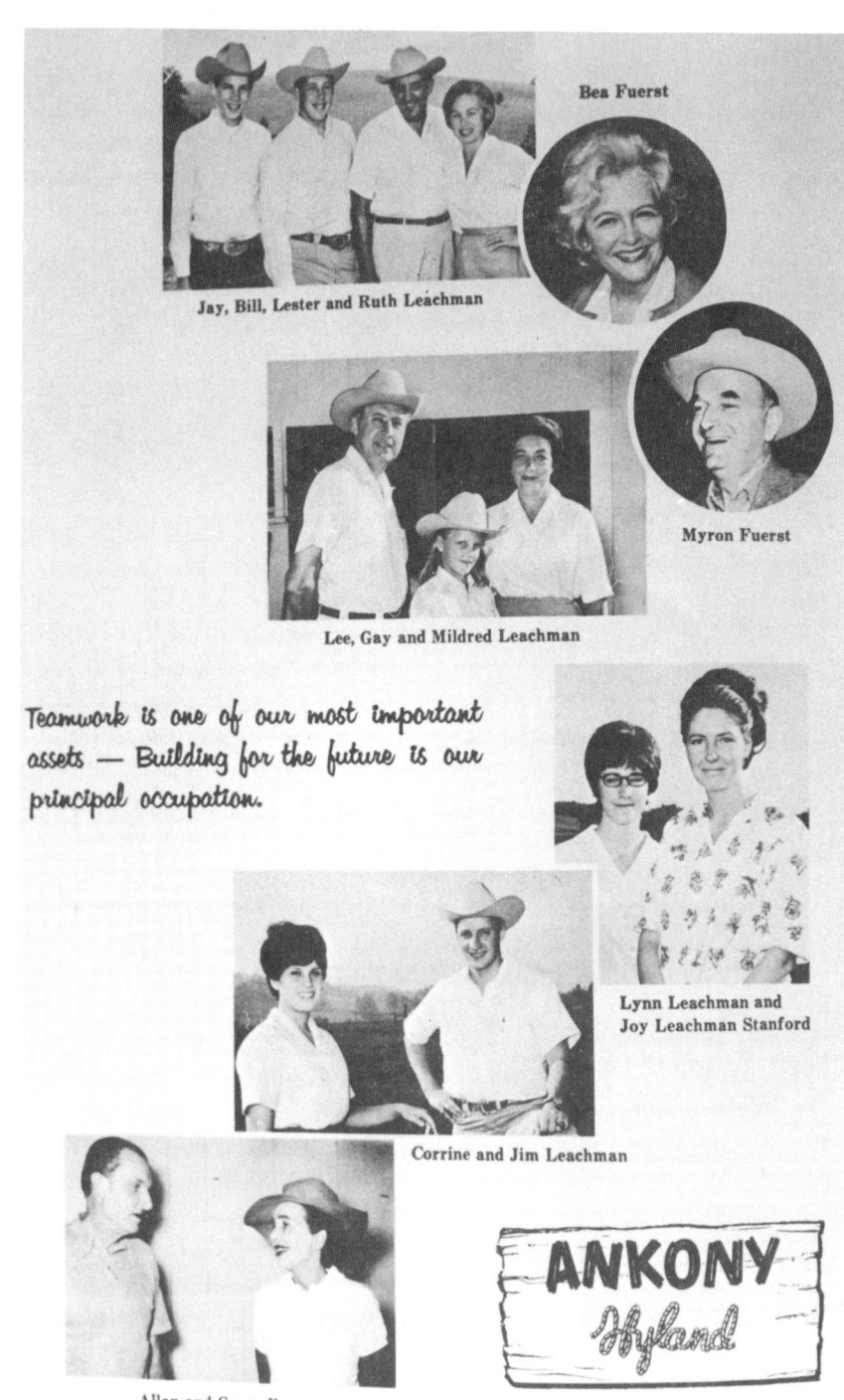

Ankony Angus Corporation of Rhinebeck, New York.

Eloise and I thought we could semi-retire. We wanted to build a place to suit us. and maintain the amount of business we desired. Then the whole family would be free to do some things we always wanted to do. We were also in the best financial condition ever in my lifetime, so we decided to make a move.

In 1963, we decided to sell all of our land, the purebred cattle, and equipment to Ankony Angus Corporation out of New York, one of the largest and best purebred breeding establishments in all America. We had done a lot of purebred business with Ankony for several years and they had indicated that they would surely be interested in our ranch, if and when we wanted to sell. They were financially sound, so we had no worries.

I had bought a lot of bulls from Ankony Angus over the past few years and their word was as good as any contract written. They planned to go right on with my breeding program and I would be in a position to be part of it, if I so desired.

We sold the ranch, purebred cattle, and all the equipment, with a good down payment, and the balance over a period of 15 years at 5% interest.

We had decided we would buy some land near a town or city we liked and build a new home and livestock handling facility and operate it to the extent we desired.

We started looking around for a place to retire, and it seemed that we could find no area that we liked as well as Highmore. We traveled all over America. We liked a lot of places, but none suited us like Highmore. This was mostly because I did not want to leave the cattle country that had been so good to me.

We bought 160 acres of land adjoining the southeast corner of the Highmore city limits. We tore down or moved out all of the buildings, except one granary and garage. We retained possession of our home on the ranch until October 1, 1964, when our home in Highmore was to be completed.

We hired some local carpenters, Robert Mason, John Williams and Loren Garrigan, who were very reputable, to do the construction of our new home. Fred Hale, local plumber and electrician, also very reputable, did all the wiring and plumbing. My eldest son, Charlie, also helped the construction crew.

Jim Jennings and Vida Blue playing pool in our poolroom.

This crew was to start as soon as they could in the spring and have the job completed as soon as possible in the fall.

The house was 80' by 48' with three bedrooms, one being the master bedroom. It had a full 80' finished basement, with two bedrooms, a pool room, utility room and a large recreation area. We also had several walk-in cedar closets in the basement. We had an attached double garage with a large overhung room over the garage that we used for an office.

These construction workers did a super excellent job from the beginning to the finish, and on October 1st, Eloise and I with our young son, Jim, plus Gloria and Charlie, moved in. I should never want anything better than this home, as it had about all the comforts and conveniences of any home.

We sodded the big lawn and transplanted about twenty-five cedar trees and lots of other trees that complemented the landscape. The place looked finished when we moved in.

That fall we remodeled and built on to the corrals and had a good set of lifetime steel rod fence. We also built some of the out-buildings and facilities. We hired Keith Aasby of Highmore as foreman of all operations. He was to take over all the incoming and outgoing cattle from my yards in Highmore. He proved to be a good foreman. He was in control of any and all cattle movements, leaving nothing to doubt.

Our new home in Highmore. The trees have not been planted or the yard sodded.

Keith Aasby—1993.

1972—New office and livestock working facilities.

Dorothy Beck, my secretary for many years, in the new office.

Our customers were very pleased with his handling of their cattle. Keith had two sons, Kent and Ben, and they helped us after school and on Saturdays. They were both very capable boys.

In 1972 we built a 48' x 80' steel building to house a really nice office, inside livestock working chutes, an inside livestock scale and bath facilities. We also had enough space left for a room that I dreamed of finishing for the entertainment and fun of my friends and customers.

Chapter 42

Black Angus Heifers by the Trainload

My friend Dave Canning was owner of Sugar Loaf Farms, a purebred Angus operation at Staunton, Virginia. He also maintained one half interest in Court Manor Plantation, an Angus breeding establishment at New Market, Virginia. At that time he had one of the most popular herds of Angus cattle. He was secretary of the Eastern United States Angus Association, an organization that he helped start years before. Dave started in the purebred Angus business in 1937. He was highly knowledgeable and successful in the field of Angus cattle. He was probably one of the greatest promoters of Angus cattle of all times. He has been known as one of the big men in the Angus shows and sales, wherever it might be.

Through my association with him at the many shows and sales, we became personal friends. It is a friendship we have cherished ever since. We had many deals of buying or selling where we were both involved. Many of the deals we made in volume dollars were done over the telephone and his recommendations and word were as good as any contract that can be drawn.

Dave Canning

We called each other on many occasions on quite a regular basis to help keep informed of the trend of markets in the purebred cattle industry.

Dave called early one morning in February 1964. He told me he had a tremendous interest in bred commercial Angus

Court Manor Plantation located on U.S. 11 in the beautiful historic Shenandoah Valley at New Market, Virginia.

heifers to go to some big ranches in Virginia. If I could get them bought, he could get them sold—on a volume basis. I had already been approached by numerous ranchers who wanted to sell some Angus bred heifers. These operators were not fixed to calve these heifers and wanted to sell them in the worst way, before they calved, which was soon. These heifers were showing heavy with calf and needed to be moved right soon or it would be disastrous to ship them while calving. I told Dave I was going to look at several bunches of heifers and would call him back in a couple of days.

I made the rounds of most of the ranchers who had bred heifers to sell and they were all willing to sell at a very reasonable price. I told them that I would be selling them to an outfit in Virginia. I would be shipping them by rail and it would be several days before the money got back here to them. They seemed willing to go on my word. I told them I would let them know about the deal—either on or off—as soon as I knew and as soon as I could get a special train of cars for the heifers to be shipped out of Miller, South Dakota.

That night I called Dave and informed him of what I had found and what they could be bought for. There were 1,250 top quality top condition Angus heifers and they would start calving about March 1st. They were a fancy set of heifers, artificially bred to Hyland Angus bulls which were some of the best bulls of the breed, and they would look good to anyone.

Dave had several buyers who would buy all of these heifers. They needed them to replace depleted herds caused by the serious drought in that area the year before. I needed to get them on the rail as soon as possible. He would guarantee his end of the deal of getting them sold at a profitable price. He was truly enthused as I was about this trainload to be shipped in a few days to a destination on the east coast. We fully believed that this was a top set of heifers, and they would easily stand the trip to Virginia and sell at a profitable price.

I made arrangments with the Chicago and Northwestern Railroad for thirty-eight carloads of these heifers to be shipped from Miller, South Dakota, to the Court Manor Plantation, New Market, Virginia, on February 7, 1964.

The sellers were advised of the day and time they should have their heifers at the railroad stockyards. Each seller was designated a certain time because the stockyards didn't have adequate facilities to hold all the heifers at one time. We had to count and load each man's heifers on the railroad cars. We followed this procedure with each rancher. All the heifers were within driving distance of the salebarn, from four to six miles, except one bunch. Don Reiman's heifers were a little too far, so had to be trucked in to Miller. The ranchers gathered them at daylight and had them in by their designated times. We got a good count on the heifers as we loaded them. These heifers were heavy with calf and were valued at nearly $400,000.00. At today's values they would be worth about one and a half million dollars! Donlin Brothers had 400 head, Paul Robinson 350 head, Robert Wagner 200 head, Donald Reiman 300 head, for a total of 1250 head. Les Leachman and B. A. Rucker, veteran cattlemen from the east coast, had come to South Dakota to inspect the heifers when we counted and loaded them. It was very enjoyable to count and load these heifers on the railroad cars. We took some pictures of the crew and the trainload of heifers. Then the engine whistled several times and headed east.

I had two caretakers ready to ride the caboose of the trainload of heifers all the way to Virginia. Dean Henson of Miller, South Dakota, and James Palon of Highmore, South Dakota, had agreed to do this. These riders were to care for the heifers at each feed station stop. They had to see that they were unloaded, fed, watered and rested for ten to twelve hours. Then they were loaded back on the cars to continue the journey. The cattle could not ride any longer than 36 hours without a stop. The first stop was at Blue Island (Chicago), Illinois, where they were fed, watered and rested for ten to twelve hours. The next stop was Pittsburg, Pennsylvania, where they were again fed, watered and rested for ten to twelve hours. The train had left Miller, South Dakota, Monday noon and arrived at the Pontiac Yards in Virginia, just outside Washington, D.C. on Saturday evening. The press took pictures. There was T.V. coverage at Senator Gore, Sr. of Tennessee, Senator Mundt and Senator McGovern of South Dakota were in attendance. From there they went on to Court Manor, New Market, Virginia. We had the best of luck with the cattle on the train. There was no death loss and no cripples and

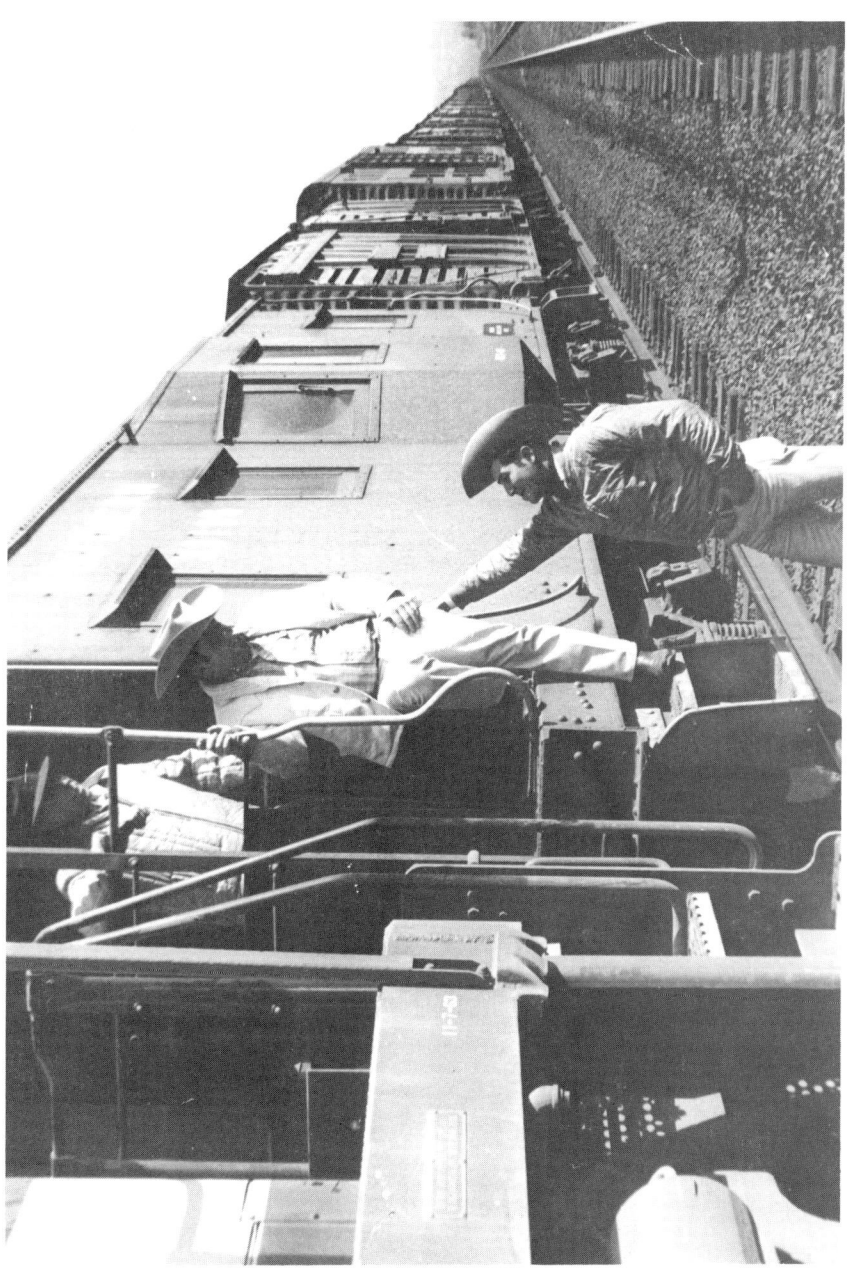

B. A. Rucker, Dean Henson and James Palon on the caboose of the trainload of heifers at Pontiac Yards outside Washington, D.C.

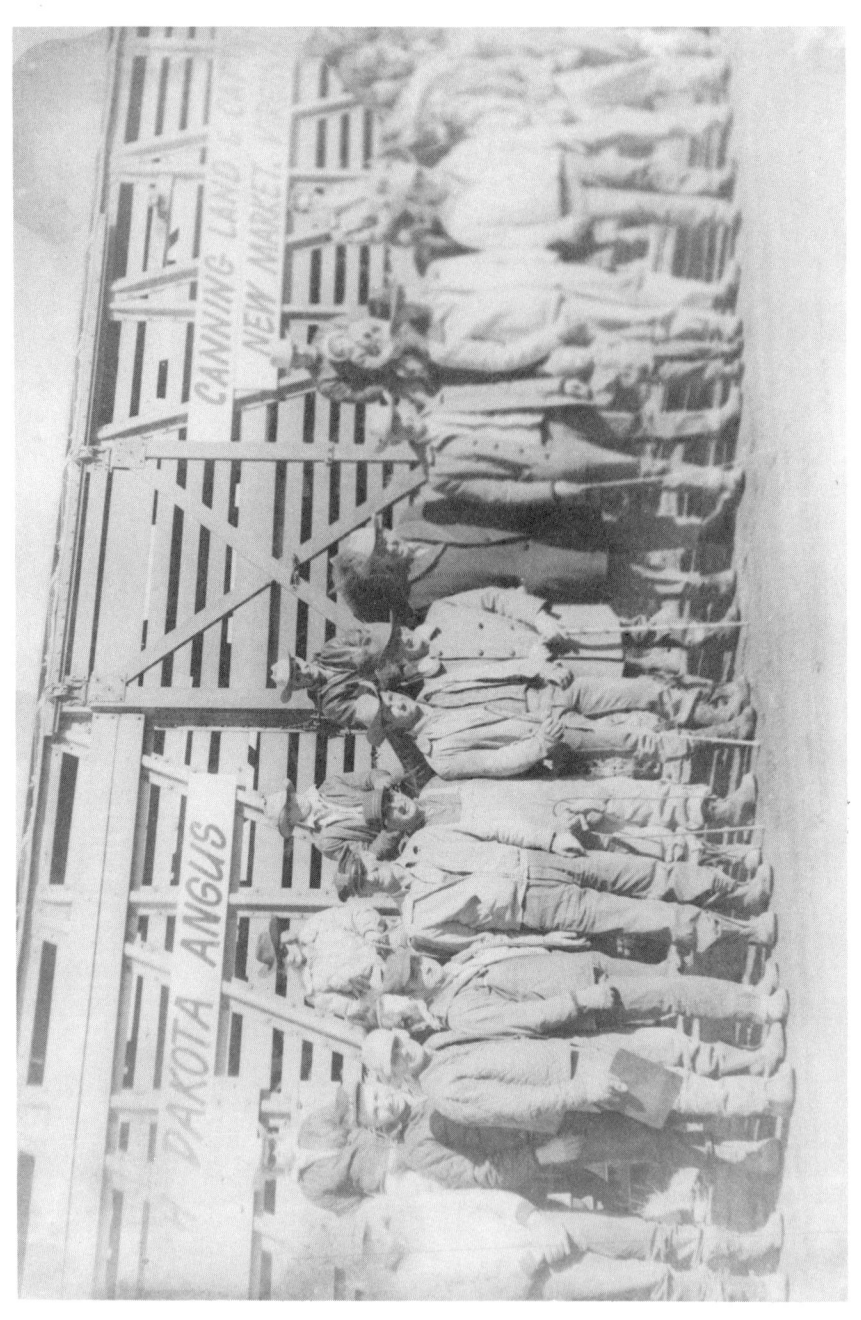

L to r: Dean Robinson, Don Rieman, Fred Meek, ? , McMurtry, Paul Robinson, James Palon, ? , Les Leachman, Clayton Jennings holding Jim Jennings' hand, B. A. Rucker, Dean Henson, Robert Wagner. On horses: Elinor Hahn, Cheryl Hahn, Mike Hahn, Melvin Fischer, Al Donlin holding Lori Robinson, ? .

L to R: ? , McMurty, Paul Robinson, James Palon, ? , Les Leachman, Clayton Jennings holding Jim Jennings' hand, B. A. Rucker, Dean Henson, Robert Wagner, Mike Donlin, Earl Mosher. On horses: Elinor Hahn, Cheryl Hahn, Mike Hahn, Melvin Fischer. Al Donlin holding Lori Robinson, ? , Ross VanBalen, ? .

within a few days, they were rested and looked as good as on their home grounds in South Dakota. My caretakers, Dean and James, did an excellent job of getting these heifers to their destination in excellent condition. They also stayed on in Virginia and calved out the heifers as no one there knew much about calving out 1,250 first-calf heifers.

The banks had heard of this transaction but hadn't seen any money from their customers' heifers. We were able to stall the bankers a couple of days at a time and promised them the money would be here shortly. I talked with the sellers by phone and assured them things were in good shape. I told them, "Just don't go to the bank to answer any questions, and the money will be here in a few days."

I talked with Don Reiman and Al Donlin several times. They had 700 good heifers on the train. We visited about the progress of the train, as the caretakers called me at each stop to keep me informed about how the trip was going. Naturally they wondered when the money would get here. I told them as best I could, but the banker had gotten Don excited and when Don gets excited he has a tendency to stutter. Don said to Al, "WWWell if ttthat mmmoney doesn't ggget here soon, III'll ggget a HHHonda and wwwhile I gggas up, you gggrab some road mmmaps. Wwwe'll put our cccaps on bbbackwards and head east. If the bbbanker sssees us, hhhe won't know if wwwe're cccoming or gggoing!!!"

The money came and everyone got paid 100% on the dollar. Everyone was happy, including the bankers! Dave Canning produced exactly as he said he would, which only verfied my confidence in him.

This was a very successful venture for Dave and me. We each enjoyed a reasonable profit.

Considering the volume of dollars involved and the distance between buyers and sellers—this ranks among the biggest deals and biggest risks of my time!

Chapter 43

J & J Ranch
Steamboat Springs, Colorado

A mountain ranch was something I had always found fascinating. I had owned thousands of acres of ranch land on the plains. Now I was intrigued with the talk of a mountain ranch—land from level to gently rolling hills and mountains with plenty of trees for shade and shelter, for year round protection, and water from the many mountain springs and streams. Beauty beyond all expectations!

While attending the Denver Stock Show in 1965, I coincidentally mentioned to Don Lufkin, an acquaintance of mine from Steamboat Springs, Colorado, my desire to own a mountain ranch. Don was a rancher near Steamboat Springs, and he knew of a pair of rancher brothers, who were getting on in years and were thinking of selling their ranch. They found it difficult to handle the weather and ranching operation, so after 55 years of operating their ranch, they had decided to sell.

As I talked further with Don, I became more and more interested. I had never been on or owned a real mountain ranch. I arranged, through Don, to meet these two ranchers and have them show me the ranch. Before going out to look over the ranch, Ruben Widmayer, my attorney, and I went to see my friend F. M. Peterson at the Denver U.S. National Bank. We were in the bank only 20 minutes. In that length of time Mr. Peterson granted me a $500,000.00 line of credit to negotiate the purchase. We left with a pad of blank bank drafts in my hand.

Don, Ruben and I drove the 150 miles northwest of Denver on Highway 40, to Steamboat Springs, in the beautiful Rocky Mountains. The headquarters ranch was about four miles from Steamboat Springs on an all-weather road. The brothers showed us around all of the ranch that could be seen from a vehicle.

Part of the ranch, you just don't see unless you are in an aircraft or on horseback.

I was really impressed with the ranch. It was very, very scenic and beautiful. It surely had the marks of a high-class grass range. The more I studied on it, the more I looked at it, the better I liked it. I didn't buy the ranch the first day that I looked at it, because I thought it was too high, and they wouldn't change. But during the conversation of another day or so, I offered to buy the entire ranch, plus all the cattle that were on the ranch. This gave them an incentive to sell and clean up their whole ranch operation. They seemed really receptive to selling the ranch on a land and package deal.

The brothers gave me a new price on the total dollars on the land machinery and about 500 cows to be delivered in the fall of 1965. We negotiated for a few hours and came to terms on the entire ranch and cattle operation and machinery.

I felt I needed a good, dependable partner, who would be the working part of the ranch. I first went to see my good friend, Stanley Johnston of Ree Heights, South Dakota, with whom I made a deal on the ranch on a year by year basis, with a financial interest to follow. I had done a lot of cattle

Stanley Johnston on his ranch south of Ree Heights, South Dakota. 1974.

business with Stanley over the past twenty years and found him to be highly capable and efficient, and his integrity was beyond question. He was very pleasant and it always felt good just to be around him. He was going to be responsible for our partnership of nearly a million dollars, and honesty is the big factor in partnership profits or losses. In any deal with Stanley, regardless of size, you could accept his handshake as absolute and final.

I remember one day, several years earlier, as I was driving a few miles south of Ree Heights, I saw Stanley riding his buckskin horse in the pasture. He waved at me, so I stopped, as I had plenty of time, especially for my friend Stanley Johnston. After a good lengthy visit, I asked him what he was doing in the pasture. He told me that this land was up for sale and he was afraid he was going to lose it. He had been renting it and needed it really bad to go with his ranch. He told me flat out he had tried to get the money but failed. I knew Stanley and I knew he was worth every dime of it, so I asked him how much money he needed, and he said it would take $30,000.00. I recall that I had my checkbook in the glove compartment of my car, which was parked in the ditch where we were visiting. I got my checkbook and wrote him a check for $30,000.00 and handed it to him over the barbed wire fence. We shook hands. I had never seen anyone illuminated so big. He was worthy of anything that I could help him with. He just said, "I'll pay you back as soon as I can." In fifteen months he paid every dollar back! Never have I ever had a better friend or business associate! Another handshake deal, that turned out right!!

Lloyd Gilroy stayed to work for me, when I bought the Colorado ranch, as he had worked for the two brothers a good many years, and he knew the mountain ranch as good as anyone living. He would work with Stanley, my new partner, the year around. I felt that I had two people as capable and trustworthy as I could find in Stanley Johnston and Lloyd Gilroy. I liked Gilroy. He was always working for my interest.

Gilroy had several teen-age sons, who worked for us during the summer months, putting up hay and fixing fence. One year, Charlie, my eldest son, and his buddy, Mick Goodrich, both about 17, worked on this ranch for the summer. They helped Gilroy's boys with the haying and fencing. They both proclaim to this day, it's the greatest experience they ever had!

Stanley and I ran the 500 cows the first year and found that it took too much hay to winter a cow, so we sold the cows after raising the calves for one year. We sold the cows on a strong market, so we realized a little profit on the original price. Then we bought steer calves each fall or winter. We could run about 1,500 steers. It took a lot less labor and feed to run the yearlings. It was a lot more pleasant, especially during the winter.

When I bought the ranch, there was a ski lift being built right next to the ranch. There didn't seem to be any really lucrative enthusiasm about this ranch, as far as price wise, because of the fact that these ski runs were being built. No one had ever been able to figure out what these ski runs would amount to, but they eventually amounted to a lot more than the whole ranch!

Stanley and Frances Johnston and Taffy on the J and J Ranch at Steamboat Springs, Colorado. 1964.

Scott Gregg and Clayton Jennings. Picture taken 1993.

Stanley and I operated this ranch until his wife became ill, and they wanted to return to South Dakota to live. I released Stanley from his responsibility and paid him off as a partner.

It didn't take long for me to discover that this ranch operation was not going to work without Stanley and his wife.

In the fall roundup of 1967, Scott Gregg of Holabird, South Dakota was head man for my transplanted crew from South Dakota. Others in the crew were Scott's daughter Lori, Eleanor Hahn, Cheryl Hahn, Leonard Aasby, and Clarence Gluhm. Scott hauled all the saddles and gear out to the Colorado ranch in his pickup. Ralph Myers flew Eloise and I out to help with the roundup.

Gilroy worked with the roundup, as he knew all the shortcuts in gathering the cattle. This summer pasture comprised over 8,000 acres of big timber, scrub oak, thick brush, and an altitude of over 7,000 feet. If you found all the cattle, you were a genius, but Gilroy was the big factor in gathering these cattle, as he had done it for years. It took several days to gather all the steers, if you were lucky. We had good luck gathering and finally quit when we were just four steers short. We took for granted they were lost or dead and would not show up. They did show up, coming down out of the mountains in the spring after the snow had thawed. We were really surprised to see the steers still alive, as they had nothing but bark and limbs to survive on, and the winter had been unseasonably cold. They were walking slowly and wobbly. We had witnessed a mircle when we saw them come down out of the mountains.

The scrub oak was thick and the cattle loved to run under it to escape the roundup. Eloise was mounted on a good horse that would follow the cattle no matter where they went. One day as they emerged from under the scrub oak, Eloise's shirt was gone. The scrub oak had ripped it right off her back! One day Lori became lost. Eloise knew she could find her, so she sang as loud as she could, as she knew Lori would hear her, and she did! All of the people on the roundup were amateurs never having worked in mountainous terrain, but they truly enjoyed their work, even though they got all scratched up and saddle sore. Scott Gregg was without a doubt as good as any hand at gathering cattle in rough country. He organized his novice crew to perfection.

After a year of operating without Stanley, I decided it was just kind of a break even deal, and maybe not quite that, especially if we had any bad luck. I put the ranch up for sale. In 1967 I had an interested buyer from El Paso, Texas. I combined a trip to El Paso with a cattle buying trip into Mexico. My wife Eloise and son Jim, and Ruben Widmayer made the trip with me. We stopped in Denver and picked up Ben Houston. He was interested in the Mexican cattle. We dropped Eloise and Jim off in Matador, Texas, (Eloise's hometown) and continued on to El Paso. Ruben was to meet with the prospective buyer and negotiate a deal for the Steamboat Springs Ranch while Ben and I went into Mexico to buy cattle. Ben and I had a successful trip into Mexico, but Ruben struck out on his mission.

Later that evening it was decided to go to the Mexican town of Juarez for supper. Juarez is located in Mexico on the other side of the Rio Grande River. There is no difficulty in crossing over on the bridge. The prospective ranch purchaser knew of an excellent eating place. We were seated at a large table on the main floor. The establishment had a balcony elevated above the place where we were dining. We were well into our meal when two young Texas border guards and their beautiful wives entered the place. They were seated on the balcony area above us. They could hear our table conversations. Apparently our table made some remarks about their attractive mates and they became quite angry. They made threatening remarks to us. The management was not happy with what was happening. They asked them to move and offered them a free drink. They refused and as a result they were asked to leave the place. As they were leaving they made threatening remarks and stated that they would be waiting for us outside. We did not want any trouble in Mexico as the history of Mexican jails was something less than to be desired. The prospective purchaser was boasting that he knew all the judges in Mexico and had no fear of any trouble and if we were incarcerated he would have us out in no time.

When we left the building, sure enough the two border guards were waiting for us. They tried to engage us in a fist fight but we as a group were able to move to our vehicles, clamor in and head for the border. Again our prospective buyer friend was boasting that we had nothing to fear. He was ready to take on the Texans. The next morning when our prospective buyer appeared on the scene he had changed his tune and exclaimed that he did not know what he was doing the previous night. Had we been arrested we would have had quite a wait in jail.

Later that year the first person out of Denver who looked at the ranch, bought it. Of course, he had insight on the fact that the real estate would be very valuable. I made a few thousand dollars on the ranch deal and turned it over to the new owner.

I kept in touch with the realtors, and followed the escalation. Less than a year later the land had increased well over a million dollars. The second year it had increased two million dollars. In the next three years it was worth well over five million more dollars than I'd received. They began selling it by the foot instead of by the acre. The price went up by leaps and bounds.

I got what I asked and was satisfied when I sold it. This was a great experience, having bought, paid for and owned a top mountain ranch, and made money on it. Even though, from my viewpoint, it could have made well over five million in five years, it was all worthwhile. It was a great experience, a great ranch and we ran good cattle.

Topography and Climate

The ranch is solidly blocked, fenced and cross fenced with many streams and springs scattered throughout. The lay of the land is level to gently rolling and mountainous. Trees for shade and shelter are scattered about for good year around protection. The average annual rainfall in this area is 29 inches.

Total Acreage

8924 acres more or less: 3424 acres deeded and 5500 Colorado State lease. This lease costs $2,031 per year and has been with the ranch for 55 years. It is renewable on a 10 year basis. There are 160 acres additional upland pasture or hay that can be leased at $750 per year and also two 80-acre tracts of irrigated meadow land adjoining the ranch at $1,000 each per year are available.

Improvements

There are two complete sets of improvements strategically located on the ranch. Each set has an all modern home, barns and corrals for easy handling of any type livestock. An ultra modern two-bedroom cabin is located at the main headquarters to provide excellent quarters for guests or the owner.

Carrying Capacity

The ranch will carry approximately 600 cows on a year-round basis or about 2000 yearlings through the summer months. It is well suited to a combination cow and yearling operation. The ranch cuts approximately 1800 tons of hay.

General Information

Two men are presently operating the entire ranch with extra help at haying time.
There is sufficient irrigation water provided by the Yampa River to irrigate the meadows and all other irrigable land for a bumper crop of hay. The ranch is capable of producing as much as three tons of hay per acre.
Electricity, phone, mail and schools and all shopping requirements are readily available.
Taxes are $2,094.97 per year.
Price. Very favorably priced for a quick sale.
Terms: Excellent terms to qualified buyer.

This ranch must be seen to be appreciated.

The J & J Ranch is an old established ranch, having been in existence some 55 years and operated as a practical cattle ranch ever since. In all these years there has never been a failure to produce feed due to a drouth.

This ranch is located in the famous Yampa Valley, which rates as the very best ranching area in the entire State of Colorado. Steamboat Springs is within a stone's throw of the ranch with the main headquarters being about four miles out on an all-weather road.

The ranch is strategically located for a purebred cattle or horse operation with over a mile of U.S. 40 Highway frontage to provide a perfect show window for the many passing motorists who travel this area in both winter and summer. The pastures are well divided with many miles of new fencing to provide adequate protection for separating the young females from the herd during breeding season. Artificial insemination could also be practiced very nicely. Cattle raised in this area produce strong bone and a beautiful coat of hair, which is a definite asset for show ring competition.

For the sports minded investor the ranch abounds with deer and elk to provide excellent big game hunting. The Yampa River which runs through the ranch and its tributaries are well stocked with trout to provide the best of fishing to be found most anywhere. Also, for the ski enthusiast it is well to note that a multimillion dollar ski area is being developed near the ranch.

The Above Statements, While Not Guaranteed Are From Sources We Believe Reliable

J and J Ranch Brochure

Cattle grazing on one of the lush meadows.

Mountain grazing—cattle near a pond in the high country.

Chapter 44

Beef Friesian Cattle From Ireland

One day in late 1969, I received a telephone call from Dave Canning, a good cattleman friend of mine from Virginia. He was excited about the greatest bull he had ever seen while on a trip to Ireland. He asked me to go see this great bull and let him know if I thought the bull was as good as he thought he was. He wanted to buy him on a partnership basis. I thought it would be a worthwhile trip, but had no intention of buying the great bull of my life. He stated that if the deal materialized and we needed more money to finance the bull, Premier Corporation headquartered at Fowlerville, Michigan, were willing to invest the necessary money.

I told Dave that he could count on me making the trip if I could get it done within the next month. I arranged the trip from South Dakota to Dublin, Ireland. I had decided to take my family with me, as I thought it would be a good education for everyone while in the line of business. I contacted the people in Ireland, and they were anxiously awaiting our visit.

We planned our trip with a little leisure time, so we could thoroughly enjoy as much humanity as we could. We landed in New York City around noon and had a layover until about six o'clock, before our trip on to Dublin. We hired a cab and had him show us as much of New York City as possible in five hours. He took us on a fantastic ride. The whole family found it unbelievably interesting.

We left New York City about six p.m. It was a beautiful flight, mostly at night. We wound up with jet-lag. Our hours for sleeping were off for several days.

Several officials from the Irish agricultural government met us at the airport in Dublin. They took us to a hotel where we had very nice accommodations. They would pick me up the next morning and take me to the various places that had

Looking at Friesian bull "Top Notch". From left: John Beatty, Irish Pedigree Livestock Agency, Clayton Jennings, South Dakota, Seamus Kelly, Ireland. The men holding the bull when photographed in Ireland were not identified.

Beef Friesian cattle. The Irish had been breeding dual purpose cattle for many, many years, and they were serving their purpose very well. They were getting a lot of percentage of beef and plenty of milk.

The first place they took me was to a great livestock breeding farm owned by Seamus Kelly. I didn't know it, but it was a climax to all the Beef Friesian in Ireland. These were all purebred Irish people and very congenial. I was highly impressed with every one of them. Seamus presented the cows in excellent condition and it was easy to see them. Then he showed me "Top Notch," and I was so impressed. He happened to be Grand Champion Sire of all bulls in Ireland. I must say that he was the best bull, fundamentally wise, that I had ever seen. You just couldn't find a flaw in any part of him. I decided right then that I was going to try to buy him.

After I had a good look at the ranch and cattle, Seamus invited us in to the kitchen, where he graciously asked us to have a little Coffee Royal (bourbon, coffee & cream) with him. I enjoyed this little courtesy very much and found that nearly all the Irish people are very sociable and you just learn to like them very much.

We left Mr. Kelly with the understanding that I would get back in touch with him in two or three days, at which time I would try to do some business with him.

We went further on the tour. We checked on several livestock operations, and they were good ones, but there was no bull or female as good in these groups, as there was in Mr. Kelly's herd. We toured for three or four consecutive days and thoroughly enjoyed every bit of our tour, but I found no bull as great as the bull, Top Notch, which I had seen on the first day of the tour.

I called Dave Canning, my potential partner in Virginia, twice during the trip and we mutually agreed that this bull, Top Notch, might be the best bull either of us had ever seen. We agreed that I should buy the bull and we would be partners on him. We had not talked any price on him, but we knew he would bring good money. We agreed that we would also buy a group of several bulls and about twenty females.

I arranged to meet with Seamus Kelly and start negotiating. He was very serious about selling us some cattle, as he knew

BIG NOTCH

Calved: 4-05-72 Tattoo: CJC-100D

Yearling weight: 1196 pounds (without creep feed)

Sire: Moneymore Top Notch HBF 295233 (3-22-64)

Dam: Knockanemore Bond Kitty 2nd HBF 2734652 (4-11-67)

One of the most popular and talked about bulls to enter the beef industry picture in a long time. True cattlemen, regardless of their breed preference, are greatly impressed with this young bull's skeletal correctness and balance. Those who have seen him declare him close to being perfect and complete in every category...frame, growth rate, structural soundness, muscle, balance and sex character. These dominant characteristics came into his possession by right of succession. His sire, Moneymore Top Notch, won every major honor in Ireland and was considered the greatest bull of the breed. His dam is a tremendous individual, also correct in her frame, structural soundness, muscling, and balance.

Big Notch was placed in the Premier Breeding Center east of Denver and semen collected on a regular twice weekly schedule started at only 10 months of age. Under this heavy work schedule, his actual yearling weight was 1196 pounds. At 18½ months, he weighed 1745 pounds.

It is the opinion of many knowledgeable cattlemen that Big Notch will rapidly become one of the most influential bulls to appear on the beef industry scene. We strongly urge you to inspect this young bull. Regardless of the kind or type of cows you are presently running, Big Notch can quickly put your cow-calf operation on the profit side of your business ledger.

Due to the popularity of this outstanding young sire, be sure to book your semen orders well in advance of your needs.

Big Notch

we would make good use of them in America. We wound up buying the great bull, Top Notch, five other bulls and 20 unrelated females. Kelly was pleased and I was well pleased with the way I had been treated in dealing and the handling of the livestock. I gave them instructions for testing and shipping. Our east coast health quarantine stations were full and would be for some time, so it necessitated us shipping the cattle to Edmonton, Alberta, Canada.

While I had been touring and inspecting the farms and cattle, my family had been enjoying themselves seeing the sights. My eldest son, Charlie went on to England and France, where he spent several days. Eloise, Gloria and Jim spent their time traveling around Ireland. They kissed the Blarney Stone! Their Irish hosts arranged to take them wherever they wished in all of Ireland. They toured many of the historic sites and places. It was a great trip!

After three months in the quarantine station, we took the cattle to a ranch in Colorado. At this place, on April 5, 1972, Big Notch, son of Top Notch, was born and he was equally as good as his daddy. We used Big Notch extensively for artificial breeding. He sired many, many top bulls and top females. He finally developed arthritis in his hind leg and had difficulty getting around. We gave him cortisone shots, but he kept getting worse. After trying every medical remedy we could, we had to sell him to the packing house for slaughter. That was a sad day, but we had collected many ampules of semen, so the Big Notch breeding would go on for many more years. We had sold a world of semen to other breeders from both Top Notch and Big Notch, which was a big asset for us.

The influence of the Beef Friesian blood has crossed over most of America and is showing up in many herds today. Tex Fulton of Miller, South Dakota is a classic example of the influence of Beef Friesian blood. The Beef Friesian and Angus cross are known as Amerifax. Genetically, purebred Amerifax are 5/8 Angus and 3/8 Beef Friesian. The cattle are polled and most are solid black.

These are some of my rancher friends who started using the Beef Friesian influence in their herds in 1971, and have continued with this program, with fantastic results. Roland, Bill and Bryan Bickel, Herb and Jerry Bowar, John Quirk,

Tex Fulton rancher (inset) and some of his Amerifax heifers on his ranch south of Miller, South Dakota.

Beef Friesian Field Day—October 1974 at Clayton Jennings', Highmore, South Dakota.

Joe Martinmaas, Tim Ohlde, Don Melius, Dean Melius, Johnson Bros., D. & R. Ogren, Bill Stolle, and John Hippen.

After over twenty years, we are still in touch with the Irish, who helped me put this deal together, and I want always to have them as my friends.

Some of the crowd at October 1974 Beef Friesian Field Day, Highmore, South Dakota.

New beef breed — the Friesian

SOUTH DAKOTA may become the U.S. headquarters for a new beef breed—the Friesian.

Clayton Jennings, Highmore, S. Dak., and Dave Canning, a Virginia businessman, are importing seven bulls and approximately 40 heifers from Ireland to establish the breed in the United States.

The Friesian is a modern-type beef animal with exceptional mothering and milking ability, according to Jennings. It is basically black in color with white markings. The Friesian resulted from generations of selection of cattle for beef production from the Holstein-Friesian breed. "But for all practical purposes, the comparison to the Holstein ends there," Jennings told THE FARMER.

The Friesian cattle are being shipped from Ireland to New York and then to New Jersey. They will remain in quarantine for at least 30 days while undergoing strict health inspection procedures. Then, animals that pass all tests will be shipped to Highmore, S. Dak., with the exception of one bull.

Extensive breeding and crossbreeding programs will be carried out with the new breed. A North American Friesian Association probably will be established, possibly based in South Dakota, Jennings reports. The association would draw up rules regarding registration and breeding for purebred stock in this country.

Backbone of the new breed in the U.S. is a bull named Top Notch. "He is the greatest bull of the breed in Ireland. He won every major honor in that country's shows. Now, his sons and daughters are winning and are producing in outstanding fashion," says Jennings.

Semen from Top Notch, who weighs more than 2,500 lbs in "working dress," was stored before the bull was shipped to the U.S. A good supply of semen should be immediately available upon arrival of the Friesian stock. This bull will be kept at a stud organization, International Beef Breeders of Denver, Colo.

Jennings and his family went to Ireland last fall to inspect this bull. The cattleman was so impressed with the breed that he expanded the purchase by six more "hand-picked" bulls plus the cows and heifers.

Jennings and Canning both are well-known breeders of Angus cattle.

"We are not thinking of leaving our breed. It is not that we love Angus less that we have made this importation, but that we love them more. We believe the Angus-Friesian cross will be ideal—to get an extra 'shot' of size, maintain beef qualities and color. Although these cattle are horned, we believe, when mated to Angus, most of the offspring will be polled," Jennings says.

From *The Farmer*—1970

The Friesian bulls will be mated with Hereford, Angus, Shorthorn, and crossbred females to test response in South Dakota. "And, as I see it, the first-cross female produced by a Friesian bull should have what every cattleman looks for: hybrid vigor, a tremendous growth factor, lots of milk and a longer milking period," Jennings comments.

The milking ability of this breed is expected to be a key selling point. Calves should get ample, if not a surplus, of milk from cows of Friesian stock. High weaning weights are the expected results.

The importers of Friesian cattle are looking forward to the day of multiple births in beef cattle. Jennings figures a Friesian can produce a crossbred cow that is able to nurse two or more calves because of high milking ability. An expanded multiple-birth research effort should produce results that commercial cattlemen can use within the next three years, he predicts.

The Friesian cow does not have the large udder and teats of a Holstein. Jennings doesn't expect such problems as teat freezing or other udder problems—even under Upper Midwest conditions. The purebred Friesian may require some protection against weather, however. Crossbreds should have no trouble, he adds.

What kind of weaning weights can be expected when calves get plenty of milk?

"Fellows who creep feed calves produced by the crossbred Friesian female should be able to send animals to slaughter at 900 to 1,100 lbs within 90 to 120 days after weaning, at an age of 7 to 8 months," he predicts.

The breed should have good carcass quality and adequate marbling, with a thin outside rind, Jennings continues. "The Friesian has smooth muscling and is not double-muscled."

The beef industry has long been interested in the dairy-beef cross animal. The Friesian promoters feel their breed will be the one to fill this gap.

There are many barriers that need to be crossed before Friesians will have won a notch in the U.S. beef industry. The cattle will have to start by passing the tough health tests on imported stock. Then, they'll have to prove themselves—after winning the battle of prejudice cattlemen show toward anything that resembles a dairy animal. They'll also have to match performance with the long time established breeds and the new ones currently becoming popular, such as the Charolais, Limousin, Maine-Anjou, Simmental and several others.

"But we can't let pride or color bother us any longer in the cattle business. You can't eat these factors," concludes Jennings. **End**

THE FARMER, March 21, 1970

Chapter 45

The Cow Palace

My dream was to fashion a room more fantastic than any one room its size anywhere including Las Vegas. Why not have this fabulous room for the enjoyment of my family, friends and business customers? We could well afford it, having placed the proceeds from the sale of the ranch and cattle on interest at the First National Bank, Miller, South Dakota. The interest gave us a steady income.

The room (which became known as the Cow Palace) was 42 feet by 34 feet. I drew up a rough sketch to figure out what all I needed to completely furnish it. I found a large warehouse with complete room displays in Denver. This warehouse had everything I needed. I was able to purchase all the furnishings for the Cow Palace in less than a half day.

Within a few days I had a potload of cattle going to the Denver area. The trucker agreed to bring my load of furnishings to Highmore as a backhaul.

I hired three carpenters to finish the Cow Palace for me. I also hired Albert and Beverly Bruce, an artistically inclined couple who could do any kind of finish necessary, including upholstery. I spent every day in the room, most of the time sitting on a sawhorse, planning every move with the workers. The most inspiring feature to me was the hip-roof ceiling made with 18 inch by 12 inch beams and cedar tongue and groove lumber. We hung large beautiful chandeliers from this ceiling. The twelve foot high walls were covered with various colored padded naugahyde and were papered with wild animal print wallpaper. We built a red horseshoe shaped bar with twelve green padded chairs. A curved stairway led to the overhanging balcony which was directly over the horseshoe bar. We had six barrel chairs that fit around an octagon table used for card playing. A large fish aquarium at the far end of this balcony room was bordered on each side with a small bed.

Clayton Jennings inspecting the progress on the finishing of the Cow Palace 1974.

The balcony room before it was completed—1974.

Clayton Jennings enjoying some of his many visitors at the Cow Palace. Picture taken from the balcony room. Note beautiful chandelier to the left.

Keith Aasby enjoying the king-sized bed in the Cow Palace.

At the top of the curved stairway, on the north side, a door opened out onto a catwalk where my customers could observe their cattle being weighed or being worked in the chutes.

On the east side of this room was a king-sized bed, flanked on each side by small beds. A large fish aquarium hung on the east wall over the head of the bed. On the west side of this room we had a small kitchen and a beautiful bathroom with another large chandelier.

When we finished the Cow Palace, I was really proud of the amount of time and money spent. The total cost of the 160 acres of land, new home, new steel building, the numerous other steel and wood out-buildings, all the concrete and steel handling facilities, and a lifetime steel-rod fence and yards totaled $550,000.00.

I feel the many people who came and enjoyed my hospitality at the Cow Palace has been a real tribute to me and my life. The visitors were men, women and children from all walks of life and of most nationalities. I am proud I can call them my friends.

The list goes on forever, here are just a few: governors, ranchers, cowboys, housewives, major league athletes, professional men and women, waitresses, state and national senators and representatives, college professors, hunters, teachers, city and county officials, clergy, brokers, bankers, cattle buyers and many many more.

South Dakota Governor Richard Kneip addressing a large group at the Cow Palace.

Dorothy Noonan, Bill Gallagher, J. C. Noonan, Pat Feeney, Bob Burnham attending one of the many functions at the Cow Palace.

Kenneth Augspurger, South Dakota Governor Richard Kneip, Tim McDermott, seated—James Brady, behind him—Jim Jennings.

Robert Aesoph visiting with Larry Pekarek at the Cow Palace.

Beverly Bruce, Eloise Jennings, Elinor Hahn, Albert Bruce and Ruben Widmayer at the Cow Palace.

Chapter 46

Cast a Little Bread Upon the Waters, And It Shall Return Tenfold

This is without a doubt, the truest of all proverbs, that I am aware of, and it has been proven to me time and time again throughout my entire life. This is a great philosophy to follow!

I had a multitude of good things come to me through my friends and business customers, and through chance. I seemed to have a guilt feeling that I had not contributed enough to my friends and customers. I seemed to feel that they had contributed so much to my welfare and my family's, that I wound up with a selfish feeling. I had the burning desire to be a part of making all of them smile and laugh and be happy.

If you can make people smile and laugh, you will find happy people.

I had attended the National Western Stockshow in Denver every year in January, except the four years I was in the service, from 1941 to 1945. The year 1974 was my 29th straight year to attend the stockshow. I stayed at the Cosmopolitan Hotel every year and was a regular preferred customer of theirs. I was in excellent standing with the management at the hotel and my credit was never questioned, and any favors were granted without question. I personally knew all of the head management, plus most of the bell boys. I had brought the hotel a lot of business during every stockshow.

I encouraged Angus people from all over America to stay at the Cosmopolitan Hotel. It was a friendly hotel, with a great atmosphere, and a big pleasant lobby, where they could see and visit with breeders and friends from any place imaginable. The lobby was an Angus and Beef Friesian beehive! It was a great meeting place for all breeders and friends. The glamour of hotels and lodging is gone, since the Cosmopolitan closed and has been torn down.

In 1974, the Beef Friesian Association had an exhibit in the stockyards that was the most fascinating to all livestock people attending the Denver stockshow. They were to have a Beef Friesian heifer sale at the stockyards at twelve o'clock noon on Sunday. As a courtesy and to promote the Beef Friesian exhibit and sale I flew thirty-three of my friends round-trip from Pierre to the Denver Stock Show. This also included twenty rooms and food and drinks for three days while they attended the stock show. I also had a three room suite for my family for ten days. This all totaled $7,500.00.

I decided to have many of my friends and customers in to a promotional Sunday breakfast at the Cosmopolitan Hotel at ten o'clock sharp. We would invite them by personal contact and put the word out to all livestock people we were having a ten o'clock breakfast at the Cosmopolitan main ballroom.

At about eight o'clock on Sunday morning I went to look over the facilities and the dining room. When I got there, one of the managers took me by the arm to show me everything. When I first walked into the ballroom, it stunned me as it was so vast that it reminded me of the vastness of the Astrodome in Houston, the first time I was there. This wasn't quite as large as a football field, but was decorated so beautifully with the high ceilings of pale blue and the white walls, with a multitude of large crystal, gold trimmed chandeliers, hanging from the high ceilings. The hardwood oak floors were highly polished. There were eight or ten rows of full length tables, adjusted with about ten foot alleys to avoid congestion. They all were covered with white linen table clothes. It was an unbelievable sight and made me tremendously happy that soon nearly a thousand friends would be seated at one time.

The menu was prime rib and Texas toast with fresh fruit of all kinds in large fruit baskets on the tables. There must have been thirty or forty waiters dressed in white, with a towel draped over one arm, ready to deliver the prime rib as soon as the people were seated.

On exhibit, as the people came into the lobby of the Cosmopoliton Hotel, we had pens for Big Banker and Irish Lady, a bull and heifer, sired by Big Notch, the Beef Friesian bull that we rated the greatest bull alive!

Big Banker, a Beef Friesian bull on display in the Cosmopolitan Hotel lobby.

Irish Lady, a Beef Friesian heifer on display in the Cosmopolitan Hotel lobby and Beef Friesian Queen Tammy Vilhauer.

Right—Wayne and Helen Peterson and son, Tom, of K. and P. Manufacturing. They furnished all the livestock panels we used for our livestock at the stock show. They also ranched south of Holabird, South Dakota and I have done lots of business with them.

I had champagne or Bloody Marys for those who wanted a toddy. There were several large flowing fountains for each of these. When I asked the caterer how much these fountains would hold, he shook his head and said, "All I know is that it took forty gallons to prime each one."

They fed 1,045 people and as simultaneously as possible. Within two hours time the people had all been watered and fed and then on to the Beef Friesian heifer sale at the stockyards. It was to begin at twelve o'clock. Everyone went and there was a packed house for the sale. Everyone was smiling and laughing, and I can assure you that they all had an experience that they had never had before. Never had I experienced such a joyous time as this!!

I had made a deal with the Hotel to serve the breakfast with all the trimmings for $15.00 a plate. They served 1,045 people and agreed to round it off to 1,000 and throw in the lease on the pens in the lobby as a courtesy to me. This $15,000.00 breakfast plus the $7,500.00 in courtesies to my friends totaled $22,000.00 – but was well worth every penny spent! Especially in lieu of the fact that I could charge it against my income as promotion, so it wasn't as bad as it sounds!

Personal thanks during this time and after were sent to me by phone and letter and many declared this was one of the most enjoyable parties of this size they had ever attended. To this day, nearly twenty years later, people remind me of their presence and they have never forgotten or seen a show to compare!

Chapter 47

Claymore Field Day

In the fall of 1978 I had been up in the Mobridge, South Dakota, area buying a lot of calves for October and November delivery to the Cow Palace in Highmore.

I had bought one big string of calves from Duane Claymore, which totalled 1,643 head of steer and heifer calves. They were sired by outstanding Limousin bulls and would catch the eye of the best judges of cattle. Duane has a beautiful sprawling ranch with twenty miles of zigzag frontage on the Missouri River. The prairie is an ocean of grass with canyons filled with lots of trees for excellent winter shelter. He has a great ranch and he is shrewd in merchandising his calves each year.

Duane and I have done lots of business together. I have bought many calves, yearlings and cows from him and I have sold on a commission basis several crops of his calves to Iowa buyers.

We decided to have a field day on the day of Duane's delivery. I asked that he get his calves down here at noon or shortly thereafter. This was a big request as that was a lot of calves to sort off the cows and load, then travel nearly 140 miles from the ranch to Highmore. He had twenty-one potloads of calves and the first loads arrived right at 12 o'clock

October 1978—Clayton Jennings, Ben Houston and Duane Claymore with Duane's calves in the background at Jennings' Yards, Highmore, South Dakota.

Trucks unloading Claymore's calves at Jennings' Yards.

and the last loads at 3 o'clock. We put out the word all around that this field day would be for all people. It was a day to see lots of great calves and a good day to enjoy the company of many other ranchers, farmers and business people. We hoped for and did have a tremendous crowd.

We served a complimentary beef lunch at noon. Our guests kept coming all afternoon. They watched the calves being unloaded, sorted for sex and size and then weighed. We passed the word that one and all were welcome in the Cow Palace to enjoy my hospitality.

I sold all of these calves by private treaty that same evening and the next day. I sold over half of them to Ben Houston of Greeley, Colorado, and the balance in smaller groups into Iowa and Nebraska.

Everyone had an enjoyable time. It was a highly successful day for all concerned.

I love South Dakota!

Chapter 48

Carol

I met Carol through my daughter Gloria. They were good friends and bowled on the same team. Carol was born and raised on a farm five miles south of Highmore, South Dakota. When I met her she was a divorced mother of two school-age children, Lisa and Joe. She was employed by Garrigan Chevrolet Company of Highmore. Gloria encouraged me to ask Carol out on a date, which I did in February of 1979.

Our first date was not what I had hoped it would be. I took her to Pierre to the Bunkhouse, a top-notch place to

Carol Lettau and children Lisa and Joel 1978.

eat. We ordered and liked to have never gotten our food. When the waitress brought it, it wasn't our dinner. We sent it back. Finally almost two hours later we got our food. We didn't enjoy our meal very much after such a long wait. I was trying to impress Carol. No ground was gained there!

All the way home I wondered what she thought of me and if she would date me again. Well, she did and we continued to date steadily. She became very familiar with me and my business. She became my part-time secretary. Then in 1981 I needed hip replacement surgery and she did everything for me, banking, secretarial work, driving me on all business trips, kept up the house and gave me moral support through some really tough times.

Clayton Jennings and Carol Lettau wedding at the Chapel in the Hills, Rapid City, South Dakota. May 23, 1990.

We were married May 23, 1990, in the Chapel in the Hills at Rapid City, South Dakota. Carol's daughter and her husband, Lisa and Dale Christensen, were our attendants. This marriage is the most rewarding experience of my life. She's lovely, she's gorgeous, she's unselfish, she's generous, she's kind, she's savvy, she's giving, she's delightful, and she's a shrewd business woman!

Togetherness is a much bigger word than I thought. Through writing this book and Carol helping so much, it gives us a constant togetherness and a depth of love that I have never known before. She has given me the inspiration I needed.

I must say that the years with Carol have been the most beautiful of my life. She is my everything!

Chapter 49

1979 Halloween Storm

I had contracted for 3,000 steer and heifer calves in the areas around Mobridge and Eagle Butte, South Dakota. Many of these calves on the Standing Rock and Cheyenne Indian Reservations were to be delivered to my yards in Highmore on October 30th.

The morning of the 30th was overcast, but nice. About noon it began to rain.

All of the calves were delivered to my yards, where my crew sorted them for sex and size, and then weighed them. They were an excellent set of quality calves.

We had really good luck all day. The calves were ready to be shipped to the various buyers which were about 25 miles southeast of Highmore. We were going to truck them out to the various places the next morning.

Late that afternoon the rain changed to sleet and snow. We were unaware of the storm that was coming. When Halloween morning dawned, we had a howling blizzard. The icy conditions and strong winds prevailed all day long, resulting in a crippled community. One only had to note the damaged fences and corrals and the broken REA poles in the country to understand the destructiveness of this storm. A thousand rural residents in the Highmore-Miller area were without electricity, some for more than a week. There were five hundred broken REA poles from the Big Bend Dam to the Ames substation.

The snow was so deep, we were unable to move a truck or a calf. I received word that this storm was centered where I was to deliver these calves. The ranchers did not have electricity, so they were unable to pump water for their own cattle, except by hand.

My crew fed the calves some hay with tractors in my small yards. We kept them fed, but it was a real mess of

Charles Gregg and Robert Hirsch sorting calves at Jennings Yards, Highmore, South Dakota.

Vince DeRouchey, vet, and his crew vaccinating the calves at Jennings Yards, Highmore, South Dakota.

mud, snow, water and hay. The calves looked pretty decent the first couple of days. Then they got stale and showed real evidence of sickness. I knew I had to make a move, but I couldn't expect these people to take these calves, when they showed a lot of sickness and staleness. I decided the loss would have to be mine because of the circumstances.

I made arrangements with numerous ranchers, not affected by the storm to feed them for me on a per head per day basis. I had every calf vaccinated for everything, before they were sent to the country.

I owned these calves about three months. The death loss was heavy—about 10%, besides all the other expenses of medicine, trucking and interest of 16¼% on $800,000.00. The calves did poorly because of all the stress and sickness they had been through. The loss on this deal was an astronomical $277,291.00.

Chapter 50

Our Little Country Ranch

Following my divorce from my second wife, Eloise, we agreed to put the house and personal property up for public auction and split the proceeds straight down the middle. We had many pieces of silver that we had bought in South America and lots of valuable pictures and glassware that we had purchased during our travels all over America and Ireland. We had many pieces of modern and western furniture and it all totaled $46,000.00. We had the house auctioned the same day and it brought $50,000.00.

All other properties were in satisfaction of our debts incurred in the big loss in the Halloween blizzard of 1979 and other losses from the depressed cattle market the last couple of years.

Sept. 20, 1981. Getting ready for the auction. Ken Wermersen, Duane Claymore, Charlie Jennings, Darcey Zilverberg, Jim Clow, Clayton Jennings, Herb Marks.

Waiting for the auction to start. Darcy Zilverberg, Ken Wermersen, Stanley Johnston, Carol and Joe Lettau.

Clayton Jennings in front of his home—1981.

Sale day was September 20, 1981 and when that day came we had a very large crowd. People came from five different states and South Dakota. These were Eloise's and my friends and I know they didn't need anything but came as a courtesy to us. We felt it was going to be a sad day, but it turned out to be a pleasant day for all concerned.

After the sale I moved out to a place that Ted and Ronnie (Ted's son) Jennings owned. It was less than a mile from where I had lived. It had a decent set of buildings, corrals and loading facilities and three small pastures, which I could use to much advantage.

One day Ronnie drove into the yard. He got out of his pickup and handed me an envelope. It contained the deed for this place for Carol and me. I said, "Ronnie, I can't pay for it now." He said, "You don't owe Ted and me anything. This is a gift from us." This was a beautiful gesture from them as we just didn't have any money. We were not only broke but worse than broke. In fact, we couldn't have paid the first installment on a free lunch!

Home of Carol and Clayton 1993.

Aerial view of our ranch—1989.

We have since had some income and have remodeled the entire house, inside and outside. We have improved and repaired all of the outbuildings.

Trains still cross South Dakota and the Dakota, Minnesota & Eastern tracks run on the south edge of our little ranch about one hundred yards from the house. When the train whistles at the nearby crossing it is reminiscent of my days in Iowa. In Livermore, Iowa, (pop. barely 500) where I spent my formative years, we lived between two railroads, the M&St.L. and the Rock Island. They were barely a half mile apart. Our living was made via these two railroads and the many, many whistles I heard each day and each night were a comfort to all the family.

We enjoy living in the country, especially for the privacy. We are near enough to Highmore to run in for the mail or have coffee with friends.

We love this little ranch and South Dakota!

Chapter 51

Fancy Bull Sale at Brown Palace

I was manager of the South Dakota Division of Lovana Farms, Clarkesville, Georgia. They had 5,000 Angus cattle on maintenance in South Dakota in 1983.

Virgil Lovell of Clarkesville was the President of Lovana Farms, an investment company that sold purebred Angus heifers as investment units to individual clients all over the United States. They started this investment vehicle in the latter part of 1978 and sold thousands of these purebred heifers. The clients were purchasing the heifers to maximize investment dollars through tax savings. When an individual purchased these heifers, they got an investment tax credit and could depreciate the animals from five to seven years. This was the average productive life of a cow. Many of the female off-spring would be kept from the heifers. The bulls were sold to cover maintenance expenses.

These cattle were to be bred by artificial insemination and then put with Angus bulls for natural service to try to get them all bred. They were managed by ranchers on a daily basis. The ranchers were being provided with a steady income as they were paid maintenance monthly with yearly bonuses.

I was associated with Lovana Farms for five years. Prior to that I was associated with several other large investment companies. They were Premier Cattle Company, Lansing, Michigan, and Caravelle, Florida. Their programs were very similar with maintenance and bonus programs.

Fancy bull sale at the Brown Palace—1983 Virgil Lovell on the far right.

Carol and I were invited to attend the Lovana Palace Ball, January 14, 1983, at the Brown Palace Hotel in Denver, Colorado. Lovana Farms was having an Angus bull and heifer sale in the lobby of the Brown Palace Hotel. We expected this show and sale to be spectacular because Lovana Farms always went first-class in all cattle endeavors. It was more than spectacular. It was an extravaganza!

"Lovana Palace," a carefully coiffed 700 pound Black Angus bull calf, was the first to make a regal debut in the lobby of the Brown Palace Hotel.

He and some of his very expensive relatives stood patiently on maroon indoor-outdoor carpet as more than 2,000 onlookers crowded around the lobby's ornate iron balconies to watch one of the slickest cattle auctions ever staged.

The West's cattle-ranching and breeding elite, many of the men in tuxedos and felt cowboy hats, the women in expensive gowns, gathered under glittering chandeliers to bid on Black Angus breeding stock offered by Lovana Farms of Clarkesville, Georgia.

It was the first time since 1954 that a live bull had stood in the historic hotel's lobby. But at that time, only a single bull was on display. By the time the auction was over, Lovana Farms had sold $1.7 million worth of cattle—seven bulls, four heifers and six unborn, genetically engineered calves (embryos).

"I've got people as far as I can see," shouted Tom Gammon after the bidding began and as he gazed up at six floors of balconies ringed with people. He was asking for quiet as he took bids on a one-third interest in the bull "Lovana Fame."

Up on the second balcony, I leaned out over the railing to make sure Tom did not miss my bid. The winning bid—$385,000.00—went to a consortium of ranchers from four states to which I belonged. Pat Feeney leaned back in his chair and smiled at me. I said, "We came out here loaded for bear, didn't we, Pat?" As proof Pat pulled from his jacket pocket a brief letter from his bank that promised he alone was good for $250,000.00.

Minutes later "Lovana Palace," only eight months old, came up for sale. He brought $82,500 and went to Mississippi. His buyer thought he got him cheap!

Befitting the grand style of the auction, a cocktail party with a country western band preceded the auction. Afterwards, guests sauntered to the Hotel's ballroom for dancing to the Tommy Dorsey Orchestra.

Clayton Jennings and Virgil Lovell—1991.

Chapter 52

Hall of Fame and Other Honors

The South Dakota Cowboy and Western Heritage Hall of Fame was established in 1974 for the purpose of recognizing and honoring pioneers and outstanding leaders from all walks of life who had contributed to the development and heritage of South Dakota.

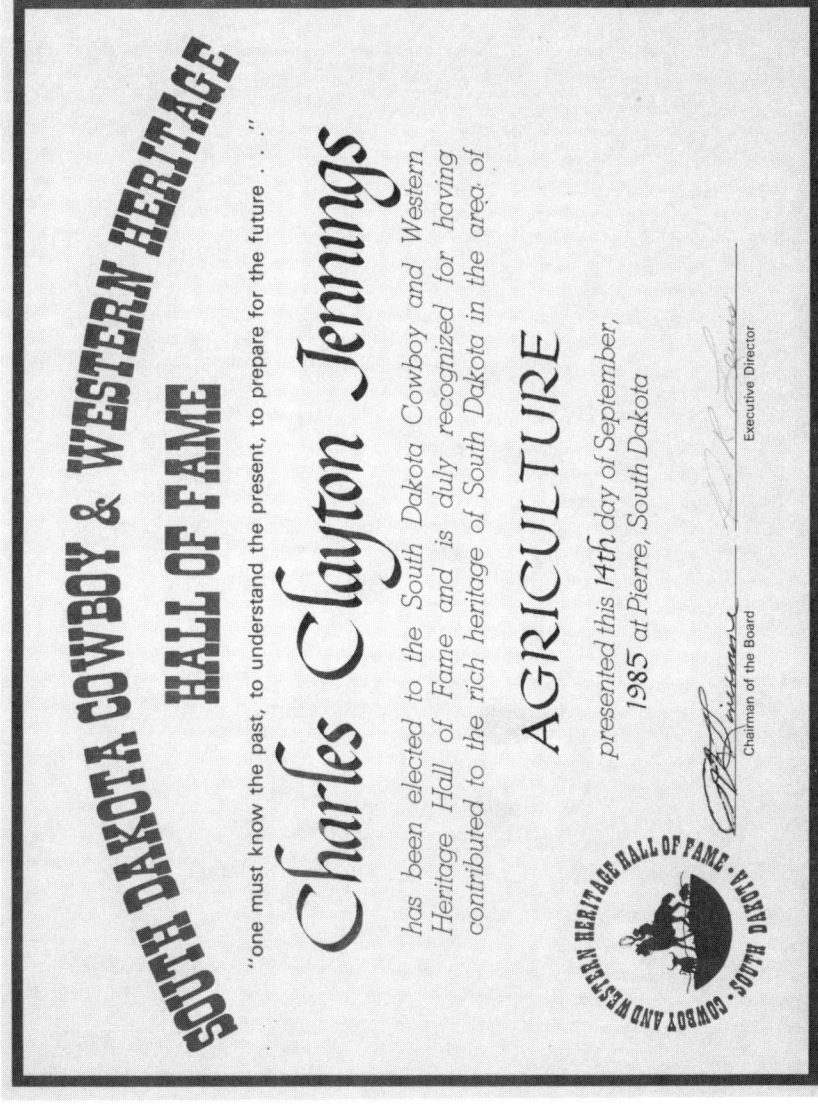

South Dakota Cowboy and Western Heritage Hall of Fame—September 14, 1985.

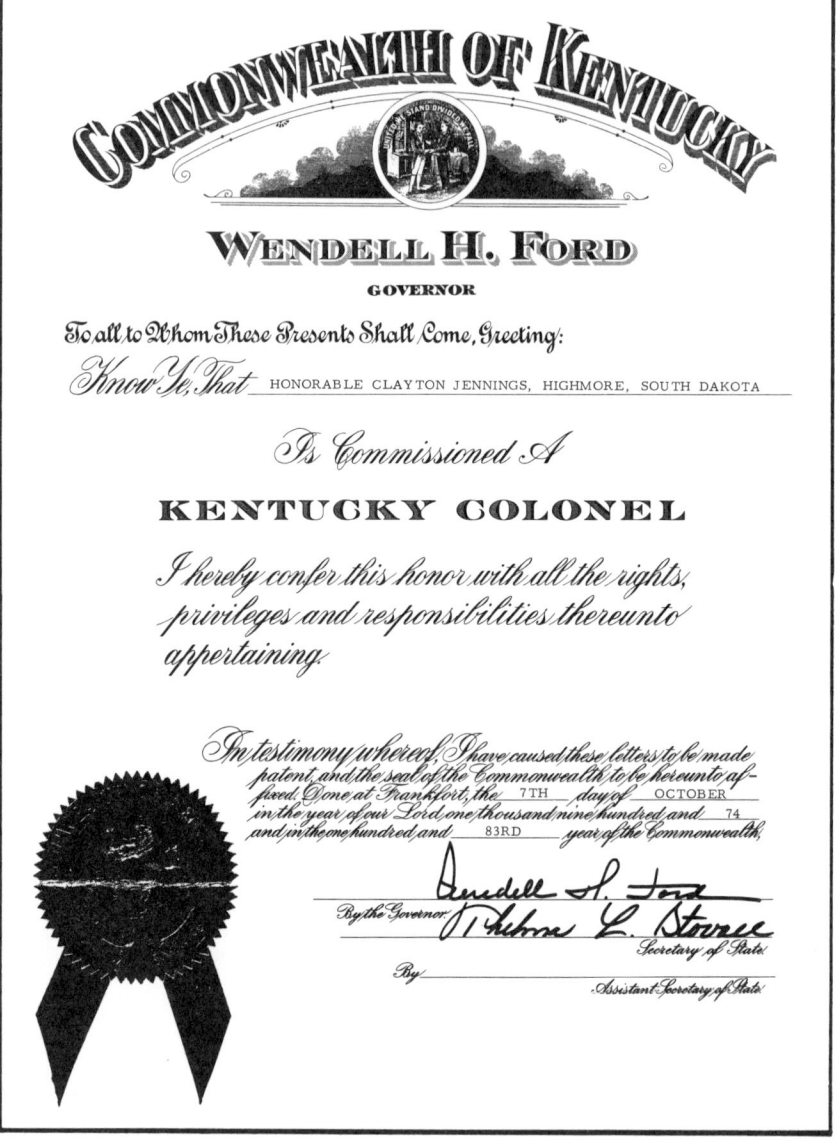

Certificate commissioning Clayton Jennings a Kentucky Colonel by the Governor of Kentucky—October 7, 1974.

A Tribute to CLAYTON JENNINGS

- For his belief in the quality, character, superiority and worth of Angus cattle and the power of the proven sire.
- For the strength of his conviction in pioneering the Angus breed in a virgin territory.
- For his courage and vision in venturing boldly and confidently into new and un-challenged areas in the development of the cattle industry.
- For his sound judgment and practical common sense in the successful building and operation of Hyland Angus Ranch.
- For his generous giving of his abilities and resources for the benefit of others.
- For his integrity, honesty and fairdealing.
- For his fulfillment of the heritage which came to him from his forebears.
- For his perseverance in the face of adversity.
- For his farsighted sensitivity to the greatness inherent in the West.
- For his compassionate concern for those in need.
- For his devotion to his family.
- For his depth of faith in mankind.
- —and for the privilege of calling him friend.

Rancher and industry leader

This tribute to Clayton Jennings appeared in the 1965 Ankony Hyland Angus Sale book and in the 1983 Lovana Hyland Heritage Sale book.

I became a Charter Life member of the Hall of Fame in 1975. I was a member of the committee for the selection of the site of the Hall of Fame. We flew around the state and looked at several locations, finally deciding on Ft. Pierre. Within the past year the Hall of Fame has been moved to Chamberlain, South Dakota.

Ted and I had the great honor of being inducted into the Hall of Fame agriculture category at their 1985 Honors Banquet held September 14 in Ft. Pierre, South Dakota. Ted and I also had the honor of being inducted in together, which was the first time ever that this award had been given to members of the same family.

In 1975/76 The Hyde County Education Association made me an honorary member of their organization.

Over the years the most gratifying and humbling honor bestowed upon me has been when many of my friends named their sons CLAYTON.

Chapter 53

Bankruptcy

BANKRUPTCY is one of the most discussed laws of our land. We must realize that we elected the officials who made this law and it needs to be respected. Every man is entitled to his opinion and anyone who has radical opinions should think of the humility that goes with it.

When a man is down and out and has no other chance to recover, he does have a chance, legally, through bankruptcy.

Through a lot of talking and agonizing with my legal council, Ruben Widmayer, we both fully agreed that this was the only way for me to go. So I filed in 1988. There could have been another chapter in this book, but the research would have been a near impossibility, as financial situations that lead to bankruptcy do not happen over night.

I'm not proud of taking bankruptcy, but I'm not ashamed either. There is a lot of humiliation and embarrassment that goes with it. I studied the response of friends of mine and when I would meet them they would smile, but it was not like previously. It was more of a disappointment sorrow. Three of the recipients showed real resentment and acted with improper conduct.

The one big cost of bankruptcy is that you lose all the credit that you have had and it takes a lot of time to regain that credit.

I'm not advocating nor do I condone bankruptcy, but each has to make his own decision in accordance to his own situation.

Now is when your true friends come in!

Chapter 54

Alberta Clipper

Don Siebrasse was a good customer of mine south of Hoven, South Dakota. I usually dealt through Gary McCloud, his cattle manager. I had made an appointment one day in February 1992 to look over their Charolais bulls for a total deal to go to Nebraska.

I told Gary we would meet him at the roadside cafe and lounge on Highway 212 for lunch, and then go to the ranch which was about five miles. They had an excellent set of Charolais and I had them in mind for some Nebraska buyers.

We went back to the roadside cafe for a short visit, when out of the bay window, we saw big snowflakes floating down and the wind was coming up by the minute. The television weather report informed us that an Alberta Clipper was on the way. An Alberta Clipper is a fast moving winter blizzard with strong cold winds and blinding blowing snow. Carol and I decided we had better get out of there now if we wanted to get home.

We started out and it seemed like every minute the storm became more intense and terrifying. We could see that we were in an old-fashioned South Dakota blizzard.

Carol was driving and the only line she could see on the highway was the white line along the edge of the road. By going very slowly we finally got to the junction of Highway 47, which we take south to Highmore. That highway was snow-packed so we lost all bearing of the white line, everything was white—road, ditches and air! We knew we were getting into some real trouble and danger. We turned around and went three miles back to Seneca, a small town with just a gas station. The station attendant wanted to close, so we filled the car with gas and bought some candy bars in case we got stalled. We talked it over and we knew that we must get shelter soon, as this was a god-awful storm.

We decided to go west on Highway 212 to Gettysburg, South Dakota as we knew they had several motels. It took us two hours to go the 19 miles. We could barely see, but we knew we were getting near Gettysburg. All of a sudden through the storm I could see a motel. I said, "Carol, turn here into the motel." She replied, "I can't see it, but I can see the Medicine Rock Cafe sign I'll pull in there!"

We thank God that we got to Gettysburg and we vowed we would not go another inch. The cafe was packed with travelers and everyone was looking for a place to camp for the night. Every motel room in town was already taken, but there was a friendly patrolman there who had foreseen the problems and had made arrangements with the county for the use of the courthouse courtroom. Most of the people at the cafe stayed at the courthouse. Each couple was given an army blanket and a pillow. We could sleep on the thinly carpeted floor or on the hard wooden benches in the courtroom.

Everyone became friends and we all felt fortunate that we had survived the storm. We were free to walk around the courthouse and I observed a prisoner in the jail cell. He had sheets and blankets on a cot with a mattress. I felt that the prisoner had more comfort than any of us. I tried every imaginable way to rest and sleep, but the benches would not let me, and the carpeted floor was even worse. Believe me I tried them all.

The storm finally subsided toward morning. We were waiting for daylight so we could get out of there. And we did!

Occasionally an episode of this nature is good for one's well-being. It will make you think and appreciate all good things during life. If I ever hear that an Alberta Clipper is coming this way, I'm locking the house and not going out until its over!

Chapter 55

Manic Depression

I have been very fortunate and have had good health all my life — except my bout with malaria, while serving in the Navy. I have also had both hips replaced.

But during the 1970's I was having periods of high euphoria, then deep depression. I had been under a lot of stress. My marriage was deteriorating.

Dr. Leander in Sioux Falls was recommended as an excellent doctor for depression. He diagnosed me as a manic depressive. This condition results in times of feeling so good that nothing, and I mean nothing, is impossible, and then periods of depression so low that it is impossible to make a decision, even the smallest one. This is a feeling that is impossible to get away from. A manic depressive cannot be cured but can be controlled with proper medication and treatment.

Dr. Leander suggested that I take electric shock treatments. This was a hairy, horrendous thought, but we mutually agreed that I should take these treatments. We scheduled several consecutive treatments in the hospital, and then every two months, a treatment as an outpatient at the hospital in Sioux Falls. The treatments, plus a drug called lithium, would control my mood swings. I'm glad now I took the treatments as I feel they helped me very much.

I still take my lithium religiously every day, I do not have any long periods of depression like I used to. I have not seen Dr. Leander for over ten years. I have been able to handle all the stress I create in business with this medication and the support of my loving wife, Carol.

Chapter 56

Religion

I was baptized in the Methodist Church in Boone, Iowa. I attended Sunday school and church regularly while we lived in Boone. When we moved to Livermore it was the same. We seldom missed as Mother saw to it that we went with no excuses.

After I graduated from high school in 1932 and moved to South Dakota, I was traveling extensively and missed numerous sermons. From 1940 on I missed many services but I did contribute to the church every year relative to my income. The only years I missed supporting my church was during my bankruptcy years.

I believe in God Almighty and seldom ever do I miss saying a little prayer at night after I turn my reading lamp off. My prayers are short and to the point.

"Thank thee, O Lord, for the many blessings you have bestowed upon me now and the days past. Give me strength and courage, O Lord, to face my responsibilities tomorrow!"

Chapter 57

South Dakota Has Been Good to Me

South Dakota has been good to me. I am grateful that I came and stayed.

I am aware that these are the twilight years of my life. I accept the fact that I cannot do things like I used to. I am semi-retired and life is very pleasant for me and my family.

I have had a wonderful and fascinating life. It has been highly interesting and meaningful. I have traveled many places and have done many things. I am happy that I was able to provide a college education for each of my children in the college of their choice.

Throughout my life I have developed friendships, near and far, that are very meaningful and important to me.

There is very little in my life that I would change, even if I had the opportunity.

Carol and I have worked tirelessly on this book. We have enjoyed the challenge. Our hope is that every reader finds it enjoyable and entertaining and that it leaves a lasting impression on all of you!

I love South Dakota and it's people!

1991—Ted Jennings, Margaret Howard, Clayton Jennings and Nadine Robinson.

1989—Charles, Clayton, Gloria, Jim and Kim (Jim's wife) Jennings. Ready to attend a Minnesota Twins game.

1992—Dale and Lisa Christensen with Laycee Jo.

Joel Lettau and Vicki Kleinsasser with Blayne Matthew—1993.

Clayton and Carol Jennings—1993.

Chapter 58

GLIMPSES
Pressure Group

The members of the PRESSURE GROUP are all prominent ranchers in this area. I have done a lot of business with each of them over the years. They are the reason for this book. They are the ones who put the most pressure on me to write this book about my life experiences. The members are Roger Gerdes, Miller, South Dakota; Robert Aesoph, Speed McCloud, Lowell and Frankie Rinehart, Highmore, South Dakota.

Roger Gerdes was the first to start the pressure. Roger even gave me a check for his book in 1989. He told me to keep it until he got his book! I still have his check! Speed McCloud probably pressured me the most. He is the one who said, "If you tell everything and tell the truth it would be a best seller!" The rest of the Group were constantly asking "How's the book coming?" I knew I had to put up or shut up! Frankie is a very talented musician and the only lady in the Group. She has an unusual personality. She has a constant smile that easily breaks into a big laugh and then into an unusual cackle that you can't ever forget!

* * * * *

HAROLD ARENDT

In 1974 I needed a partner. I was running myself in every direction. I desperately needed someone to take over part of my business. The man who came to mind was Harold Arendt. He was raised on a North Dakota livestock and grain farm. He started his career from absolute scratch. He had desires and visions. As a kid he clawed his way up a notch for every year until he was made manager of the Ankony Hyland Ranch in South Dakota in 1965. When Ankony sold out he went to Platte City, Missouri, and worked for a going concern there.

Pressure Group

Robert Aesoph
Breeds Angus replacement heifers

Speed McCloud
Raises Angus and Charolois cattle

Roger Gerdes
Chianina and Chiangus breeder

Lowell and Frankie Rinehart
Simmental breeders

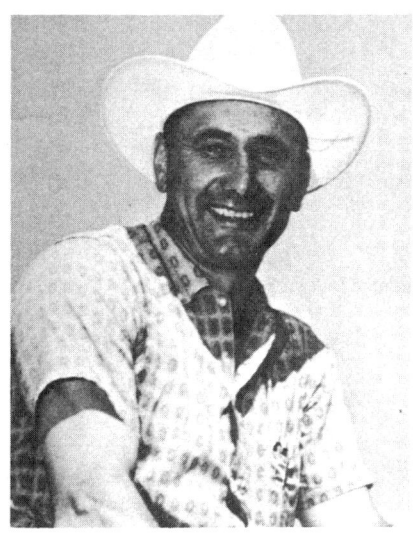

Harold Arendt

I needed a man of his calibre, if I could find such a man and if I could hire him. Harold had gotten himself up in life to where I was doubtful I could pay the kind of money it would take to get him. I called him one evening and told him what I had in mind. He said he would be interested, so I chartered a light plane to fly me from Highmore to Platte City. We both agreed that it could be a really good and pleasant deal. I didn't hire him but I did make a partnership deal (A and J Cattle Company) with him of 50/50 right down the middle of the road. Our business was good and enjoyable. His untimely death in 1978 prevented him from unaccomplished heights. He was a great man and I lost a good friend!

* * * * *

BRUCE MILLER

I have had a beautiful relationship with Bruce Miller of Spearfish, South Dakota, since 1975. Bruce deals in bulls and feeder cattle and as a bullman he is unsurpassed. The first time I sold him bulls he came to Highmore and we looked at them together and he bought what I showed him. Since that time I have sold him acres of bulls and each year it is done over the phone. Each time after the bulls arrive he calls

Bruce Miller

and gives me complimentary reports. This guy is what I call a natural in the cattle business. Most years I send him one hundred or more bulls. Besides being a bull specialist he is a gentleman deluxe and my friend!

* * * * *

PAT FEENEY

I met Pat Feeney at the Houston House Hotel in Ft. Pierre, South Dakota, in 1937 and we made friendship on our first acquaintance and have maintained that up to this day.

Pat has been in the bull leasing business for thirty-two consecutive years. I rate him, without question, the "King of the Bull Leasers!" Most of his bulls are leased at auction the first Monday in May and he always has a packed house. Pat says he doesn't know which is worse, an upper bowel exam at Mayo Clinic or having another bull lease sale!

Pat bought a lot of Haakon County land in the low price period of South Dakota history. He bought this land at fifty cents an acre with ten cents an acre down payment and the balance to be paid over five years. When I asked Pat why he didn't buy more of that land at that time he replied, "I just didn't have the ten cents to pay down!"

Pat Feeney

Pat says, "Credit is what broke me, twice. Credit can turn on you!"

All through the years we have often partnered on cattle deals even though we have always been competitors in the bull business. For me it feels good just to be in his company. I am sure we both cherish each others friendship!

* * * * *

AL DONLIN

The Donlins were a big family around Miller, South Dakota. I knew the entire family and did a lot of business with them over the years. Al is the oldest and in the 40's and 50's he owned Donlin's Trucking Service. He had two 14 or 16 foot trucks. His motto was "Not the biggest but the best." He was a superb trucker and was always available with one or the other truck. He knew the entire territory and was extra cooperative in trucking or helping with the sorting of the livestock. We were and still are the best of friends.

I recall an occasion where Al had hauled some cattle for me and needed his money, so I told him I would match him double or nothing. He replied, "I won't match you, but I will wrestle you on that stack of hay to see who goes down first." I thought he was bluffing, so I called him, but he climbed

Chuck and Al Donlin

up on the stack of hay so I had to put up or shut up! We shoved and pushed each other around for some time. Then he grabbed my arm. We went round and round and he threw me down on the hay and won. He got a great chuckle out of it when I wrote a check for double the bill of $110.00.

* * * * *

WILLIAM SCHUETTE

Bill is a classic example of a self-made man. He has fought his way up, slowly but surely. Today he is a prominent rancher northeast of Highmore. Through lots of turmoil, toil and sweat he now has 460 cows, 150 yearlings and 24 herd bulls, both Hereford and Angus, on his 7,000 acre ranch, which is all free and clear. Bill also has a beautiful new home in Highmore, plus other investments.

Bill has confided in me and told me all about his life. He is my valued friend and business associate. I have sold him numerous bulls over the years and he needs no help in choosing the bulls he wants out of a large group.

Bill always works for the betterment of his community. He was honored in 1969 as SDREA Man of the Year, in 1986 as Range Manager of the Year, and in 1991 Eminent Farmer for a lifetime of service to agriculture and rural life in South

William Schuette

Dakota. In 1993 he was honored by the S. D. Hereford Association. He has been active as a 4-H leader, served on the church council and has been clerk of township and school boards.

It has been my privilege to make a friend of him!

* * * * *

WILLIAM C. GALLAGHER

I have known Bill Gallagher since the late 1950's. I've had lots of deals with him, buying, selling or trading bulls, cows, yearlings and calves. Bill has been a wonderful source of entertainment for me. Numerous times when I was in a state of depression, medium or heavy, I would look him up and just through an hour or two of grassroots talk and being in his presence it gave me a feeling of security and well-being.

Bill has many talents that have not yet been tapped. He is past president of the South Dakota Stock Growers Association, is currently Chairman of the National Cattleman's Association Cow-Calf Stocker Council (1992) and is presently secretary of the Advisory Committee on Foreign Animal and Poultry Diseases for the U. S. Department of Agriculture.

Bill's physical make-up, mustache and all makes you think of a cowpoke from the "old west." His Irish wit makes him distinguished and unforgettable. I would say that if he was

William Gallagher

given just a few lessons in song and the guitar he would be another Johnny Cash—possibly better.

Bill's handshake is 100% as demonstrated by this deal I had with him. About three years ago I bought his steer and heifer calves on a per head basis. It was a big price, well over $500 a head on most Charolais calves with a few blacks and they were excellent. I sold them at a real advantage. They made so much money I could hardly count it. There was no complaining from Bill. He stuck with the deal, so as a courtesy to him I gave him a yearling Angus bull valued at $1,500.00!

* * * * *

DAVID STRUCK

One day in 1975 a good friend of mine Duane Struck of Wolsey, South Dakota, asked me if I would help his eleven-year-old son David get started in a few good cows. I told him it would be a pleasure.

In November David and I attended an Ankony Hyland sale at their headquarters near Highmore. This was probably David's first lesson in buying purebred cattle. David sat with me all day long, and I explained to him every pro and con

David Struck

about each cow sold. For being only eleven-years-old he made an excellent student. We sat through the entire sale and bought eleven good purebred Angus cows. This was his foundation for a good purebred herd. Later David and I flew by private plane to Bloomfield, Nebraska where Ankony Angus was having a dispersal of that operation. Again David sat on the seats with me all day long. Of course we talked cows. We bought twelve purebred Angus cows for Vida Blue, the baseball pitcher for the Oakland A's. Vida and I had a good friendship. He wanted to invest a little money in cattle. We made a deal for David to take care of them on a percentage of income basis.

David has kept his top heifer calves each year until he now has 131 cows with calves and six top herd bulls. His operation consists of 1,120 acres owned land and 700 acres leased, both grass and farm ground.

I have bought David's bull crop in its entirety nearly every year and his bulls are in real demand. The first years David just had a few bulls, so I bought them myself. Then for three years I sold them to Howard Philpot in Nebraska. Bruce Miller of Spearfish, South Dakota, has gotten them the past eight

Vida Blue and Clayton Jennings

years. He has repeat buyers waiting for them each year. This year, 1993, Bruce purchased 42 yearling and two-year-old bulls from David. David has come along in the purebred Angus business. He is a classic example of a young kid making good and he has just begun!

* * * * *

WILLIAM MARSDEN

Last November 1st, 1992, Carol and I decided to lease our little ranch and all the facilities on a year-to-year basis to our closest neighbor, Bill Marsden. This did not include the house. We retained that for our home.

Bill has a purebred Angus herd of between 100 and 200 cows. His cows are ultra modern and he uses ultra modern bulls on them. His cows are as long as a freight train and as leggy as a Tennessee walking horse. They were a beautiful sight when he drove them from his yards to our ranch.

Bill always gets up plenty of feed and as well as I have ever seen. He has a lot of equipment and most of it is new. I have had several deals with him and each one came out as it was supposed to. Besides doing everything as he agreed on our small deals, he has done me numerous favors without me even knowing about them at the time. I won't be here to do it, but it will take twenty or thirty years to evaluate him totally. As to his future I would at this time bet my money that he would be among the top cattlemen in whatever cattle country he prefers!

* * * * *

RICHARD MOTT

Dick Mott possesses some over 500 head of registered purebred Angus cows on a ranch at Maher, Colorado. For my money if I had a chance and opportunity to pick 500 registered Angus cows out of any one herd in America I would take Dick Mott's. I have applied the trial and error on his bulls for over ten years and they have proven superb in all ways. All but two years I have bought his bulls over the telephone and talking with Dick on the phone is as good as any handshake! He is a class man and I have always enjoyed dealing with him. He knows when to give and when to take. He's the kind of guy you will admire and like right soon after you meet him.

* * * * *

Richard Mott, Clayton Jennings and Bruce Miller making a deal.

Vivian and
Don Neuharth

DUSTY ACRES RANCH

The Neuharths, Don and his mother Vivian, were an excellent test plot for me over the years. They have an excellent ranch with good facilities and super equipment and always get up an abundance of feed. They were willing to gamble and experiment on nearly everything I suggested and our working relationship was beautiful. I think we all truly enjoyed every deal and experiment that we tried. We had many laughs but no cries.

Neuharths were strong with Beef Friesen bulls and developed a top herd of black cows. They kept their heifer calves for replacements until about 95% of their herd was Beef Friesen. These cows put them in a new dimension of the cow/calf business.

Neuharths would always help me out. When I had cattle to put out I always looked to Neuharths as they had the best quality feed and best yards and were always willing and able. I called them one morning at 3 a.m. from North Dakota. I needed a place for a potload of cattle I had bought at a sale. I already had them plugged with cattle, but I told them I just needed a place for a few days. Don said, "We took them. One way or the other we were either damn good friends or damn fools!"

* * * * *

Don Reiman

DONALD REIMAN

I have been dealing with Donnie of Ree Heights, South Dakota, since he was feeding 4-H calves in high school. I've found that he is psychic in his cattle deals. In this book you will read that I bought 300 Angus heifers from him as part of a trainload that I sent to Virginia. Donnie has given me an order on several occasions to buy him a thousand or more calves at weaning time in October or November. He would put them on a growing ration for sale the following spring. I got him steer and heifer calves at a cost of $226.80 each. The following spring there was a good demand for black baldie breeding heifers. I sold 500 to a buyer in Wyoming for $500.00 to be picked up at Donnie's loading chute. This has got to be one of his better cattle deals in his lifetime. Don said, "It put me over the top!" Since then he has done nothing but good in his operation. He has been a regular bull customer over the years and I'm really proud to call him my friend. He is one of my friends who I look up when I have a case of depression. By just being with him and hour or two, he changes my attitude about life!

* * * * *

PEKAREKS

Joe Pekarek and his sons, Ron and Larry have ranched south of Highmore for many years. When we had the first sale at the Miller Livestock Auction on July 20th, 1939, we

Larry and Joe Pekarek

hired Joe Pekarek to handle the salebarn door for cattle coming into the sale-ring. He was very efficient and dependable in his job. Joe had a really good ranch 14 miles southeast of Highmore. He raised a lot of oats and had a program to fit his job and his ranch to perfection. He would buy light weight calves of about 300 pounds. He would winter and summer them and sell them the next fall. Through his persistence he put a lot of calves together with a low dollar cost and grew them on the oats he raised. He had a knack of growing these calves that made him a nifty profit each year. Joe always said, "Buy light and sell heavy. That's the name of the game!"

RONNIE PEKAREK took over after his dad retired and has practiced a program similar to his dad's and has done exceptionally well. One day in 1979 Ronnie came to the Cow Palace and we talked about the calves he would like to buy. We decided he needed calves that were light weight of decent or better quality. I told him that I had over 10,000 calves bought on the Standing Rock Indian Reservation in northwest South Dakota. Delivery of these calves was to start in early October and we could sort the light end off each bunch. I told him the price would be from $200 to $250 per head depending on each group's weight. We agreed that this would make a nice deal for both of us. He was to stay ready on

Ronnie and Janet Pekarek

all days. I would notify him when calves were being delivered. He came two or three times a week for calves, sometimes helping with the sorting, until he had 1,000 steer and heifer calves. When he got all through we agreed on a price per head. Even with an 11% winter death loss, these calves more than doubled their money the next fall when he sold them. He sold the 500 steer calves for $500 per head to Bruce Miller of Spearfish, South Dakota. We have had many buy and sell deals since, but none as lucrative as this group of calves.

LARRY PEKAREK owns a ranch adjoining Ronnie. I have made many cattle sales to Larry. One of the sweetest sales

Larry and Bonnie Pekarek

was in 1982 when I sold him 252 three-year-old Angus cows bred to Angus bulls from Big Timber, Montana. These cows cost Larry $517.00 per head and at today's price they would be valued at $1,200.00. He claims they are the best set of cows he ever owned! It's not easy finding a set of cows that performed as well as these. I have bought, sold and traded many bulls, cows and calves over a period of years with Larry.

* * * * *

GLENN DAWSON

One of the most interesting humans that we had on our ranch was Glenn Dawson, who was loved and admired by our entire crew.

Glenn called me one evening as he was passing through Highmore. He was looking for a job. I invited him out to the ranch to interview him. He was tall and lanky and had a superb sense of humor. We visited about his position and I told him he would be working under several different foremen that we had until I found out what he was qualified to do. I recall that we started talking about wages and privileges and I made mention that I would pay him what he was worth. He interrupted me and said, "I will have to have more than I'm worth!" His dry humor captivated me. I hired him on the spot and he went to work the next day.

Glenn turned out to be not only as good a hand as we ever had but kept the whole crew feeling good with his humor and crazy antics. If anyone on the whole crew had been underpaid it was Glenn Dawson!

* * * * *

HAROLD RINEHART

I knew Harold Rinehart of Highmore, South Dakota, back in the 1960's, but got better acquainted with him when I owed him a favor, so I took Harold and Jap Gadd to a cattle symposium in Las Vegas in 1969. It was a great show of the new exotic breeds that had just come over from Europe. Harold became enthused over the Limousin cattle. He bought a lifetime membership in their organization and a breeding interest in

Harold Rinehart and Clayton Jennings—1993.

Prince Pompadour, receiving fifty viles of his semen at that time. He received his percentage of the semen every year thereafter. Harold bred artificially to the Pompadour strain of cattle and at one time had 1,100 purebred Limousin females. Harold is now semi-retired, but this has been an exciting experience for over 20 years. The highlights of every year were Rinehart's bull sales in the spring and the carload bull shows every January in Denver!

* * * * *

NORM FUEGEN

I have know Norm and his wife Hazel of Reliance, South Dakota, for over 20 years. I have done an enormous amount of bull, cow and calf business with them. I would rate them as experts in all phases of cattle business. Several years ago when in a financial pinch they diversified and started bronze sculpture work and have become nationally known. This relieved the financial pressure on the cattle operation. This year he is breeding 700 black Angus heifers to bulls that I furnished him. It is a real pleasure to do business with them as they are class people.

* * * * *

Hazel, Norm and Mike Fuegen

Dan Weber and Clayton Jennings—1993

DAN WEBER

Dan Weber of Raymond, South Dakota is a relatively young fellow and is basically in the bull leasing business. He is aggressive and shrewd in his deals. Dan calls me often for my opinions and advice. During our conversations I tell him that he will made good in this business because of this youth and persistence.

* * * * *

ALBERT HERMANN

Albert Hermann of Draper, South Dakota was a legend in his area. He had a big ranch that would run about 2,000 cows. At least twice during the 50's or 60's he elected to sell Ted and me 1,000 cows to take advantage of the capital gains on income tax. Capital gains was applicable only on female breeding stock and ½ of the sale amount was tax free. It was the best thing ever to happen to the rancher. Albert would sell nothing more that year. He would keep all his calf and yearling crop to sell a year later. Then if the capital gain law was still in effect he would sell another 1,000 cows (never 999 or 1,001 but 1,000). This plan worked to his advantage.

Albert was a good customer as well as a good friend. It was a sad day for me when I was asked to be a pallbearer at his funeral.

* * * * *

HERMAN GEPPERT

Herman Geppert was an eccentric rancher from Buffalo County, South Dakota. He was discussed for good, for bad, and for indifferent. Herman was a millionaire and in his will it is well-known that he left $5.00 to each of his relatives and the balance to the Catholic priests at Highmore, Stephan and Harrold.

Herman's ranch was south west of my ranch. In his later years I stopped to visit him often and he always made me feel good. The last time I visited him, he was very ill and in bed, but wanted to visit. He had a quart of Old Fitzgerald

Herman Geppert
holding a rattlesnake.

under his bed. He reached under for the bottle, removed the cap, and offered me a drink right out of the bottle.

Many stories have been out that there was a going feud for years with Geppert, Boots Gregg and the Knippling Bros. That simply is not true. It is certain that each of the three envied each other, but I would say that they had a mildly friendly relationship.

Herman was a Hereford man, one whom I could not crack. I tried on several occasions to sell him some black Angus bulls, but he wouldn't crack.

Herman had a famous saying when he lost calves in the spring he would always say, "Well, they shouldn't have been born anyway!"

* * * * *

KNIPPLING BROTHERS

Lambert and Joe Knippling, two brothers very similar to the Jennings Brothers, ran a big spread southeast of the Indian Mission at Stephan, South Dakota. They ran between 1,000 and 1,500 commercial Hereford cows with efficiency to the maximum. Both brothers had large families, mostly boys, who fit right into their operation.

I did a lot of business with the Knippling Brothers, mostly through Lambert. I sold them many yearling steers that I bought out of the Midland, Monahan and Odessa, Texas areas. One day when I was in this area receiving the yearlings that were destined for Knipplings, Lambert wanted me to buy him two palomino stallions. The palomino color was all the rage at that time. Lambert had about sixty really good sorrel and bay mares that he wanted to breed to palomino stallions. I

Lambert Knippling

found two nice coming two-years-old for $150.00 each. They were named Bronze Warrior and Gold Dust. I loaded them with the yearlings destined for Knippling's ranch. Lambert really liked these young stallions and the next spring he had nearly all palomino colored colts. They developed into a string of top-notch ranch horses. They kept a lot of the off-spring for their own use and sold the balance at a first-come first-served basis. Their colts were always in demand.

Lambert and Joe were both tall and raw-boned, real cowboys. I would say the Knippling Brothers were a great crew to deal with and do business with. They knew when to give and when to take. They made sure their customers were satisfied.

Before Lambert's death I took the privilege of stopping by to visit him. He was in bed most times that I stopped. I would take a quart of Canadian Club and we would enjoy another drink for old times sake. If I could have had a second father, it would have been Lambert. With Lambert's death I lost a great friend!

* * * * *

RUBEN WIDMAYER

One blizzardy day in March 1964 I had a situation arise that required an attorney, who could make a quick trip with me. I asked Ruben Widmayer of Heidepriem and Widmayer of Miller, to make this trip. He had done some legal work for Ted and me when we divided our partnership. Upon our return to Highmore, we had lunch at Namanny's Cafe. Ruben told me that he thought I needed an attorney on a retained basis, one who could be available when the need arose.

After Ruben explained the duties of a retained counsel, I was interested and asked him what his fee would be. He said he would act as my retained attorney for $100.00 a month. I thought that was a little high and counter-offered with $50.00 per month. He did not agree so I said, "Let's flip for it." If he won I would pay him $100.00 a month and if I won I would pay him $50.00 a month. We flipped a coin and Ruben won. He served as my retained counsel for approximately 25 years.

Ruben Widmayer

Over the years I have developed a great trust and confidence in Ruben because of his sincerity and honesty. His work was always accurate and above reproach. His presence and knowledge added much to the deals I made. He went with me on many trips all over the United States and Mexico. He became known as my "flying attorney."

Ruben and I remain the best of friends today and he is still doing legal work for me.

* * * * *

LARRY BERG

Larry Berg is owner of Larry's Smart Fashions in Huron, South Dakota, a lady's clothing store often frequented by all three of my wives, especially if they needed something very outstanding and stylish.

Larry and I had had numerous cattle deals involving feeder cattle and fat cattle. One year at the Denver stock show when he was my special guest, I asked him to go on a mission for me.

I had four very good Angus customers from Polo, South Dakota, that I owed a favor. I asked Larry to call a cab and take these four ranchers to Gross Tailors. I wanted him to see that each one got a western dress suit of the finest material and styling that existed. I told him to check everything to make sure that they got the very best. I knew he would as he was an expert in this line. Then he would have Gross Tailors put the suits on my account.

Larry has done many favors for me over the years. He is my good friend!

* * * * *

K LAZY K RANCH INC

Max Kusser founded this ranch many years ago. Following World War II he purchased some land and developed it into a thousand cow operation. Two of his boys, Simon and Joe, have stayed on the ranch and they both have large families with their boys also staying on the ranch to help develop one of the finest crossbred operations I have witnessed.

From the beginning this ranch was a straight Hereford operation (no exceptions), with their cattle rated among the best. Finally I was able to convince Max that he should use black Angus bulls on his heifers. I made this sale personally to Max and this developed into a good relationship. Eight or ten years ago, Max passed on and I started dealing with Joe and his son, Jerry, and I'm still dealing with them. They have sixty two-year-old Angus breeding bulls that are a sight to behold. They have a cross-breeding program that is working to perfection for them. They keep perfect identification on the females by ear-tag and brand. They have improved their calves with each generation, raising their weaning weights by 150 pounds per head and have moved them up to a premium price basis. Seeing is believing! I have sold them bulls every year and I am really proud that they have allowed me this opportunity to work and counsel with them in their breeding program. I have bought, sold and traded a lot of bulls and heifers with them.

Several years ago I needed to make a trip to Maher, Colorado, to receive a bunch of Angus bulls that I had bought from Dick Mott. I had done business with him for ten or twelve years. This was the greatest source of top bulls that I had ever found. I wasn't able to drive too far because of an ailing hip that was giving me a lot of difficulty. I talked Jerry Kusser into going with me to help me drive. After arriving in Maher,

John, Jerry, Simon, Joey and Joe Kusser.

Dan & Tim Kusser

it didn't take long to complete the bull deal. Dick then took us in his pickup and showed us his entire herd of cows. We enjoyed looking at his cowherd and his mountain ranch. I'm sure it opened Jerry's eyes to see this magnificent set of full-blood Angus cows. Because Jerry saw this cowherd, I was able to help Kussers purchase about 200 full-blood Angus bred

Branding time at Kussers. Max is doing the branding with Simon holding the calf and with Joe under his arm holding the calf.

Joe Kusser, Marvin Beranek, Simon Kusser, Bill Stephens, Ed Kusser, Leland Siverten, Gene Shaw, Ross VanBalen and Jack Gallagher on the ground.

heifers from Dick. I truly got acquainted with Jerry on this trip. He is multi-talented with both cows and bulls.

I predict that the K Lazy K Ranch Inc will continue to be prominent with their crossbred cattle and gain much prestige with their full-blood Angus cattle! Simon and Joe have produced a fine group of young men to continue this tradition! They all know what toil and sweat are and they are willing to pay that price for accomplishment!

* * * * *

SALEBARNS

I have done a tremendous amount of business with these central South Dakota sale barns over the years, both buying and selling. These sale barns have been very active and have given their communities an economic stability.

1993—Highmore Auction Barn, Karen Hemminger, Gary McCloud, Nathan Shaull—owner, Mike Cook, Hoss Roseland, Bennie Snodgrass, Delmas Meek—foreground, Dean Duxbury in ring.

Original owners of the Highmore Livestock Exchange. Jess Shaull, John Heezen, Jean Dehaven, Ross VanBalen and Elwood Redick.

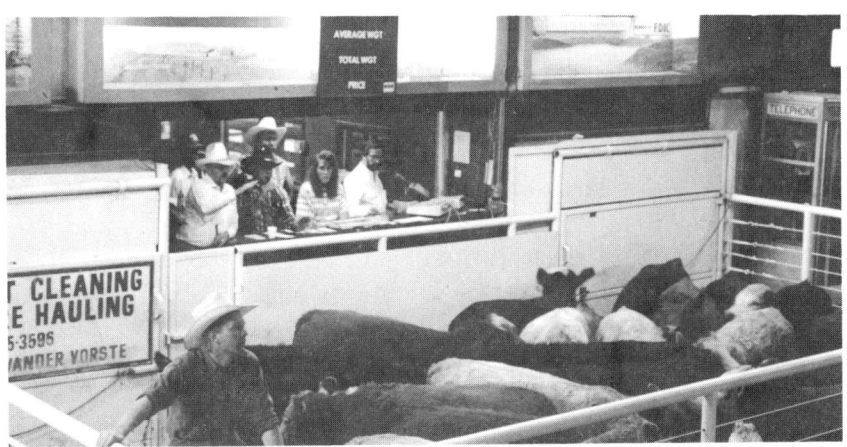

1992—Mobridge Livestock Exchange Inc. Dale Christensen, in foreground—owner, Gene Christensen—owner, Preston Droog, Jerry Green—behind, Lisa Christensen—owner, Tom Keller.

1993—Ft. Pierre Livestock Exchange, John Smith, Dennis Hanson—owner, Don Bourk, Alisha Andersen, Billy Markwed and Steve Foth.

Chapter 59

Reminiscences From Old Friends

My first knowledge of the Jennings Brothers and quality Angus cattle was on a visit to Karl Hoffman's feedlot at Ida Grove, Iowa. Karl fed top quality Hereford and Angus calves to the optimum prime grade for major cattle shows including Chicago, and won!

Clayton and Ted Jennings sold Karl these top Angus calves and they were prize winners! The cattle had good frames, were big cattle for the times—mid 50's.

A couple of years later Clayton came to Great Falls, Montana to judge the Angus show at the state fair. The Angus breed was invading Hereford country and the Angus show at the state fair was very popular with the name breeders around the country. Clayton had an eye for cattle. Not only did he do a good job of placing cattle, but his reasons made sense, were articulated clearly and were believable!

Clayton had a creative mind; he was a "deal maker." Buyers who went to the ranch to buy bulls had a big selection from which to choose. While driving through the pastures one could look at several hundred bulls or females in their "working clothes" and Clayton was right there telling about the animals' strengths and weaknesses. Hidden Valley Ranch (Sam Dawson) and Willow Creek Ranch (John Marne, mgr.) were two Montana outfits that come to mind that changed over from Hereford to Angus. Both Sam and John became friends and customers of Clayton early on. The calves produced in these two herds were some of the best to be found. While the Angus breed was foremost in his mind, Clayton saw opportunities with the European (exotic) breeds. While these breeds never dominated his cattle business, the potential for cross-breeding really raised his curiosity as to what might be done. In the late 60's and 70's when the exotics were "hot" Clayton always said, "There's a place for these cattle in our industry, but remember you should always keep some Angus in their bloodlines." He had a strong influence in maintaining the integrity of the Angus breed; he held to a strong advocacy for size, scale and smoothness in the breed.

Never was there a more hospitable person than Clayton Jennings. I don't believe Clayton ever "met a person he didn't like!" Friends were welcome at his home for business and relaxation. He was good-hearted (almost to a fault) and had a high trust level in his fellow man; a person's word was good until he was shown otherwise. He helped many a friend. Gene Holzing told me of the encouragement and help Clayton gave him after the death of his father. This gave Gene the heart and the knowledge to build his own Angus cattle herd and be a better cowman.

If anyone ever devoted his/her life to the cattle industry it was Clayton Jennings. As one of the top breeders and leaders in the Angus cattle industry, today's breeders and customers alike can thank him for persevering through the years for a type of cattle that would do commercial breeders the most good—we have that type today!

Thanks Clayton!
Buck Moore
Norwest Bank

* * * * *

...I have heard of you, Clayton, since I was a boy barely able to read Angus Journals. The Hyland Angus Ranch was a legend in the West and I often heard stories told by cattlemen of the Jennings' fame.

I shall never forget one day when we were driving from Miller to Highmore in January 1984. It was cold as hell and you said that our lives were alike in many ways. You said, "Both of us can make a lot of money but we need to hide a little where we can't get it ourselves because sure as hell, we'd spend it for another deal!"

Virgil Lovell, President
Ankony Angus Corporation

* * * * *

...started buying bulls from Clayton Jennings after we purchased a cowherd from him in 1954. In the late 50's and 60's, Sam Dawson and I would go down to his ranch in South Dakota in November. We would buy the bulls right out of the lots. We'd pick out the bulls we wanted, but he wouldn't price them until we played poker all night and drank some Scotch. Then just before we went to bed, he'd tell us the price. It was always within reason!

Clayton bought the Willow Creek Ranch calves for many years. He would come out to the ranch in Montana, drink some Scotch with us, and buy the calves, sight unseen. He always paid premium as he knew they were good. I would sort and weigh them. Then I would call him to see when he wanted them shipped. No contracts, no down payments. It all worked on trust!

John R. Marn
Willow Creek Ranch, Montana

* * * * *

...about your ranch house, I remember those beautiful backlighted color photographs, side by side, across a whole wall. There were terrific pictures and I always remember one of the bucking horse with the horse's hind legs clean up in the air and the rider just being bucked off!

Clayt, you were an outstanding manager. I always remember how efficiently you ran the ranch with very little help. I particularly remember the calving barn and how well it was arranged with the lots for close-calving cows not too far away and the shed for the cows with their baby calves also close by.

The famous Sale Barn with "Hyland Angus Ranch" inscribed in the shingles of the roof was always impressive.

I remember the complete circle of marketing which you and Ted worked out. You operated the purebred ranch and sold the bulls to commercial breeders. In turn, when the calves by those bulls were ready to wean, Ted purchased them and marketed them very successfully, thus giving your bull customers a real market for their calves.

One of the things I remember about you, Clayt, was your ability to make a quick decision. You made up your mind and it was either "Yes" or "No." Not many people have the ability to do that the way you did over the years.

I always remember that in contrast to much cattle business in the East, cattle business in the West was on a "cash or check on delivery basis." You always had your checkbook with you and when a deal was struck, you were there with the money.

Okay, Clayt. all the best!
Myron M Fuerst
Rhinebeck, New York

* * * * *

There are times when an unforgettable person crosses one's path in life, who unselfishly counsels, shares, advises and provides friendship. That situation happened to me over twenty years ago and that man was you, Clayton.

Our introduction was when you and Larry Berg of Great Plains Feed Lot in Huron, South Dakota came to the Minneapolis Athletic Club in your satorial splendor: Silk cowboy suits, hand-tooled boots and Stetson hats.

Each year Denver is the site of the cattle industry's "world series." The "who's who" of this colorful event included the Jennings Brothers of South Dakota, domiciled at the Cosmopolitan Hotel, where memories were made, and probably more cattle changed hands there than "on the hill."

Carl Nelson at the Minnesota State Angus Sale in 1983. This bull brought $25,000.00.

I look at you, Clayt, as a visionary and a pragmatic cattleman and businessman. You were a master breeder, promoting the Emulous line which improved the traits so essential to profitable beef production and popularized the type cattle demanded by the American housewife. Serious cattle breeders traveled to the Hyland Angus Ranch at Highmore just to gaze on your great bull, Dynamo.

I was your "cattle hedging specialist." Some positions worked, and some didn't, but you were a professional, and handled all transactions like the square-shooter which you are.

You're probably Dakota's number one Twins fan. I have fond memories of you attending games with Gloria, Jim and Charlie. You also were like a security blanket to me when I would look up into the crowd at a cattle sale, and you and Carol would give me "thumbs-up!"

If I had to sum up my experience with you in only three words, I would say, "What a man!"
Carl F. Nelson
Senior Vice President
Dean Witter Reynolds, Inc.

* * * * *

Without a doubt, Clayton, you more than any one person have contributed to the spread of the Angus breed throughout the West. There's no question, you're the biggest "bull shipper" in the country. In addition you convinced many Hereford breeders to use Angus bulls. I'll never forget the 42 car loads of black bald-faced heifers you sent me for a promotional sale I put on at New Market, Virginia, some years ago. You hand picked them for me from a lot of your bull customers. They were even better than you described them over the phone. You're the only man I'd have ever thought of spending that much money with without looking. But I knew I could depend on you 100% as so many cattlemen have through the years. Your word was always, and still is, your bond.

I remember you telling me about that train-load of heifers over the phone. You said you had picked the ones with black pigment around their eyes to avoid pink-eye. You said they looked like a bunch of pretty women with mascara, and that they did.

You served admirably as a judge. You not only did a great job of judging, but there never was any complaining about your work. The consignors knew they were under the presence of a "master."

Well, it's time to wind this up. A lot of our "mates have already headed out to the 'Big Roundup' in the sky, and I hope one day we all get together for what the mountain men of the West used to call "Rendezvous."
Dave Canning
Canning Land and Livestock

* * * * *

Index

A

A & J Cattle Co., 174
A. I., 106
Aasby, Ben, 195
Aasby, Keith, 192, 193
Aasby, Kent, 195
Aasby, Leonard, 207
Aberdeen, South Dakota, 35
Adams, Bill, 121-25
Aesoph, Robert, 259
Alberta Clipper, 252, 253
Alberta, Canada, 58, 157
Algona, Iowa, 25
Amerifax, 216,
Anderberg, Jay, 65
Angus Journals, 290
Ankony Angus Corporation, 112, 191, 267, 290
Ankony Hyland Ranch, 259, 266
Arendt, Harold, 259
Artesian Well, 118
Australia, 108

B

Babcock, Nels, 69, 70, 71, 72, 73
Baloun, Ray and Reg, 56
Bar Bolster Brand, 100
Becker, George, 167
Beef Friesian Cattle, 214, 216, 219, 220, 227, 228, 230, 270
Bell Boy, 161
Bell Fontaine Angus Farms, 161
Belt, Montana, 164
Belvidere, South Dakota, 36
Berg, Larry, 281, 282, 291
Bernard, Chuck, 19
Berry, Tom, 36
Bickel, Bill, 216
Bickel, Bryan, 216
Bickel, Roland, 216
Bietz, John, 103
Big Banker, 228
Big Bend Dam, 185, 236

Big Notch, 216, 228
Big Springs, Texas, 73
Big Timber, Montana, 274
Billings, Montana, 55
Bismarck, 157
Blair, Jim, 100, 111, 175
Blarney Stone, 216
Bloomfield, Nebraska, 267
Blue Island, Illinois, 198
Blue, Vida, 267
Bode, Iowa, 22
Boone, County, 1, 254
Boone, Iowa, 3, 4, 5, 6
Borundo, Teofilo, 121, 122, 123, 124, 125
Bowar, Herb, 216
Bowar, Jerry, 216
Bradgate, Iowa, 34
Branding Iron Bar, 153
Bronze Warrior, 280
Brown Hotel, 42, 45, 56
Brown Palace, 245, 246
Brown, Frank, 42, 43
Browning, Montana, 58
Bruce, Albert, 221
Bruce, Beverly, 221
Buffalo County, 277
Bull Ranch, 103
Bunkhouse, 233

C

Cahalan, Art B., 10, 45, 52, 53, 54, 55, 56, 57
Canada, 58, 108
Canadian Club, 280
Canning, Dave, 195, 196, 197, 202, 212, 214, 219, 293
Caravelle, 244
Cassius Clay, 68
Cayou, O. J., 16
Cedar Rapids, Iowa, 1, 8, 22, 23
Chamberlain, South Dakota, 250
Chapel in the Hills, 235

Cheyenne Indian Reservation, 69, 236
Cheyenne Indians, 61
Cheyenne River, 36
Chicago & Northwestern RR, 28, 30, 36, 63, 197
Chicago Stockyards, 8, 9
Chihuahua, Mexico, 121, 122
Christensen, Dale, 235
Christensen, Lisa, 235
Clarkesville, Georgia, 243
Claymore, Duane, 231
Cody, Nebraska, 173
Colorado, 203, 216
Columbia Sheep, 55
Cook, Jack, 109
Copenhagen, 174
Cosmopoliton Hotel, 153, 154, 156, 227, 228
Court Manor Plantation, 195, 197, 198
Cow Palace, 221, 224, 233, 272

D

Dakota, Minnesota & Eastern, 243
Davenport Angus Ranch, 173
Dawson, Floyd, 165
Dawson, Glenn, 274
Dawson, Sam, 164, 166, 290
Dean Witter Reynolds, 293
Denver, 74, 125, 126, 153, 155, 156, 157, 180, 183, 186, 208, 245,
Denver US National Bank, 203
Diagonal, 16
Diamond A Ranch, 69
Dinklage, Louis, 73, 74, 75
Dittman, Fred, 103, 173
Dittman, Jim, 173
Dolliver Ranch, 43, 44
Donlin Bros., 198
Donlin Trucking Service, 263
Donlin, Al, 202, 263, 264
Draper, South Dakota 277
Dublin, Ireland, 212
Dusty Acres Ranch, 270
Dwyer, Eloise, 180
Dynamo, 292

E

Eagle Butte, South Dakota, 69, 236
Eastern US Angus Ass'n, 195
Edmonton, Canada, 157, 216
El Paso, Texas, 121, 122, 123, 125, 208
Emirau, 83

Emulous, 292
Enger, Caryl, 99
England, 108
Erb Ranch, 44
Eureka, South Dakota, 35
European Allies, 75

F

Faith, South Dakota, 69
Farmers Savings Bank, 23
Faulkton, South Dakota 167
Fawcett Bros., 106
Fawcett, Ed, 103
Federal Land Bank, 43, 44, 52
Feeney, Pat, 245, 262, 263
Fernow, Marvin, 99
First National Bank, Denver, 129, 133
First National Bank, Miller, 45, 52, 53, 54, 129, 133, 221
Fischer Bros. Merchandise Store, 41
Fish, Dorothy, 116, 117, 118
Fowlerville, Michigan, 212
France, 108
Frazier, Charlie, 66, 67, 68, 69
Ft. Pierre, South Dakota, 2, 36, 37, 38, 41, 66, 74, 250
Ft. Thompson, South Dakota 185
Ft. Worth, Texas, 157
Fuegen, Hazel, 275
Fuegen, Norm, 275
Fuerst, Myron, 291
Fulton, Tex, 216

G

Gadd, Jap, 274
Gallagher, William C., 265, 266
Gannon, Tom, 245
Gard, Bob, 83
Gardner, Charlie, 44, 52
Garrigan, Loren, 191
Geppert, Herman, 277, 278
Gerdes, Roger, 259
Gerlach, John, 177
Germany, 75
Gettysburg, South Dakota 252
Gilroy, Lloyd, 205, 206, 207
Gluhm, Clarence, 207
Gold Dust, 280
Goldendale, Washington, 173
Goodrich, Mick, 205
Gore, Al, Sr., 198
Grable, Melvin, 127

Grand River Stock Farm, 163
Great Atlantic Bull Sale, 185
Great Falls, Montana, 157, 164, 288
Great Plains Feedlot, 291
Greeley, Colorado, 233
Gregg, Boots, 27, 28, 30, 31, 32, 278
Gregg, Lori, 207, 208
Gregg, Scott, 207, 208
Gross Tailors, 126, 281
Grosz, Theodore, 100
Guadalcanal, 82, 83
Guinness Book of World Records, 51

H
Haakon County, 262
Hahn, Bud, 103, 111
Hahn, Cheryl, 207
Hahn, Elinor, 207
Hale, Fred, 191
Halloween, 238
Hand County, 44, 109
Hansen, Hans, 24, 25
Hanson, Lyman, 100
Hardin, Montana, 55, 56
Hardy, Iowa, 22
Harrold, South Dakota, 27, 28, 31, 277
Harry Robinson Ranch, 173
Hawarden, Iowa, 58
Hawkinson & Quirk, 106
Healey & Lackey, 103
Heenan, Ben, 127
Heidepriem & Widmayer, 280
Hendren, J. J., MD, 163
Henson, Dean, 198, 202
Hermann, Albert, 277
Hidden Valley Ranch, 164, 289
Highmore, South Dakota, 56, 99, 100, 106, 127, 129, 159, 191, 198, 231, 233, 252, 261, 274, 277
Highway 14, 99, 121, 129, 130
Highway 212, 251, 252
Highway 40, 203
Highway 47, 252
Hippen, John, 218
Hoffman, Karl, 288
Holdman, Gloria Jennings, 178
Holzing, Gene, 289
Hop Scotch Bar, 66
Houston Astrodome, 228
Houston House Hotel, 262
Houston, Ben, 208
Hoven, South Dakota, 251

Huron, South Dakota, 61, 65
Hyde Co. Education Association, 250
Hyde County, 109
Hyland Angus Ranch, 99, 106, 107, 108, 112, 124, 127, 134, 167, 173, 183, 188, 290, 291, 292
Hyland Angus Ranch Crew, 109, 112
Hyland Bardalier 151, 167

I
Ice, Cecil, 122, 159
Ida Grove, Iowa, 288
Ingomar, Montana, 55
International Beef Breeders, 219
Iowa, 35, 36, 65, 72
Ipswich, 35
Ireland, 108, 212, 214, 216
Irish Lady, 228
Isburg & McIntosh, 100
Italy, 75

J
J. and J. Ranch, 203
Jack Daniels, 122, 123, 124
Japan, 75, 76, 82, 83, 90
Jennings Bros. 45, 46, 106, 107, 108, 134, 186, 288, 291
Jennings, Carol, 235, 245, 252, 255, 268, 292
Jennings, Charles Clayton, 117, 118, 179, 191, 192, 205, 216, 292
Jennings, Charles McClellan, 1, 91, 92, 93, 95
Jennings, Dorothy, 124, 130, 176
Jennings, Eloise, 156, 157, 180, 183, 191, 207, 208, 238, 240
Jennings, Gary, 176
Jennings, Gloria Jean, 118, 179, 192, 216, 233, 292
Jennings, James Ted, 179, 183, 192, 208, 216, 292
Jennings, Margaret, 11, 23
Jennings, Mary L. Vogler, 1, 91, 95, 96
Jennings, Ron, 100, 176, 240
Jennings, Ted, 22, 23, 24, 25, 32, 34, 35, 36, 44, 45, 65, 73, 74, 75, 76, 98, 100, 108, 109, 111, 129, 130, 164, 240, 250, 288
Jennings, W. O., 8, 10
Jewett Angus Ranch, 161
Johnson Bros., 218
Johnston, Frances, 189, 207

Johnston, Stanley, 189, 204, 205, 206, 207, 208
Juarez, 208

K

K Lazy K Ranch, Inc., 282, 286
Kelly Seamus, 214
Kemp, Angus Farms, 161
Kluge, Lefty, 186
Knapp, Kenneth & Pete, 65
Knippling Bros., 278, 279, 280
Krick, Jimmy, 100, 111
Kusser, Eddie, 127
Kusser, Jerry, 282, 283
Kusser, Joe, 282, 286
Kusser, Max, 282
Kusser, Phil, 127
Kusser, Simon, 127, 282, 286

L

Lander, Wyoming, 54
Langley, James, 173
Lansing, Michigan, 244
Larry's Smart Fashions, 281
Las Vegas, 221, 274
Leachman, Les, 198
Leander, Dr. 253, 254
Lennep, Montana, 186
Leola, South Dakota, 35
Lettau, Carol, 233, 234, 235, 240
Lettau, Joe, 233
Lettau, Lisa, 233
Lingscheit, Frank, 100
Livermore, Iowa, 8, 9, 22, 23, 25, 28, 30, 76
Long Lake, South Dakota, 35
Lovana Farms, 243, 244, 245
Lovana Palace, 245
Lovana Palace Ball, 245
Lovell, Virgil, 243, 290
Lufkin, Don, 203

M

M & St. L Railroad, 8
Madison Square Garden, 69
Magness, J. M. (Jim), 61, 63
Maher, Colorado, 269, 282
Manning, John, 103
Marion, Iowa, 99
Market Street, 86
Marn, John, 165, 290
Marsden, William, 268

Martin, Mr., 72
Martinmaas, Arnold, 167
Martinmaas, Joe, 218
Mason City, Iowa, 16
Mason, Robert, 191
Matador, Texas, 208
Mayo Clinic, 262
Mays Department Store, 126
McBride, Charles, 100
McCloud, Gary, 251
McCloud, Speed, 259
McGovern, Senator George, 198
McKown, Jim, 50
Medicine Rock Cafe, 252
Melius, Dean, 216
Melius, Don, 216
Methodist Church, 254
Mexico, 108, 125, 281
Meyer, Alfred, 177
Michigan, 118
Midland, Texas, 58, 73, 279
Miles City, Montana, 63, 173
Milk River, 58
Miller Livestock Auction Co., 63, 76, 271
Miller, Bruce, 261, 267, 268
Miller, South Dakota, 1, 32, 42, 43, 44, 46, 56, 57, 61, 65, 71, 76, 83, 85, 116, 117, 124, 163, 176, 197, 198, 216, 221, 280
Milwaukee Railroad, 71
Minneapolis, 90
Minneapolis Athletic Club, 291
Mission Ridge, South Dakota 36, 41
Mississippi, 245
Missouri River, 27, 185, 231
Mobridge, South Dakota, 231, 236
Mogelson, Sonny, 55
Monahan, Texas, 73, 279
Montana, 54, 56, 58, 164, 166, 167
Montana State Fair, 164
Moore, Buck, 164, 165, 166
Mossman Yards, 71, 73
Mossman, C. A. (Cap), 69, 71, 72
Mott, Richard, 269, 282, 283, 286
Mundt, Senator Karl, 198
Myers, Ralph, 159, 207

N

National Western Stock Show, 74, 153, 186, 203, 227, 228
Nedved, Harold, 100

Nelson, Carl, 209
Neuharth, Don, 270
Neuharth, Vivian, 270
New Caledonia, 82
New Georgia, 82, 83
New Market, Virginia, 195, 197, 198
New York, 191, 212
Newell, Wes, 100
Nicolls, O. C., 99
Niederauer, George, 185
Nora, 153, 154, 155, 157
North Ranch, 100

O

O Bardoliermire 2nd, 167
O'Brien, Gene, 118
Oakland A's, 267
Odessa, Texas, 73, 279
Ogren, D & R., 218
Ohlde, Tim, 218
Okinawa, 90
Old Fitzgerald, 277
Old Grand Dad, 31
Omaha, Nebraska, 76
Orcutt, Bruce, 173

P

Pacific Fleet, 75
Pacific Ocean, 80, 82
Paine, Roger, 103
Palon, Bud, 48, 63
Palon, James, 198, 202
Parade, South Dakota, 71
Parlin, Harold, 111, 179
Parlin, Phyllis, 112
Peaches, 97
Pearl Harbor, 75, 76
Pekarek, Joe, 271, 272
Pekarek, Larry, 271, 273, 274
Pekarek, Ron, 271, 272, 273
Peterson, F. M. 129, 130, 131, 133
Philpot, Howard, 267
Pierre, South Dakota, 27, 36, 72, 122, 159, 233
Pittsburgh, Pennsylvania, 198
Platte City, Missouri, 259, 261
Polo, South Dakota, 281
Pontiac Yards, Virginia, 198
Port Hueneme, California, 80
Premier Cattle Company, 244
Premier Corporation, 212
Pressure Group, 259

Prince Pompadour, 275
Prostrollo, J. M., 103

Q

Quinn, Faye, 173
Quirk, John, 216

R

Radisson Hotel, 155, 156
Ranches, 99
Raona Angus Farms, Lansing, Michigan, 161
Raona Herd, 162
Rawhide, 177
Raymond, South Dakota, 277
Redfield, South Dakota, 61
Reding, Frank, 35
Ree Heights, South Dakota, 99, 100, 106, 204, 205, 271
Reiman, Don, 198, 202, 271
Reliance, South Dakota, 275
Renner, John, 103
Rhinebeck, New York, 291
Richmond, Virginia, 185
Rinehart, Frankie, 259
Rinehart, Harold, 274, 275
Rinehart, Lowell, 259
Rio Grande River, 208
Roanoke, Virginia, 157
Robinson, Dale, 103
Robinson, Harry, 103
Robinson, Nadine, 34, 65, 85, 92
Robinson, Paul, 34, 85, 198
Rock Island Railroad, 22
Rocky Mountains, 203
Rose, Orville, 99
Ruark, LeRoy, 127
Rucker, B. A., 198
Rural Credit, 43, 45

S

Sacramento, California, 157
Salebarns, 286
San Angelo, Texas, 46
San Diego, California, 76, 77
San Francisco, California, 86
Sandcamp, Otto, 100
Schaub Ranch, 127
Schuette, William, 264
Scotland, 108
Scott, Millard, 43, 44, 45
Seattle Naval Station, 77

Seattle, Washington, 117
Selective Service Act, 75
Seneca, South Dakota, 252
Sheldon, North Dakota, 167
Sheridan, Wyoming, 55
Siebrasse, Don, 251
Silver Dollar, 15
Sioux City, Iowa, 19, 32
Sioux Falls, South Dakota, 24, 253
Snell, Frank, 127
Solomon Islands, 80
Sonnenschein, Earl, 36, 37, 66, 67
South America, 108
South Dakota, 19, 24, 25, 32, 35, 43, 45, 57, 90, 98, 106, 109, 125, 161
South Dakota Hall of Fame, 246, 250
South Pacific, 80, 82, 83, 84, 85
South Ranch, 99
Spearfish, South Dakota 261, 267
St. Lawrence, South Dakota, 61
Standing Rock Reservation, 236, 272
State Fairs, 157
Staunton, Virginia, 195
Steamboat Springs, Colorado, 203, 208
Steers, Buck, 100, 103
Steinlitner, Herman, 52
Stephan Indian Mission, 279
Stephan, South Dakota, 99
Stockman's Cafe, 55
Stockman's Store, 125
Stolle, Bill, 218
Struck, David, 266, 267, 268
Sugar Loaf Farms, 195
Sugar Loaf Scot 913, 186
Suhn, Ernest, Jr., 100, 103, 111
Suhn, Loretta, 111
Sykes, Jack, 16

T

Tennessee, 198
Texas, 74
Thermopolis, Wyoming, 55
Thunder, 176, 177
Tibbs, Casey, 41
Tommy Dorsey Orchestra, 246
Tompkins, Leo, 103

Top Notch, 214, 216, 219
Trammell, John, 99
Treasure Island, 86
Tumble Inn, 67, 68

U

United States, 75, 76
USS Cabott, 86, 90
USS California, 90
Utah, 58

V

VanDervoort, Rand, 106
Virginia, 197, 198, 212, 271
Vogler, Mary L., 1
Voldseth Bros., 186

W

Wagner, Robert, 198
Wagon Mound, New Mexico, 69
Washing Machine Charlie, 83
Washington, D.C., 198
Weber, Dan, 277
Wermersen, George, 57, 58, 164
Wermersen, Ken, 57
West Hotel, 69
West Texas, 58
Western Contracting, 185
WHO Radio, 24
Widmayer, Ruben, 203, 208, 250, 280, 281
Williams, John, 191
Willow Creek Ranch, 165, 289, 290
Wilson Packing Company, 1, 8, 22, 23, 27
Wilson, Phil, 22
Wind River Reservation, 61
Wisner Improvement Corporation, 74
Wisner, Nebraska, 73
Wolsey, South Dakota, 173, 266
Wonderly, John, 12, 13, 14
Worland, Wyoming, 55
WPA, 121
Wurts, Dale, 127
Wyoming, 54, 56, 57, 61